# CLIMATE CHANGE AND THE CONTEMPORARY NOVEL

Climate change is becoming a major theme in the contemporary novel, as authors reflect concerns in wider society. Given the urgency and enormity of the problem, can literature (and the emotional response it provokes) play a role in answering the complex ethical issues that arise because of climate change? This book shows that conventional fictional techniques should not be disregarded as inadequate to the demands of climate change; rather, fiction has the potential to challenge us, emotionally and ethically, to reconsider our relationship to the future. Adeline Johns-Putra focuses on the dominant theme of intergenerational ethics in the contemporary novel: that is, the idea of our obligation to future generations as a basis for environmental action. Rather than simply framing parenthood and posterity in sentimental terms, the climate change novel uses their emotional appeal to critique their anthropocentricism and identity politics, offering radical alternatives instead.

ADELINE JOHNS-PUTRA is Reader in English Literature at the School of Literature and Languages, University of Surrey. She is the author of *Heroes and Housewives: Women's Epic Poetry and Domestic Ideology in the Romantic Age* (2001) and *The History of the Epic* (2006). She is also the editor of *Process: Landscape and Text* (2010) and *Literature and Sustainability: Concept, Text, and Culture* (2017).

CAMBRIDGE STUDIES IN TWENTY-FIRST-CENTURY
LITERATURE AND CULTURE

*Editor*
Peter Boxall, *University of Sussex*

As the cultural environment of the twenty-first century comes into clearer focus, Cambridge Studies in Twenty-First-Century Literature and Culture presents a series of monographs that undertakes the most penetrating and rigorous analysis of contemporary culture and thought.

The series is driven by the perception that critical thinking today is in a state of transition. The global forces that produce cultural forms are entering into powerful new alignments, which demand new analytical vocabularies in the wake of later twentieth century theory. The series will demonstrate that theory is not simply a failed revolutionary gesture that we need to move beyond, but rather brings us to the threshold of a new episteme, which will require new theoretical energy to navigate.

In this spirit, the series will host work that explores the most important emerging critical contours of the twenty-first century, marrying inventive and imaginative criticism with theoretical and philosophical rigor. The aim of the series will be to produce an enduring account of the twenty-first-century intellectual landscape that will not only stand as a record of the critical nature of our time, but that will also forge new critical languages and vocabularies with which to navigate an unfolding age. In offering a historically rich and philosophically nuanced account of contemporary literature and culture, the series will stand as an enduring body of work that helps us to understand the cultural moment in which we live.

## Forthcoming Books in This Series

Joel Evans *Conceptualizing the Global in the Wake of Postmodernism*
Caroline Edwards *Utopia and the Contemporary British Novel*

# CLIMATE CHANGE AND THE CONTEMPORARY NOVEL

ADELINE JOHNS-PUTRA

*University of Surrey*

CAMBRIDGE
UNIVERSITY PRESS

# CAMBRIDGE
## UNIVERSITY PRESS

University Printing House, Cambridge CB2 8BS, United Kingdom

One Liberty Plaza, 20th Floor, New York, NY 10006, USA

477 Williamstown Road, Port Melbourne, VIC 3207, Australia

314–321, 3rd Floor, Plot 3, Splendor Forum, Jasola District Centre,
New Delhi – 110025, India

79 Anson Road, #06–04/06, Singapore 079906

Cambridge University Press is part of the University of Cambridge.

It furthers the University's mission by disseminating knowledge in the pursuit of
education, learning, and research at the highest international levels of excellence.

www.cambridge.org
Information on this title: www.cambridge.org/9781108427371
DOI: 10.1017/9781108610162

© Adeline Johns-Putra 2019

First published 2019

Printed and bound in Great Britain by Clays Ltd, Elcograf S.p.A.

*A catalogue record for this publication is available from the British Library.*

*Library of Congress Cataloging-in-Publication Data*
NAMES: Johns-Putra, Adeline, 1973– author.
TITLE: Climate change and the contemporary novel / Adeline Johns-Putra,
University of Surrey.
DESCRIPTION: Cambridge, UK ; New York, NY : Cambridge University Press, 2018. | Includes
bibliographical references.
IDENTIFIERS: LCCN 2018024050 | ISBN 9781108427371 (hardback)
SUBJECTS: LCSH: Climatic changes in literature. | American fiction – 20th century – History
and criticism. | American fiction – 21st century – History and criticism. | English
fiction – 20th century – History and criticism. | English fiction – 21st century – History
and criticism.
CLASSIFICATION: LCC PS374.C555 J54 2018 | DDC 813/.60936–dc23
LC record available at https://lccn.loc.gov/2018024050

ISBN 978-1-108-42737-1 Hardback

*For Matthew, for everything*

# Contents

# Figures

# Acknowledgements

This book has been several years in the making, and has been aided and encouraged by exchanges and conversations with many others. Its beginnings lie in an interdisciplinary research project at the University of Exeter called 'From Climate to Landscape: Imagining the Future', the brainchild of Matthew Evans, funded by the European Social Fund from 2009 to 2012. I am pleased to acknowledge the input of my co-investigators, Catherine Leyshon and Robert Wilson, and research fellows, Adam Trexler, Hilary Geoghegan, and Ilya Maclean. In particular, some of the initial ideas for this book were born out of discussions that I had with Adam.

My research has been sustained by the interest and enthusiasm of many fellow scholars in the environmental humanities, especially Lucy Burnett, Brycchan Carey, Greg Garrard, Terry Gifford, Axel Goodbody, Richard Kerridge, Agnes Kneitz, John Parham, Kate Rigby, Libby Robin, and Catriona Sandilands. Thanks go also to Astrid Bracke for sharing the manuscript of her monograph, *Climate Crisis and the Twenty-First-Century British Novel*, and to Alexa Weik von Mossner, whose recent book, *Affective Ecologies: Empathy, Emotion, and Environmental Narrative*, appeared too late, unfortunately, for me to incorporate its many rich insights. I am particularly grateful to Hannes Bergthaller, Dana Phillips, and Louise Squire for their friendship and for many fruitful exchanges, and to Claire Colebrook for her mentorship and ready advice over the years.

For invitations to present or publish my work and thus for opportunities to shape my thinking further, I thank Marco Amiero, Gerry Canavan, Lena Christensen, Paul Crawford, Niamh Downing, Petra Fachinger, Sina Farzin, Rebecca Ford, Thomas Ford, Ruth Heholt, Emanuel Herold, David Higgins, Eva Horn, Mike Hulme, Robert Markley, Kym Martindale, Isabel Pérez Ramos, Michelle Poland, Kim Stanley Robinson, Tess Somervell, Molly Wallace, Jason Whittaker, and Glenn

Willmott, as well as: the Association for Literature, Environment and Culture, Canada (ALECC); the Association for the Study of Literature and Environment, UK and Ireland (ASLE UKI); the Department of Foreign Language and Literature at National Chung Hsing University in Taichung, Taiwan; the Environmental Humanities Lab at KTH Royal Institute of Technology in Stockholm; and the Lund University Centre for Sustainability Studies (LUCSUS).

Some of the material in this book first appeared elsewhere, and has been substantially revised for this book. A version of the Introduction appeared as 'Borrowing the World: Climate Change Fiction and the Problem of Posterity', *Climate Change, Complexity, and Representation*, a special issue of *Metaphora* (2017) edited by Hannes Bergthaller and Arndt Niebisch. Some of Chapter 2 is drawn from '"My Job Is to Take Care of You": Climate Change, Humanity, and Cormac McCarthy's *The Road*', *Modern Fiction Studies*, Volume 62, Issue 3 (September 2016) © Purdue University. Parts of Chapter 4 and the conclusion were published as 'The Unsustainable Aesthetics of Sustainability: The Sense of No Ending in Jeanette Winterson's *The Stone Gods*', *Literature and Sustainability: Concept, Text, and Culture*, which I edited with John Parham and Louise Squire (Manchester University Press, 2017). I am grateful to Mary Engelbreit and MECC, LLC for permission to reproduce Ms Engelbreit's artwork in the Introduction.

A visiting fellowship at the Humanities Research Centre of the Australian National University in 2012 gave me a congenial setting in which to clarify many of my ideas; I am grateful to the Centre and its then-director, Debjani Ganguly. A substantial amount of research time was also enabled by two periods of research leave from the University of Exeter and the University of Surrey, respectively. I appreciate the assistance of my former Exeter colleagues and, most especially, the enduring friendship of Robert Mack and Shelly Windsor. For their collegiality and willingness to share the load, I owe much to colleagues past and present at Surrey, including Lucy Bell, Holly Luhning, Donna McCormack, Stephen Mooney, Bran Nicol, Beth Palmer, Neema Parvini, Greg Tate, Paul Vlitos, and Marion Wynne-Davies. I am especially grateful to Diane Watt, former Head of the School of English and Languages at Surrey, for her abiding support.

At Cambridge University Press, Ray Ryan has been a generous editor and Peter Boxall an encouraging series editor. My manuscript was substantially improved by the perceptive and detailed suggestions of an anonymous reviewer, though any flaws in the final work are my own.

Deepest thanks go to my family: to my parents, my sisters, and my brother-in-law for their love and support; to Jenny, Chris, and Jeremy Evans for their encouragement; and to Isabel and Sam, for being part of my life and making me think so very carefully about the meaning of posterity. The dedication to this book acknowledges a debt of gratitude to the one who has been by my side from its beginnings and who made it all possible.

# Introduction

Ever since I have known him, my ecologist husband has owned a well-worn cardboard bookmark; I first came across it tucked, appropriately enough, into his copy of the Brundtland Commission's report, *Our Common Future* (1987).[1] The bookmark was a gift from his parents and its pencilled inscription is still just visible on its reverse: this is also appropriate, not only because of the familial sentiments it expresses, but because my in-laws' commitment to self-sufficient life helped to lay the foundations for my husband's professional, academic, and personal commitment to the environment, which have, in turn, encouraged mine. I noticed the bookmark, a now somewhat tattered strip of cardboard, for its faded epigram: 'We have not inherited the Earth from our fathers; we are borrowing it from our children.' Described as a 'Native American saying', these words are accompanied by a banner featuring a pastiche of indigenous American art (now torn off from my husband's well-used bookmark) and an illustration of three people in a canoe (Fig. 1). Of course, clad in the fly-fisherman's uniform of khaki fishing vest and bucket hat, the paddlers are not themselves characterised as indigenous; indeed, their apparent whiteness identifies them as 'mainstream' Americans enjoying their country's wilderness while managing, in their bark canoe, to exemplify a romantic, 'noble savage' wisdom. That said, the bookmark's folksy sense of Americana is intended to be decontextualised as far as geography goes (my in-laws no doubt purchased it in a bookshop in Wales, where they live) and its three illustrated figures (a grandfather, father, and child) signify the three generations of 'fathers', 'children', and the text's inclusive 'we' who inhabit the middle ground. The main point of the keepsake is to locate its modern reader, wherever she may be, in intergenerational terms, reminding her of her part in a bargain of posterity.

[1] World Commission on Environment and Development, *Our Common Future* (Oxford University Press: 1987).

Figure 1: Mary Engelbreit, 'We Have Not Inherited the Earth from Our Fathers'
© Mary Engelbreit Enterprises, Inc.

It is not the bookmark's quaint and cutesy appeal but its self-consciously wise aphorism that is so striking. The cynic who suspects that it is not a Native American saying would be right. The special attraction of these words has meant that they have been quoted and requoted in various forms over the past three decades, and their provenance has proven surprisingly portable. Meticulous research by the writer who blogs as Garson O'Toole shows that the sentiments were first expressed by activist-author Wendell Berry; writing in 1971 about protecting the Red River Gorge in his beloved Kentucky, Berry declared: 'I speak of the life of a man who knows that the world is not given by his fathers, but borrowed from his children; who has undertaken to cherish it and do it no damage, not because he is duty-bound, but because he loves the world and loves his children.'[2] The publication of Berry's words in *Audubon* magazine soon after led to its misattribution to John James Audubon, and when Dennis Hall, an official at Michigan's Office of Land Use, adapted them without citation in 1973, he was erroneously credited also.[3] Similarly, Australian Environment Minister Moss Cass's use of it in a speech to OPEC in 1974 – inserting the grander phrase 'inherited the Earth' to replace the idea of being 'given' the world – meant that the adage has sometimes been ascribed to him.[4] From the 1980s onwards, the phrase was quoted in speeches and reprinted on book jackets and in report bylines – by, among others, representatives of the United Nations Environment Programme and the World Wildlife Fund.[5] Paul and Anne Ehrlich attributed it to the International Union for the Conservation of Nature and an article in the *Christian Science Monitor* assigned it to environmentalist Lester Brown of the Worldwatch Institute.[6] The *Los Angeles Times* asserted that it was an Amish saying; US Secretary of State James Baker named Ralph Waldo Emerson as its author; and the US Council on Environmental Quality claimed the source to be Chief Seattle.[7] If Mary Engelbreit, the artist responsible for the bookmark along with countless other epigrammatic adornments of greeting cards and calendars, chose sometime in the 1990s to describe this as

[2] Garson O' Toole, 'We Do Not Inherit the Earth from Our Ancestors; We Borrow It from Our Children', *Quote Investigator: Exploring the Origins of Quotations*, http://quoteinvestigator.com/2013/01/22/borrow-earth/#note-5296-1; Wendell E. Berry, *The Unforeseen Wilderness: An Essay on Kentucky's Red River Gorge* (Lexington: University of Kentucky Press, 1971), p. 26.

[3] Wendell E. Berry, 'The One-Inch Journey', *Audubon* (May 1971), 4–11; Dennis Hall, 'The Land Is Borrowed from Our Children', *Michigan Natural Resources*, 44.4 (1975), 2–3.

[4] O'Toole, 'Inherit the Earth'.

[5] United Nations Environment Programme, *Annual Review 1978* (London: UNEP Earthprint, 1980); Lee M. Talbot, 'A World Conservation Strategy', *Journal of the Royal Society of Arts*, 128.5288 (July 1980).

[6] Paul and Anne Ehrlich, 'The Politics of Extinction', *Bulletin of the Atomic Scientists*, 37.5 (1981), 26; Ed Jones, 'Saving the Soil – by Private Initiative', *Christian Science Monitor* (5 January 1983), 23.

[7] Frank Riley, 'John Muir's Legacy Still Strong in Glacier Country', *Los Angeles Times* (14 Aug. 1988), 5; Ralph Keyes, 'Some of Our Favorite Quotations Never Quite Went that Way: Did They REALLY Say It?' *Washington Post* (16 May 1993), L10.

Native American, one can only assume that her decision was partly a matter of canny merchandising and partly the same kind of genuine, unchecked error made by many others.[8]

At first glance, the sentiment seems to strike a chord of environmental concern, and it is easy to see why differing versions have proliferated even as they have been attributed to sufficiently venerable and quotable sources. The idea that our relationship with the biosphere is automatically a matter of posterity is a powerful one, and this quotation in particular achieves several important rhetorical tricks. It collapses a web of obligations – primarily, between species – into a single intergenerational strand of time. We are not construed as guardians of the environment for the environment's sake but are explicitly called on to steward it for a vastly distant future, even as we are reminded of our debt to those in the past; we are thus placed in a grand historical chain of obligations. More importantly, this version of environmentalist posterity brings future generations into the immediate purview of parental love. Even as the call to stewardship seems to trail off into the reaches of time, its use of synecdoche – the modelling of our attitude to future generations on our responsibilities to our offspring – replaces the terror of sublime infinity with the sentimentality of parental caring, sheltering, and nurturing. From Berry's original expression of it through its many incarnations, the primal, emotional punchline is that (every)man loves his children.

Such rhetorical manoeuvres are discernible in a wide range of late twentieth- and twenty-first-century cultural texts and artefacts, from media reportage to cinema, from popular science to poetry. Indeed, this parental rhetoric of posterity is possibly one of the most prevalent tactics in contemporary environmentalist discourse. Unsurprisingly, this rhetoric has turned ubiquitous with the deepening sense of global environmentalist crisis in this century in the face of anthropogenic climate change, part of an age of unprecedented human impact on the biosphere increasingly referred to as the Anthropocene. It is, therefore, simultaneously an expression of and response to the worries called forth by climate change. It frames our climate change concerns as a fear for future (human) generations and particularly for the most immediate of those – our offspring. It seems, too, that it allows us to convince ourselves that parental care is the obvious

[8] Mary Engelbreit, www.maryengelbreit.com. But Engelbreit should not be readily dismissed as racially insensitive: she gained attention for producing an anti-racist (and parentally themed) image in response to the police shooting of Michael Brown in Ferguson, Missouri, in 2014; Diana Reese, 'Michael Brown's Mother Inspires Controversial Artwork by Mary Engelbreit', *Washington Post*, 25 August 2014.

and most effective solution to climate change: if we just cared more about our children, we would be motivated to save them and everything would be all right.

The discourse of environmentalist crisis in the Anthropocene is peppered with such references to parental obligations to posterity, creating a sense of transcendence and timelessness on the one hand and conjuring up elemental feelings of care and love on the other. It is what, for example, gives especial power to British poet Ruth Padel's haunting climate change poem, 'Slices of Toast' (2007), an effective piece of environmentalist poetry thanks to its evocation of the poet's parents and child. The poem's lyrical description of environmental crisis is occasioned by a warm winter's day that is 'almost too warm'; it begins with memories of the colder winters of childhood and ends with worries about the future world.[9] Anxieties about disruptions in ocean flows, melting polar icecaps, and deadly weather events segue into the poet's memory of events at a public lecture by environmentalist James Lovelock: 'A woman in the auditorium asks: *If all you say / is true, what should we be teaching our children?*, to which Lovelock's deflated and defeated response is simply, '*I don't know. I really don't know.*'[10] All then turn out to be addressed, along with a final, unanswerable plea, to the poet's daughter. For if, indeed, all Lovelock says is true, then, 'the only answer is *commando skills. / Fight to the death for any high ground you're standing on / my darling.*'[11] The poem ends, self-aware but helpless all the same: 'I know the Thames Barrier, small waters / of our particular rivers, and this terrible readiness / to worry about your own family first, may be the least / of our problems but I think *my daughter, my daughter, / how is she going to deal with this?*'[12] The shift from planet to child may in rational terms be an abrupt one – it is 'a question' that Lovelock 'hadn't faced before' – but it flows, affectively speaking, with utter ease.[13] The repetition of '*my daughter*' strikes a note with the reader because of what the poet realises is everyone's 'terrible readiness' to think of the environment in terms of posterity.

The question that haunts Padel's Lovelock is evident in many other popular calls to environmental action. It is transformed in such rhetoric into a reason to act, a rationale for changing our ways in the present to make a better life for those in the future. The film *An Inconvenient Truth* (2006) ends with Al Gore's affecting words to the audience: 'Future

---

[9] Ruth Padel, 'Slices of Toast', *London Review of Books*, 29.5 (8 March 2007), 31.
[10] Ibid., 31; original emphasis.    [11] Ibid., 31; original emphasis.    [12] Ibid., 31; original emphasis.
[13] Ibid., 31; original emphasis.

generations may well have occasion to ask themselves, "What were our parents thinking? Why didn't they wake up when they had a chance?" We have to hear that question from them, now."[14] Meanwhile, climate scientist James Hansen has titled his book on global warming *Storms of My Grandchildren* (2009) and includes photographs of those grandchildren at various points in the book. In his preface, beneath an image of his granddaughter at two, he opines: 'I did not want my grandchildren, someday in the future, to look back and say "Opa understood what was happening, but he did not make it clear".'[15] More recently, Hansen has joined with a group of twenty-one young people in Eugene, Oregon, to take legal action against the government of the United States; *Juliana v. United States* is a suit against governmental inaction on climate change on the grounds that this represents a violation of the constitutional rights of future adults (and, indeed, future humans, as Hansen's status as a plaintiff is both on behalf of his granddaughter and as guardian for future generations).[16] For Gore, Hansen, and others, 'we' have a parental duty to not just one generation but to countless many.

The affective appeal of parenthood gives a seeming common sense to environmentalist attitudes to posterity; hence the rhetorical certitude of Gore's closing remarks, Hansen's concerns, and Padel's pathos. But, as I hope to show in this book, the use of posterity as environmentalist rationale is not without its logical inconsistencies and ethical conundrums. The elision of non-human environment with human posterity is not something to be done lightly. For one thing, there are conflicting needs at stake: not just between the non-human biosphere at large (if such a thing can indeed be imagined) and the human species in its entirety, but among diverse non-human and human populations of the world. For another, even if these differences were somehow magically accounted for, there exists considerable difficulty in apprehending and measuring our obligations to fellow humans into the distant future, not to mention balancing present needs against these. The framing of posterity as parenthood – not just the expression of environmental obligations as a matter of posterity but the alignment of these with the language and norms associated with parenthood – is both an ethical response to these complexities and

---

[14] *An Inconvenient Truth*, dir. David Guggenheim, perf. Al Gore (Lawrence Bender Productions, 2006).

[15] James Hansen, *Storms of My Grandchildren: The Truth about the Coming Climate Catastrophe and Our Last Chance to Save Humanity* (London: Bloomsbury, 2009), p. xii.

[16] 'Landmark U.S. Federal Climate Lawsuit', Our Children's Trust. www.ourchildrenstrust.org/us/federal-lawsuit

a rhetorical overlay that glosses over their difficulty. That is, this rhetoric and the ethics that underpin it place the seemingly irresolvable questions around the environment and the future, and the anxieties that ensue from these, within the comforting frame of affection, love, and responsibility, distilling them down to the ostensibly universal concerns of parenthood. They attempt to transform, in other words, the unknowable into the knowable.

In spite – or perhaps because – of this, the parentally charged rhetoric and ethics of posterity are vulnerable to critique for their shortcomings and shortcuts. And, thus, even as it affords expressive space to parental accounts of posterity, the creative and cultural discourse around climate change (art, literature, film, and so on) is also the place where these might be open to critique. Probably one of the most prominent strands of such discourse is now being called climate change fiction, the novel being, even in an age of visual and digital media, an enduringly popular art form. In novels that deal with climate change, there are certainly instances in which representations of parental care are employed for their psychological purchase on the reader. At the same time, however, rather than celebrating such a position, many novels reveal this rhetorical manoeuvre to be based on a problematic ideal, riddled with ethical inconsistencies and bearing the burden, unsuccessfully, of collective climate change anxiety. That is, such fiction does not simply use the child as a convenient signifier for the future; it just as often actively interrogates this symbolic use of the child and the norms it calls forth, particularly scrutinising the narrowness of these expectations and showing them to be predicated on anthropocentric and politically conservative stereotypes to do with gender, sexual orientation, race, and economic privilege.

Thus, while the rise of 'posterity-as-parenthood' rhetoric is the premise – and, indeed, spur – for this book, its main argument is that contemporary climate change fiction does not necessarily reproduce this rhetoric unquestioningly, nor does it utilise it merely to assuage climate change anxiety (though, importantly, it does this to some extent). Rather, a striking number of climate change novels take the opportunity to query the adequacy of the parental response to a climate-changed world and, in some instances, replace this with radical versions of posterity that might be fitter for purpose in such a world. For climate change and other manifestations of this epoch have engendered something like a loss of innocence towards notions of selfhood, identity, care, and sympathy. But the critical knowledge that climate change has disclosed – the disruption it brings to humans' place in the world – is knowledge that is not confined to academic critique and philosophical esotericism. This new knowledge is discernible in the conversations, representations, and entertainments to be found in that relatively vernacular form of art, the climate change novel. I therefore suggest that it pays to scrutinise such fiction for the insights it yields. What this book seeks to achieve, then, is a critical consideration of the climate change novel and the self-reflective light that it sheds in the shadow of the Anthropocene.

# CHAPTER I

# The Ethics of Posterity and the Climate Change Novel

A study of the climate change novel and its response to environmentalist idealisations of posterity and parenthood – or, more accurately, idealisations of posterity *as* parenthood – requires an initial analysis of the intricate links that connect ethics, literature, and environmental crisis. This involves, first, an overview of intergenerational issues in environmental ethics, and, then, a comparison of these conventional ethical accounts of posterity-as-parenthood with more radical conceptualisations of posterity, with an eye to whether conventional intergenerational ethics and their vision of posterity are now adequate to the demands of this epoch of anthropogenic, global, environmental depredation we have taken to calling the Anthropocene. And, finally, it necessitates a discussion of the ethical role of literature, framed also within the terms of the Anthropocene.

I therefore begin with a section on how twentieth-century environmental ethics has treated of intergenerational obligations. The next section sketches out directions for a more radical posterity than the parenthood rhetoric on offer in contemporary discourse. Approaching the Anthropocene as both the setting for a rhetorical upturn in parental framings of posterity and the reason that they bear scrutiny, a third section turns to the Anthropocene's effects on our understandings of time and posterity, as well as to the challenge this mounts to art, literary or otherwise; this includes a brief delineation of the literary category of climate change fiction. Because this book is chiefly concerned with the ways in which climate change fiction reassesses parental care as an ethical position, a fourth section explores the relationship between literature (here, specifically, the novel), ethics, and emotion. In this fourth and final section, I also set out a mode of reading the climate change novel that allows us to understand its potential both as an intervention into the rhetoric and ethics of posterity-as-parenthood and as a resource for alternative understandings of posterity.

## Posterity-as-Parenthood: Debates and Dilemmas in Environmental Ethics

Though it seems a rough and ready response to the Anthropocene, the idea of parental care as an environmentalist position properly emerges out of ethical debate and discussion in the twentieth century. Questions of posterity are implicit in early statements of environmental ethics as well as in the discourses of environmental awareness and activism that occur more or less in tandem with the rise of environmental ethics in the mid-twentieth century. As I have already indicated, the alignment of present humans' obligations not to damage ecosystems and the species that live in them with a set of moral obligations towards future humans is a powerful idea; yet, it introduces a range of ethical conundrums. One might argue that all philosophy – moral philosophy included – deals in the arcane; nonetheless, to introduce posterity to environmental ethics is to raise questions of moral need and rights particularly premised on the virtually unknowable: far-distant future humans, diverse and innumerable non-human species and complex ecosystems, and the balance to be struck not just among these but with human moral agents in the present.

In what follows, I briefly chronicle the development of posterity positions in environmental ethics, paying particular attention to their success or failure in meeting the challenge of establishing the moral status of the unknown and unknowable, future human and non-human others, and in proposing a rationale for ethical action towards them. In doing so, I retell a particular history of a gap in intergenerational and environmental ethics in order to show how the imagery of parenthood emerged as an apparent solution and rationale for action. I then interrogate parental care ethics, before considering more radical possibilities for a future-oriented ethics.

### Intergenerational Ethics

The legacy of environmental damage is a key concern of environmentalist activism from its beginnings in the mid-twentieth century; in the tradition of American environmentalism, for example, it underpins such pioneering works as Rachel Carson's *Silent Spring* (1962) and *The Limits to Growth* (1972) commissioned by the Club of Rome.[1] Broadly speaking, mid-twentieth-century environmental discourse introduced an alternative

---

[1] Rachel Carson, *Silent Spring* (first published 1962; London: Penguin, 2000); Donella H. Meadows, Dennis L. Meadows, Jorgen Randers, and William W. Behrens, *The Limits to Growth: A Report on the Club of Rome's Project for the Predicament of Mankind* (New York: Universe Books, 1972).

view of posterity to the prevailing view of progress. The dominant idea of a future of humans' ever-increasing material comfort and wealth drawn from unchecked economic growth and technological improvement was confronted with two truisms: first, that such so-called progress would end in disaster for human and non-human species alike and, second, that changing course – ethically, culturally, and politically speaking – would secure an alternative future for humans and non-humans. Such a reframing of posterity is latent in Carson's ironic reference to our 'obligation to endure', which may seem to describe the conventional path to progress but turns out to signal our moral duty to ensure the preservation of the biosphere.[2] One could characterise environmentalist calls to action in the mid-twentieth century as a rallying cry to revolutionise humans' beliefs and behaviours in the present in order to ensure the well-being of humans and non-humans in the future.

Perhaps by little coincidence, the 1960s and 1970s also saw the emergence in the West of the serious philosophical study of posterity that is now called intergenerational justice or ethics.[3] This is not to say that references to posterity in Western philosophy did not exist before this: among others, David Hume and Henry Sidgwick speculated on the possibility of expanding considerations of rights and utility – that is, usefulness, value, or even happiness – to those not yet born; further, as I will show later in this chapter, there exists a very different, but no less important, set of ideas concerning posterity in the work of Hannah Arendt.[4] Overall, however, the innovation of intergenerational ethics in the mid-twentieth century was to grant to the concerns of future generations their place in a branch of moral philosophy. It subjected to formal scrutiny the implications of endowing future humans with moral standing or, in Kenneth Goodpaster's phrase, 'moral considerability'.[5]

---

[2] Carson, *Silent Spring*, p. 30.

[3] Although I use the words justice and ethics interchangeably here, I do note that ethical questions specifically concerned with justice represent a subset of the larger field of ethics or moral philosophy; ethics deals with right or wrong conduct, and justice with the rights of the agents and patients of such conduct. As Claire Andre and Manuel Velasquez point out, 'Justice is not the same as moral or ethical behaviour, though, of course, it is a central part of it'; see 'Justice and Fairness', *Issues in Ethics* 3.2 (1990), https://legacy.scu.edu/ethics/publications/iie/v3n2.

[4] David Hume, *An Enquiry Concerning Human Understanding*, ed. Stephen Buckle (first published 1748; Cambridge University Press, 2007); Henry Sidgwick, *Practical Ethics: A Collection of Addresses and Essays* (first published 1898; Oxford University Press, 1998); Hannah Arendt, *Between Past and Future: Eight Exercises in Political Thought* (first published 1954; Harmondsworth: Penguin, 1977).

[5] Kenneth E. Goodpaster, 'On Being Morally Considerable', *Journal of Philosophy* 75 (1978), 308–25.

The first thoroughgoing theory of intergenerational ethics was set out by John Rawls in his 1970 *Theory of Justice*.[6] Rawls's theory explicitly counters the emphasis on meeting only the needs and wishes of the present that is found, for example, in the narrative of progress. Specifically, Rawls – drawing in part on Hume – revises the dominant philosophical and economic view that is utilitarianism, whose primary measure in ethical decision-making is how much utility an individual derives from a decision or action and whose logic of the 'social discount rate' assumes that the more immediate the consumption of goods or the effect of the decision, the greater the utility.[7] Rawls argues that no treatment of justice could be complete without accounting for justice to future generations (although he notes that 'the question of justice between generations . . . subjects any ethical theory to severe if not impossible tests').[8] Rawls proposes a set of principles for just social and political decision-making: first, that all members of society should have equal and basic liberties; second, that there should be equality of opportunity, with the specific notation that any inequalities of wealth should give greatest advantage to those who are least advantaged. Importantly, Rawls insists that this last point – the 'difference principle' – applies across generations; it involves 'the long-term prospects of the least favored extending over future generations'.[9] This leads to the 'just savings principle', whereby the present generation saves enough for future generations to live within institutions that make the fundamental principles of justice possible.[10] That is, Rawls assumes a contractualist rather than utilitarian position, in which 'each generation receives its due from its predecessors and does its fair share for those to come'.[11]

Rawls's framework is notable not only for what it includes (the considerability of the future) but for what it leaves out (the question of what would motivate this consideration and the significant action or change in behaviour it requires). Rawls's theory is not an ethical framework per se since it refuses to offer any rationale for why we should provide for, or are even obligated to, those in the future; in David Heyd's critique, Rawls's theory is 'not a principle *of* justice but only a statement about the *value* of

---

[6] John Rawls, *A Theory of Justice* (Cambridge, MA: Harvard University Press, 1971).

[7] Robert Proctor, *Value-Free Science? Purity and Power in Modern Knowledge* (Cambridge, MA: Harvard University Press, 1991), pp. 184–90.

[8] Rawls, *Theory of Justice*, p. 251.      [9] Ibid., p. 252.

[10] Ibid., p. 252; see also Rawls, *Justice as Fairness: A Restatement* (Cambridge, MA: Harvard University Press, 2001), p. 189.

[11] Rawls, *Theory of Justice*, p. 254.

justice and the duty to maintain or promote it'.[12] Rawls's principles emerge from a hypothetical 'original position', a scenario in which 'rational men' – the 'parties' – decide on these principles from behind a 'veil of ignorance', unaware of the class, social status, and abilities of the others, using 'fair agreement or bargain'.[13] Because this original position of anonymity cannot adequately explain any future-oriented motivation (the parties are ignorant of how much, if at all, past generations have saved for them, and thus are not necessarily motivated to save at all for future generations), Rawls posits a 'motivational assumption': he assumes that the parties are also heads of 'family lines', who would therefore 'care at least about their more immediate descendants'.[14] Notably, in later work, Rawls retracted the motivational assumption and did not speculate further on it, identifying such questions as belonging to the realm of 'non-ideal theory', which deals with existing conditions, and clarifying that his 'ideal' theory of justice was concerned with ideal states.[15]

It is worth briefly comparing Rawls's position to that in *Our Common Future*, the 1987 report of the United Nations World Commission on the Environment and Development led by Gro Harlem Brundtland. While not a formal theory of justice or ethics, the report offers an important perspective on intergenerational ethics from the point of view of environmental thinking. This is encapsulated in its now-famous definition of sustainable development: 'development that meets the needs of the present without compromising the ability of future generations to meet their own needs'.[16] To some extent, this statement resembles Rawls's principle of just savings for future generations (though Brundtland gives what some have identified as a 'sufficientarian' – rather than Rawls's egalitarian – account of intergenerational justice).[17] Like Rawls, however, Brundtland does not provide a new moral rationale for behavioural change or action on behalf of future generations. Despite their implicit critique of simple utilitarian assumptions such as the social discount rate, the version of the future

---

[12] David Heyd, 'A Value or an Obligation? Rawls on Justice to Future Generations', in Axel Gosseries and Lukas H. Meyer (eds.), *Intergenerational Justice* (Oxford University Press, 2012), p.172.

[13] Rawls, *Theory of Justice*, p. 11.     [14] Rawls, *Theory of Justice*, p. 255.

[15] Rawls, *Political Liberalism* (New York: Columbia University Press, 1993), p. 274.

[16] World Commission on Environment and Development, *Our Common Future* (Oxford University Press, 1987), p. 43.

[17] As Nicholas Vrousalis points out, the sufficientarian position is that 'justice is not equality. All that matters is that *every generation has enough*'; Vrousalis, 'Intergenerational Justice: A Primer', in Iñigo González-Ricoy and Axel Gosseries (eds.), *Institutions for Future Generations* (Oxford University Press, 2016), p. 53, original emphasis; see also Gosseries, 'The Egalitarian Case against Brundtland's Sustainability', *GAIA*, 14.1 (2005), 40–6.

envisioned by Rawls and Brundtland is akin to that captured by the myth of progress. Rawls assumes that future benefits are ensured through capital accumulation and the preservation of culture and technology, while Brundtland expresses the hope 'that people can cooperate to build a future that is more prosperous, more just, and more secure; that a new era of economic growth can be attained, one based on policies that sustain and expand the Earth's resource base; and that the progress that some have known over the last century can be experienced by all in the years ahead'.[18] That is, both are invested in a relatively conservative account of the future in terms of economic growth.

In a 1995 response to Rawls's theory of intergenerational justice, Avner de-Shalit explicitly sets out a different kind of motivation for the future, one that begins with a shift in dominant ideologies and behaviours.[19] De-Shalit opens with the argument that 'in our context the moral dilemmas derive from the very fact that the harm caused to future persons is the by-product of a genuine, albeit sometimes mistaken, desire to improve (in terms of a certain ideology) the standard of living of contemporaries'.[20] De-Shalit argues that we should, instead, consider ourselves part of 'a transgenerational community'.[21] This concept rests on a notion of community as defined by both 'cultural interaction' and 'moral similarity', that is, by the sharing of customs, codes of communication, values, and experiences.[22] Importantly, the basis for such a community is a common outlook that shapes and is shaped by debate: 'In every genuine community some values and some attitudes towards moral and political questions are common to most people and serve as a background or as a framework when the members engage in discourse on their political and social life. These values and attitudes are, in fact, spectacles through which a member looks at the world around her. Each member of the community shares these values, ideas, and norms with the other members.'[23] When this sense of community is expanded to include unborn generations, it seems that we are motivated by something like 'moral sympathy' with those in the future (a term that de-Shalit appears to use, with echoes of Adam Smith, to suggest sympathy as an emotional response necessarily supplemented by a rational response).[24] Thus, moral sympathy and shared moral values

---

[18] World Commission on Environment and Development, *Our Common Future*, p. 28.
[19] Avner de-Shalit, *Why Posterity Matters: Environmental Policies and Future Generations* (London: Routledge, 1995).
[20] Ibid., p. 6.   [21] Ibid., p. 13.   [22] Ibid., pp. 21–31.   [23] Ibid., p. 28.
[24] Ibid., p. 52; for more on Smith and moral sympathy, see Robert C. Solomon, *In Defense of Sentimentality* (Oxford University Press, 2004), p. 31.

mutually reinforce each other: because we share values, we sympathise; because we sympathise, we pass down values to be shared.

Promising as it is, de-Shalit's theory falters when applied to humans distant in time and thus in conditions virtually unknowable and unimaginable to those in the present. After all, de-Shalit confines his model to a given community: his transgenerational community seems to refer to generations of societies already defined in the present by shared cultural and moral ties; hence, this is no all-encompassing vision of a single assembly of humanity. Moreover, and related to this, the transgenerational community is likely to diminish over time. De-Shalit is at pains to point out that the communitarian motivations of moral sympathy and the sharing of values do not extend to the remote future: as 'communities and traditional values fade away over time', our 'obligations to remote future generations fade away, although not all our obligations to them completely vanish'.[25] Future generations remote in time are subject to issues of 'humanity' rather than of 'justice', that is, to abstract questions of why we should prevent the suffering of fellow humans rather than to more definite motivations of sympathy; of such abstract questions de-Shalit declines to partake.[26]

Why should we be prompted to act on behalf of those in the distant future, whom we do not know? Rawls's contractualism and Brundtland's sufficientarianism suggest that we owe future humans a just or 'decent life', but only as part of an enlightened expansion of our current commitment to economic progress; yet, this hardly seems a robust response when ways of life in the present might need to be radically transformed to allow such an obligation to be met.[27] De-Shalit's communitarian framework, meanwhile, is, in the context of the Anthropocene, a relatively short-term view of intergenerational obligation. In the face of such a question, the framing of posterity in terms of parenthood seems a promising alternative. It answers the question by analogy: future humans resemble our children, and we should be motivated by something like a parental duty of care to them. Indeed, Rawls's brief mention of 'family' and 'care' gestures at kinship as a motivation and model for intergenerational obligation and demonstrates its appeal as a possible rationale, though he does not develop

---

[25] De-Shalit, *Why Posterity Matters*, p. 54.

[26] Ibid., p. 63; for the distinction between humanity and justice, made in the context of contemporary global society, see Brian Barry, 'Humanity and Justice in Global Perspective', in J. Roland Pennock and John W. Chapman (eds.), *Ethics, Economics, and the Law* (New York University Press, 1982), pp. 219–52.

[27] World Commission on Environment and Development, *Our Common Future*, p. 41.

this. Moreover, the political efficacy of couching posterity in the rhetoric of parenthood should not be underestimated (a potential already suggested by the early successes of the *Juliana* v. *United States* suit, which was first filed in 2015 and is being heard through 2016 and 2017, as I write).[28] Nonetheless, it is a position that is not without its inconsistences as a rationale for ethical behaviour.

## Parental Care Ethics

A recent attempt to introduce parenthood models to intergenerational and environmental ethics demonstrates, by way of case study, both how parenthood comes to be supplied as a moral solution to environmental crisis and the risks that attend such an ethical intervention. In a 2014 study, Christopher Groves sets out a normative ethical basis for fulfilling our obligations to future generations, an ethics he explicitly relates to the far-reaching effects of climate change.[29]

At the outset, Groves establishes his ethics as a way of dealing with the future's unknowability, a condition he labels 'reflexive uncertainty'.[30] Though Groves never properly defines this term, he makes clear that it is indebted to Arendt's insights into humans' imperfect knowledge of the future as a fundamental aspect of the human condition. Specifically, Groves echoes Arendt's observation that the world in which we act is conditioned by us as much as it conditions us: 'In addition to the conditions under which life is given to man on earth, and partly out of them, men constantly create their own, self-made conditions, which, their human origin and variability notwithstanding, possess the same conditioning power as natural thing.'[31] Groves paraphrases Arendt's stance thus: 'what human beings create through subjective effort takes on an objective form that then conditions their own existence and that of contemporaries and successors in unforeseen ways'.[32] He therefore interprets Arendt's analysis to mean that our actions produce uncertainty, in that they have unpredictable consequences, and this uncertainty cannot help but condition our existence; he argues that this is exacerbated in a technological

[28] 'Landmark U.S. Federal Climate Lawsuit', Our Children's Trust. www.ourchildrenstrust.org/us/federal-lawsuit

[29] Christopher Groves, *Care, Uncertainty, and Intergenerational Ethics* (Basingstoke: Palgrave–Macmillan, 2014).

[30] Ibid., p. 15.

[31] Hannah Arendt, *The Human Condition*, 2nd edn. (first published 1958; Chicago University Press, 1998), p. 9.

[32] Groves, *Care, Uncertainty, and Intergenerational Ethics*, p. 16.

society and it finds ironic expression in the environmental declension that is the Anthropocene. His ethics aims to provide a rationale for our obligations to the future while accepting that we cannot know it – that, indeed, our actions cause its unknowability. Thus, Groves critiques existing accounts of intergenerational ethics for disregarding the condition of reflexive uncertainty, challenging Rawls's theory, for example, for viewing future needs and wants through the prism of present needs and wants; according to Groves, such approaches simply ignore the profound unknowability attached to the future.[33] In their stead, Groves offers an intergenerational ethics of care. Groves argues that care provides a robust ethical motivation for our obligations to unknown and unborn others, where, in contrast, de-Shalit explicitly rules out emotional response as a basis for ethical action towards future generations because he sees it as relevant to intimate rather than intergenerational relationships.[34]

Of course, care ethics is not in itself an original proposition, having first emerged in the 1980s and since become an increasingly accepted alternative to utilitarian thinking, justice perspectives, and Kantian ethics; thus, it is worth briefly outlining it here.[35] Care was initially posited as the basis for an alternative female perspective and principle of conduct by Carol Gilligan in *In a Different Voice* (1982), a psychological study of cognitive development that showed that women conceptualise morality as care rather than fairness, and that women's moral development is built on 'responsibility and relationships' rather than an 'understanding of rights and rules'.[36] In 1984, Nel Noddings's normative ethics of care developed Gilligan's identification of care and relationality into distinct components of moral understanding that are 'characteristically and essentially feminine'.[37] For Noddings, 'an ethic of caring arises out of our experience as women, just as the traditional logical approach to ethical problems arises more obviously from masculine experience'.[38] Noddings explicitly theorises care as based on emotion rather than on reason, finding that it

---

[33] For Groves, one 'problem with these responses is the strains that are evident between their claims to universal applicability, and the suspicion of historical and cultural particularity that attaches to the list of needs and goods they provide'; *Care, Uncertainty, and Intergenerational Ethics*, p. 47.

[34] De-Shalit, *Why Posterity Matters*, pp. 31–4.

[35] Virginia Held, *The Ethics of Care: Personal, Political, and Global* (Oxford University Press, 2005), p. 9.

[36] Carol Gilligan, *In a Different Voice: Psychological Theory and Women's Development* (Cambridge, MA: Harvard University Press, 1982), p. 19.

[37] Nel Noddings, *Caring: A Relational Approach to Ethics and Moral Education*, updated edn. (first published 1984; Berkeley: University of California Press, 2013), p. 29; the updated edition includes a revision of the original title, *Caring: A Feminine Approach to Ethics and Moral Education*.

[38] Ibid., p. 29.

originates in the 'initial, enabling, sentiment' of 'natural caring', a sentiment that in its turn arises from the experience of caring and the memory
of being cared for.[39] Noddings counters too the concern with reciprocity
that characterises justice perspectives such as Rawls's contractualist position. So disdainful is she of theories grounded in reciprocity and reason
that she rejects the notion of empathy in favour of the concept of 'engrossment', that is, a kind of holistic reception of the other's needs and wants.[40]
Empathy signals a 'peculiarly rational, western, masculine way of looking
at "feeling with"', privileging 'projection' over 'reception'; whereas, in the
act of engrossment or caring, 'I do not project; I receive the other into
myself, and I see and feel with the other.'[41]

Though Groves invokes several care ethicists, his ethics of care is
identifiable primarily as an ungendered version of Noddings's model,
inflected by phenomenological understandings of selfhood; Arendt's
thinking on posterity provides a motivation for, but barely informs,
this ethical position. Groves's argument is not that we should care
despite the future's unknowability; it is that we care because of it – or,
more precisely – as a way of making sense of it. Focusing on the way
in which relationships with 'objects of care' impact on the 'conative
self', Groves argues that we are motivated to care because care is of
direct benefit to the self, possessing 'constitutive value' to the individual.[42] Here, one should note, Groves is indebted not just to the
attachment theories of object-relations psychoanalysts such as Donald
Winnicott but to environmental philosopher John O'Neill's argument
that 'the flourishing of many other living things ought to be promoted
because they are constitutive of our own flourishing' (O'Neill's premise is itself drawn from Aristotle's locating of *eudaimonia*, or human
well-being, in the act of 'living or faring well').[43] For Groves,
'Relationships with constitutive values *hold* … the self together.'[44]
Care, it would seem, holds together both moral agent (or what
Noddings calls the 'one-caring') and moral patient (the 'cared-for')
in the face of reflexive uncertainty, for Groves finds both that care is 'a
way of rendering an uncertain future liveable in the present … for the
subject' and that it creates a 'secure space' for the cared-for to 'clarify

[39] Ibid., p. 95.    [40] Ibid., p. 49.    [41] Ibid., p. 49.
[42] Groves, *Care, Uncertainty, and Intergenerational Ethics*, pp. 102, 139.
[43] John O'Neill, *Ecology, Policy and Politics: Human Well-Being and the Natural World* (London:
Routledge, 1993), p. 24; Aristotle, *The Nicomachean Ethics*, trans. David Ross, rev. J. L. Ackrill and J.
O. Urmson (Oxford University Press, 1980), I.8, 1098b5-28.
[44] Groves, *Care, Uncertainty, and Intergenerational Ethics*, p. 143; original emphasis.

what he or she can do in the world, and thus who s/he is, in the face of an uncertain future'.[45]

In expanding the private and direct mode of care into a rationale for political and indirect care for the future, Groves's argument does not rely on a simple alignment of prospective generations with children, but emphasises nonetheless the importance of immediate attachments and explicitly models these attachments on parental ones, pointing out that care must 'be directed towards a particular kind of object' – most often in his analysis, this is the child.[46] According to Groves, because we are motivated to care for immediate attachments, we care about the practices, traditions, and material circumstances that support them. The secure space, as it were, is thus expanded. Then, because our acts of caring for this enlarged secure space become institutionalised and capable of extending through time, care is applied to unborn others. As Groves states, somewhat gnomically, 'we are enjoined, by the activity of caring, to expand our concern towards the wider social and biophysical worlds, and to extend it in time in the attempt to become more adequate to the timescapes of the objects of our direct and indirect care'.[47] In other words, this is not about framing a moral obligation to those in the future whom we do not know; it is about the achievement of a positive outcome for them, almost incidentally. We care about those in the present whom we do know; those acts of caring become part of an infrastructure of caring, which in turn is of benefit to those in the future. Groves's account, then, is a vicarious version of the posterity-as-parenthood analogy: though he does not place future generations in the guises of our children, Groves nevertheless aligns these with each other indirectly when he aligns acts of immediate parental care with institutionalised practices of care.

Groves's model demonstrates the challenges that ethical models of care face in dealing with our obligations to an uncertain future, challenges it meets with varying success. A consideration of these helps to delineate the shortcomings of parental care ethics more generally. First, such arguments tend to ignore how parental care is not automatically a positive disposition and act, and is not always productive of certainty, security, and good for the cared-for. Private conduct does not translate so easily to the public realm, and care relationships are imbricated with, even inseparable from, less-than-ideal emotional and psychological states and acts. Indeed, parental care is often also a relationship of power. Even Groves acknowledges

---

[45] Noddings, *Caring*, p. 24; Groves, *Care, Uncertainty, and Intergenerational Ethics*, pp. 112–13, 125.
[46] Groves, *Care, Uncertainty, and Intergenerational Ethics*, p. 128.   [47] Ibid., p. 182.

briefly in his analysis that 'caring and being cared for can lead to power-lessness and an erosion of agency in particular circumstances (and as part of some attachment styles)', though he does little with this particular pro-blem.[48] As Joan Tronto notes in her detailed consideration of the risks attendant in any reckless scaling up of the private activities of care, the 'two primary dangers of care as a political ideal', which 'arise inherently out of the nature of care itself', are 'paternalism or maternalism, and parochial-ism'.[49] Of paternalism or maternalism, Tronto notes that 'care-givers may well come to see themselves as more capable of assessing the needs of care-receivers than are the care-receivers themselves', and, of parochialism, she warns that those who are 'enmeshed in ongoing, continuing, relationships of care are likely to see the caring relationships that they are engaged in, and which they know best, as the most important'.[50] Neither position, states Tronto, is productive of democratic political or ethical action: the first risks developing 'relationships of profound inequality' and the second produces the assumption 'that everyone should cultivate one's own garden, and let others take care of themselves, too'.[51] In other words, a private position that depends on authority and familiarity is potentially undemocratic and even unethical when it becomes a model for public, moral action.

Such paternalism and parochialism are connected to another shortcom-ing of parental care ethics – its distillation of ethical agency to the perspective of the parent or, in other words, its exclusionary identity politics. As Catriona Sandilands notes, 'an obvious result of identity politics is an exclusionary logic – "you can't speak about this because you do not belong to the group"'.[52] When (private) identity is placed at the crux of public action, individuals are collectivised into a broader public identity on the assumption that they share an essential set of experiences and activities, which grant them insight into the material reality of human relations. This, as Sandilands notes, is the power of the standpoint.[53] Much depends on the maintenance of the standpoint through the policing of rhetorical boundaries, in, for example, claims to specialness and even superiority: 'The solidification of identity results in politics of exclusion.'[54] In other words, the idealisation of care very easily becomes the

---

[48] Ibid., p. 117.

[49] Joan C. Tronto, *Moral Boundaries: A Political Argument for an Ethic of Care* (New York: Routledge, 1993), p. 170.

[50] Ibid., p. 170.     [51] Ibid., pp. 170–1.

[52] Catriona Sandilands, *The Good-Natured Feminist: Ecofeminism and the Quest for Democracy* (Minneapolis: University of Minnesota Press, 1999), p. 5.

[53] Ibid., pp. 38–41.     [54] Ibid., p. 47.

exceptionalism of care and of those who are seen to care, such as women, mothers, or parents.

Moreover, the identities that inform parental care ethics tend to reify certain cultural norms, and a politicisation of care is in danger of either replicating or ignoring the damaging biases that attend care as a private disposition. Early iterations of care ethics, such as Noddings's, depend on an association of women with motherhood as a prerequisite for ethical action: this both relegates moral responsibility to women and reduces women's agency to a stereotypical image of domesticity and maternity. Chris Cuomo reminds us that such values jeopardise the political potential of care, for these norms carry with them the history of women's – and carers' – disempowerment, one that is not to be so simply set aside or transformed into a collective political power and agency: 'Individuals who have been socialized or constructed, to their moral detriment, to behave or to *be* in certain ways, cannot easily, individually transform the social meanings and roles propagated by that being. The significance of values such as caring, mothering, and non-violence is embedded in their current meanings, as well as in the genealogy of their meanings.'[55] Many of the dispositional aspects of care that are so celebrated for their ethical promise, such as 'ego denial', are also idealised characteristics that have informed historical patterns of women's oppression.[56] In Sandilands's description of 'motherhood environmentalism', such a construction of ethical agency emerges from, and in turn shores up, conservative norms in the political and cultural sphere.[57] Writes Sandilands of motherhood environmentalism, the 'neoconservative aroma of this discourse should be quite noticeable: a return to patriarchal and heterosexual "family values" will restore not only a healthy (natural) family but a healthy (natural) planet. ... It is a naturalized morality tale of private women embodying particularistic, nuclear-family-oriented, antifeminist, heterosexist, and ultimately apolitical interests.'[58]

Certainly, one should not be too comforted by the seemingly 'gender-neutral' parenthood of more recent expressions of parental care ethics, such as Groves's moral framework, whose apparent universality potentially elides not just the problematic legacy of gender norms in care ethics but assumptions to do with sexuality, race, and

---

[55] Chris J. Cuomo, *Feminism and Ecological Communities: An Ethics of Flourishing* (London: Routledge, 1998), p. 130.
[56] Cuomo, *Feminism and Ecological Communities*, p. 129.
[57] Sandilands, *Good-Natured Feminist*, p. xiii.  [58] Ibid., p. xiii.

class. As Nicole Seymour notes of such 'sentimentalized rhetoric' as parental ethics, it 'suggests that concern for the future qua the planet *can only emerge*, or *emerges most effectively*, from white, heterosexual, familial reproductivity'.[59] In this, Lee Edelman's critique of what he terms 'reproductive futurism' and its attendant phenomenon of 'pronatalism' – the equation of the future with posterity and the emphasis on parenthood that accompanies it – is highly relevant.[60] For Edelman, the figure of the child is 'the perpetual horizon of every acknowledged politics, the fantasmatic beneficiary of every political intervention'.[61] As Edelman argues, the child is the tool of a heteronormative hegemony, which he reads in Lacanian terms as exploiting our universal desire for Imaginary wholeness, an impulse towards teleology that is easily fooled by invocations of a never-achievable future. The child (and the political model it invokes) beguiles the subject (here, Edelman focuses on the queer subject) into both assuming a parental posture that is inherently heterosexist and investing in a political hegemony that serves higher socioeconomic and political interests. The secure space imagined by parental care ethics such as Groves's is a domestic interior based on far from universal expectations around nuclear family units, material comfort, and class privilege.

Thus, parental care ethics as a moral outlook for the future, with its idealisation of care as an ethical disposition and its problematic identity biases, lays itself open to critique on several counts. Among other things, the exclusionary tendencies of identity politics and the parochialism and paternalism that undermine positions of care have the potential to lead to a narrow concept of posterity as genetic survivalism, that is, the privileging of one's own legacy over others'. Moreover, motherhood environmentalism results in a reductive and nostalgic conceptualisation of ethical agency to the future as one of procreation and parenting, one that comes into direct conflict with some of that future's starker realities, such as resource scarcity and human overpopulation. Such a critique, as I shall show in chapter 2 and chapter 3, is mounted in a number of climate change novels.

---

[59] Nicole Seymour, *Strange Natures: Futurity, Empathy, and the Queer Ecological Imagination* (Urbana: University of Illinois Press, 2013), p. 7; original emphasis.
[60] Lee Edelman, *No Future: Queer Theory and the Death Drive* (Durham, NC: Duke University Press, 2004), pp. 2, 17.
[61] Ibid., p. 3.

## Radical Posterity

These problems in parental care ethics – its idealisation of care as an ethical disposition and its problematic identity biases – are part of its wider (mis) conceptualisation of moral agency and identity as fixed and as focused on human wants and concerns. Alternative, radical conceptions of posterity, then, often rest on reconfigurations of both the profoundly identity-oriented, or identitarian, logic and anthropocentricism that tend to inform ethics of parental care, reconfigurations that I outline here.

### *Non-Identitarian Possibilities*

To begin with, the ethics of parental care is predicated on an identitarian view of ethical agents and patients. Interestingly, what Groves misses in his invocation of Arendt is the emphasis in much of her writings on the instability of identity, and the arena of social and political interaction as the space in which identity is made and remade. Yet, the construction of moral agents and patients as ontologically stable, identifiable, and knowable beings problematises rather than clarifies any ethical basis to our responsibilities to the future (though the suggestive imagery of caring and affectionate parenting attempts to reassure us otherwise).

Part of the problem lies in a fundamental misconception of the condition of the moral patients of a future-oriented ethics – that is, future humans – and their identities. This Derek Parfit has labelled 'the non-identity problem'.[62] First, according to Parfit, future individuals cannot be treated in ethical terms as known individuals, since any actions made in the present for future people would likely change the time and manner of their conception and birth and thus their specific identities. To construe them as knowable is to commit an ontological error as well as to be drawn into making inconsistent or morally indefensible statements.[63] Future others are inherently unknowable, not only because we in the present cannot

---

[62] Derek Parfit, *Reasons and Persons* (Oxford University Press, 1986), p. 351.

[63] In Parfit's 'depletion' scenario, for example, those in the present decide to deplete rather than conserve resources, as a consequence of which quality of life in two centuries' time will be much diminished. 'The great lowering of the quality of life must provide some moral reason not to choose Depletion', notes Parfit. At the same time, however, depletion does not necessarily make life *worse* for anyone. The depletion decision causes those specific future people to suffer, but a different decision would change the timing and manner of their conception and thus produce different people. Because Parfit assumes that the existence of those future people is worth having, he is forced to conclude that depletion cannot be said to be 'bad for' anyone at all. There is thus no coherent moral reason not to choose depletion if we define future others in terms of their identity; Parfit, *Reasons and Persons*, p. 363.

travel into the future to know them, but because, as Parfit would have it, by dint of their very futurity, their identities are fluid and are changeable by the actions of those in the present. As Robin Attfield usefully puts Parfit's argument, 'morality is in part impersonal'.[64] Our obligations to the future are to persons not in particular but in the abstract. In other words, the contingency of personal identity necessitates a reframing of the future recipients of ethical action as unknowable entities (both human and non-human) in unknowable circumstances, though no less deserving of attention than the immediate attachments and objects of care. Indeed, it is, perhaps, that very unknowability that should motivate our vigilance, concern, and responsibility.

Like the contingency of the identity of the future moral patient, the ontological fluidity of the moral *agent* also has profound implications for conceptualising ethical behaviour. Here, again, Parfit is relevant. Parfit argues that identity is something of a chimera: what we think of as personal identity consists of 'nothing more than the occurrence of an interrelated series of mental and physical events'.[65] He defines identity as the connectedness and continuity of a person's experience, united by causality; the existence of a person comprises merely these causal experiences, along with his or her brain and body.[66] If identity is simply this, then a single person's identity can become less connected over time (an argument that leads Parfit to some important conclusions about autonomy, responsibility, and justice, including the view that an individual is less responsible for a crime he commits the further away in the past it was committed, as well as the condoning of some paternalistic attitudes to certain individuals, not out of anything so identity-dependent as care but in circumstances where it might lead to the prevention of moral wrongs committed against others).[67]

If one acknowledges, with Parfit, that identity is contingent and unstable, then one must attend to the process by which so-called identity is made and remade if one is to take full account of the nuances of ethical agency. In her analysis of ecofeminism's potential as a democratic project, Sandilands sharply critiques the reliance on essentialist notions of selfhood found in certain versions of ecofeminist theory and politics. The context of her critique is a concern with the fallacy of essentialism that underlies identity politics in general: 'most ecofeminist writing is imbricated in a cultural feminist logic of identity politics in which ontological claims to an

---

[64] Robin Attfield, 'Non-Reciprocal Responsibilities and the Banquet of the Kingdom', *Journal of Global Ethics* 5.1 (2009), 34.
[65] Parfit, *Reasons and Persons*, p. 341.    [66] Ibid., p. 261.    [67] Ibid., pp. 321, 326.

essence ... are understood necessarily to precede political claims'.[68] Thus, Sandilands argues for what she terms a 'radical democratic politics', which would challenge the very case for identity.[69] Her analysis is grounded in a Lacanian understanding of subjectivity and, strikingly, adopts language that recalls Parfit's description of personal identity. Sandilands describes the process of identity-making, contingent as it is, as 'the intervention of a nodal point that collects a certain set of interpreted experiences and produces from them a sense of coherence as if the identity in question emerged from somewhere else', that is, from some wished-for originary point.[70] 'It is not', writes Sandilands, 'that identity doesn't exist, it is that it is an intra-social process that actually masks the impossibility of its completion.'[71] What is crucial about Sandilands's analysis of both political and personal identity is her recognition of the occurrence of a 'nodal point', a nub in a network of memories, experiences, and so on (that is, identity as Parfit would have it) where some of these meet and are interpreted as a coherent sense of self (that is, what we mistake as identity).

One could say that, for Sandilands, because it is fluid, identity is always partial; because it is partial, identity finds its potential in affinity with others. Sandilands's position echoes the cyborg feminism of Donna Haraway (which posits that identity is always hybrid) and aligns with the new materialism of Karen Barad (according to which agency is formed in interaction with others). Haraway's 'cyborg myth is about transgressed boundaries, potent fusions, and dangerous possibilities which progressive people might explore as one part of needed political work'.[72] While the 'recent history for much of the US left and US feminism has been a response to this kind of crisis by endless splitting and searches for a new essential unity', 'there has also been a growing recognition of another response through coalition – affinity, not identity'.[73] Meanwhile, Barad has argued that agency is established in what she names 'intra-action', the process by which objects encounter each other, and which depends on both separability and apprehension of the other.[74] Most importantly for a consideration of ethical conduct, Sandilands's analysis is invested in Arendtian theories of the human condition, particularly Arendt's

---

[68] Sandilands, *Good-Natured Feminist*, p. xix.    [69] Ibid., p. xx.    [70] Ibid., p. 84.
[71] Ibid., p. 84.
[72] Donna J. Haraway, 'A Cyborg Manifesto: Science, Technology, and Socialist-Feminism in the Late Twentieth Century', *Simians, Cyborgs and Women: The Reinvention of Nature* (London: Free Association Books, 1991), p. 154.
[73] Ibid., p. 155.
[74] Karen Barad, 'Posthumanist Performativity: Toward an Understanding of How Matter Comes to Matter', *Signs* 28.2 (2003), 813.

description of this as the *vita activa*, divided into three components: work, labour, and action.[75] It is in the sphere of action, through dialogue with others, that the self is formed, Arendt argues.[76] That is, identity is produced in public and political action and the spaces between political actors. The ethical implications of such an approach are usefully drawn out in recent climate change fiction, as I show in chapter 4.

The implications of a specifically Arendtian conceptualisation of identity and time for a future-oriented ethics are also worth sketching out here. Arendt theorises the modern condition as a time in which the true meaning and moral weight of traditional concepts, such as freedom and authority, have been lost. Unable to understand the lessons of the past but desiring a better future, the modern individual finds himself trapped in a clash between these two forces.[77] Specifically, the present becomes a 'gap between the past and future'; at this point, the 'two antagonistic forces are both unlimited as to their origins, the one coming from an infinite past and the other from an infinite future; but though they have no known beginning, they have a terminal ending, the point at which they clash'.[78] At this meeting point, or 'parallelogram', of conflicting forces labours the human subject.[79] But, of course, a third force exists, for, in Arendt's philosophy, the human in the present has his own capacity for thought and action (a fluid and changeable capacity not to be mistaken for identity per se). This produces another force, coming diagonally at the two antagonistic forces of past and present: 'This diagonal force, whose origin is known, whose direction is determined by past and future, but whose eventual end lies in infinity, is the perfect metaphor for the activity of thought.'[80] Without the activity of thought, the individual risks clashing fruitlessly with the powers of past and future, that is, an incompletely understood history on the one hand and an unknowable posterity on the other. What Arendt proposes is a critical awareness of the provisionality of this position, so that the individual is able to achieve a 'settling down into the gap between the past and future' rather than becoming 'worn out under the pressure of constant fighting'.[81] Some climate change fiction, as I shall suggest in Chapter 4, enables just such a critical acceptance of the imperfectly remembered past along with what one could call the imperfectability of the future; in the process, it asks how such a critical awareness of the

---

[75] Arendt, *The Human Condition*, pp. 7–8.    [76] Ibid., pp. 175–81.
[77] Arendt, *Between Past and Future*, pp. 3–15.    [78] Ibid., p. 12.    [79] Ibid., p. 12.    [80] Ibid., p. 13.
[81] Ibid., p. 13.

irrecoverability of the past might best inform an ethical relationship with posterity.

## *Ecocentric Possibilities*

At the same time, parental care ethics, along with most models of inter-generational ethics, possesses deeply anthropocentric tendencies, constru-ing the future of the biosphere as relevant primarily in relation to human survival and well-being. Even de-Shalit, who locates his proposal in the context of environmental ethics, dismisses 'biocentric' approaches and prefers to place environmental issues 'within the framework of moral relations among human beings . . . as a matter of distribution of access to goods (natural resources, forests, clean air, as well as capital and informa-tion)'.[82] The logic of parental care ethics, with its interest in the welfare of future humans, is predicated on a similarly dismissive approach to the non-human environment. This is unsurprising, given the anthropocentric focus of care ethics more generally: so much does Noddings focus on the kind of relationality and responsiveness found between humans that she contends that it is difficult to imagine the 'cared-for' as a non-human animal, apart from, perhaps, as a household pet.[83] Groves, building on Noddings's model, finds that the non-human is relevant only when it is a direct object of care ('from pet cats and domesticated horses to the common or rare species the attentive botanist or zoologist studies') or when it is considered as part of the support system of the cared-for (since the 'practices, narra-tives, traditions, institutions and infrastructures' he discusses may be 'either human or natural in origin').[84] Groves's ethics is an example of how, even in an environmentally conscious framework, the temptation remains to view the non-human as a service to humans' moral considerability.

The apparent solution is an ecocentric ethics of posterity, that is, the application of moral considerability to the future of ecosystems and their species. Yet, even so, one must beware the trap of identitarianism. Many influential ecocentric ethical attempts have tended to enforce a holistic view that subsumes ecological diversity within the rubric of 'nature'. So Aldo Leopold's land ethic, laid out in his *Sand County Almanac* (1949), proposes that, if ethics depends on the premise that 'the individual is a member of a community of interdependent parts', an environmental ethics

---

[82] De-Shalit, *Why Posterity Matters*, p. 8.    [83] Noddings, *Caring*, pp. 159–69.
[84] Groves, *Care, Uncertainty, and Intergenerational Ethics*, pp. 170–1.

simply expands 'the boundaries of the community to include soils, waters, plants, and animals, or collectively: the land', which deserve to have recognised 'their right to continued existence'.[85] Going further, deep ecology, particularly as defined by Arne Næss, argues not only for a '*relational, total-field image*' of all organisms, but also for their '*equal right to live and blossom*'; paramount to the deep ecology movement is the idea that the 'flourishing of human and non-human life on Earth has intrinsic value'.[86] As laudable as this widening of ethical concern is, Næss and Leopold commit what Attfield identifies as the error of holism common to ecocentric, as opposed to biocentric, approaches (where ecocentric approaches view whole ecosystems as moral objects and biocentric approaches are concerned with the individuals that inhabit those ecosystems).[87] The ecocentric emphasis on ecosystems risks eliding the very different conditions and needs of organisms and species under a convenient marker of identity. These differences represent both important ecological dynamics (relationships of competition, predation, and so on) and potential ethical complexity (the question, for example, of what individuals, populations, or species take priority when not all can be equally benefitted); these differences necessarily pertain to any concern for posterity for all.

The very construction of nature as nature points to a further identitarian error in environmentalist ethics: that of insisting on the existence of the non-human voice. This leads to the 'dilemma', as Sandilands puts it, of discerning 'the authentic "voice" of nature', the problem of providing, assuming, or assigning 'authentic speech for nonspeaking nature'.[88] While both ecocentric and biocentric ethics, and the rhetoric that surrounds them, tend to extol the act of 'hearing' or attending to the 'voice' of nature or of its creatures, they do not always acknowledge that that voice is radically distinct from human language or that it is a mediated composite of many signs at many levels. For Sandilands, this is not just about the problem of human ventriloquising of the non-human, though this is certainly something that is too often ignored: 'Rendering nature knowable involves a process of subjectivation; constructing nature as a subject . . . is

---

[85] Aldo Leopold, *A Sand County Almanac: With Essays on Conservation*, illustrated edn. (first published 1949; Oxford University Press, 2001) p. 171.

[86] Arne Næss, 'The Shallow and the Deep, Long-Range Ecology Movement: A Summary', *Inquiry* 16.1–4 (1973), 95–6, original emphasis; Arne Næss and David Rothenberg, *Ecology, Community, and Lifestyle: Outline of an Ecosophy* (Cambridge University Press, 1989), p. 29.

[87] Robin Attfield, *Environmental Ethics: An Overview for the Twenty-First Century*, 2nd edn. (London: Polity, 2014), pp. 39–40.

[88] Sandilands, *Good-Natured Feminist*, p. 79.

the task of environmentalism.'[89] This is, more importantly, also about how such ventriloquism usually involves translation, a sleight of hand that transforms the inaudible into the (humanly) audible, the unknowable into the (readily) knowable. As Sandilands warns: 'The "I" that speaks in environmentalist discourse . . . is always already something else, subject to a process of translation through other identities, through myriad relationships and interactions, through other forms of language.'[90] The problem, Sandilands suggests, is the fetishisation of authenticity, as though the human medium of voice is the only way in which 'nature' might communicate and count as an ethical other.

This realisation calls for a coming to terms with the difference between human and non-human species, inasmuch as non-human beings possess a radical unknowability that is different from humans' unknowability to each other. Acknowledging this has two crucial effects: it avoids the trap of attempting to speak for and thus, in Sandilands's terms, subjectivating nature, and it does not shirk the responsibility of moral agency possessed by humans rather than non-humans. What this suggests, then, is a posterity ethics that attends not simply to non-human and human species, but to difference in at least two senses – not just ecological diversity (differences within) but the otherness of non-human beings from human beings (difference from). While difference might sound pejorative and exclusionary in an identitarian framework, where knowability and identity are everything, a non-identitarian ecocentric ethics would acknowledge that what we call nature is just as radically contingent as human identity, as well as different from the human, while still locating non-human and human beings within the same ethical universe.

Just such an ethical possibility – an ecocentric rather than anthropocentric account of non-human posterity – emerges in some climate change fiction, as I shall suggest in chapter 5. As I shall also show in that chapter, the ethical model of interspecies affinity and coalition put forward by Cuomo is particularly helpful in analysing such radical ethical solutions for posterity. Cuomo's is an ethics of flourishing, inspired in part by Aristotle's terms of eudaemonia, but differing in crucial ways from it and from other posterity ethics that draw from it, such as Groves's.[91] Cuomo's model keeps in mind the moral considerability of non-human others, while preserving a sense of the important difference between humans and non-

---

[89] Ibid., p. 79.   [90] Ibid., p. 80.
[91] Cuomo, *Feminism and Ecological Communities*, pp. 62–80.

humans, namely the ethical responsibility that humans bear towards non-human organisms and systems.

## Time and Art in the Anthropocene

Although the ethical stance and the rhetorical strategies that foreground our parental duties to posterity may seem a useful response to the Anthropocene, they are, as I have begun to suggest, inadequate to this epoch's demands for radical new understandings of human ontology. Central to interrogations of human ontology in the Anthropocene are questions of scale: spatial and temporal scale. The very concept of the Anthropocene as a *geological* time period is a reminder that human agency has assumed non-human proportions. Climate change and other Anthropocene events make clear that the effect of humans on their environment will far outlast anthropocentric dimensions of individual lifetimes, civilisation expansions and declines, and even historical epochs. Some of the impacts of human activity – for example, species depletion and polar ice melt – are, if not irrevocable, then reversible only over more immense durations of time. Indeed, some effects might take thousands of years just to emerge, this being the case with so-called millennial timescale events such as ocean anoxia, oxygen depletion, and disruptions to thermohaline circulation.

Thus, the mid-twentieth-century environmentalist call for political action and change has become, in the light of the twenty-first century's Anthropocene awareness, not just an ethical but an existential revolution. The past decade or so has seen a tendency in ecocriticism to consider the environmental upheavals of the late-twentieth and twenty-first centuries as a moment of the deconstruction of the human condition generally. What has sometimes been called 'climate criticism' or 'critical climate change' – a term that was first employed by Tom Cohen in founding the Institute of Critical Climate Change, or IC³, at Albany, was subsequently used in Cohen's *Telemorphosis*, and is now identified with Timothy Morton, Timothy Clark, and Claire Colebrook, among others – construes the contemporary environmental crisis as the transformation of once esoteric notions about the contingency of human agency and ontology into something of a lived reality.[92] Alongside this, other ecocritical investigations

---

[92] Tom Cohen, ed., *Telemorphosis: Essays in Critical Climate Change* (Ann Arbor, MI: Open Humanities Press, 2012); see also Timothy Clark, *Ecocriticism on the Edge: The Anthropocene as a Threshold Concept* (London: Bloomsbury, 2015); Tom Cohen, Claire Colebrook, and J. Hillis

have been made into the permeability of human–non-human boundaries and the interconnectedness of human with non-human agency, particularly in the way in which the discursive and material are interlinked (as in the work of Barad and Stacy Alaimo).[93] Increasingly, these varied conceptualisations of contemporary environmental crisis are concerned with how 'the Anthropocene' names a point in history in which the fallacy of human exceptionalism – the assumption that humans are outside and not subject to the laws of 'nature' – has been exposed, even as humans are forced to consider whether that myth might be appropriable into some kind of ethical action. Most recently, the existential force of the problem has been powerfully described by novelist Amitav Ghosh. Writing of the 'deification of the human that gave [Nature] an illusory apartness from ourselves', Ghosh warns: 'Now that nonhuman agencies have dispelled that illusion, we are confronted suddenly with a new task: that of finding other ways in which to imagine the unthinkable beings and events of this era.'[94]

## *Time in the Anthropocene: Posterity*

These enlarged matters of scale and corresponding shifts in conceptualisations of human ontology are, of course, of import to the issue of posterity, for one of the Anthropocene's challenges is its demand that we readjust the dominant logic of the immediate, the individual, and the intimate in order to account for humanity's effect on a vastly distant – and therefore vastly *different* – future. As I have already suggested, one could say that the rhetoric of posterity-as-parenthood is an attempt at such readjustment, but, equally, one must ask just how adequate such a rhetorical move, with its insistence on relationality and identity, is to the task of apprehending the radically unknowable future conjured up by the Anthropocene. Here, two recent and prominent critical considerations of the Anthropocene, both depicting

Miller, *Theory and the Disappearing Future: On De Man, on Benjamin* (New York: Routledge, 2012); Colebrook, *Death of the Posthuman: Essays in Extinction* (Ann Arbor, MI: Open Humanities Press, 2014); and Timothy Morton, *Hyperobjects: Philosophy and Ecology after the End of the World* (Minneapolis: University of Minnesota Press, 2013). See also Adeline Johns-Putra, 'A New Critical Climate', *symplokē* 21.1–2 (2013), 9–12.

[93] Barad, *Meeting the Universe Halfway: Quantum Physics and the Entanglement of Matter and Meaning* (Durham, NC: Duke University Press, 2007); Stacy Alaimo, *Bodily Natures: Science, Environment and the Embodied Self* (Bloomington: Indiana University Press, 2010).

[94] Amitav Ghosh, *The Great Derangement: Climate Change and the Unthinkable* (University of Chicago Press, 2016), p. 33.

its wholesale ontological disruption as a matter of scalar dislocation, are relevant for their reflections on the (im)possibility of knowing the humans and non-humans that inhabit the distant future. In *Hyperobjects* (2013), Morton has dubbed climate change and other markers of the Anthropocene 'hyperobjects', defined as 'things that are massively distributed in time and space relative to humans', whose effects, in terms of their magnitude and human–non-human hybridity, undo any easy division of the world into human subjects and the objects they perceive; this simplistic division is what Morton and others term 'correlationalism'.[95] For Clark, in *Ecocriticism on the Edge* (2015), meanwhile, the Anthropocene results in what he terms 'Anthropocene disorder', in which the placing of thoughts and acts in human-to-human terms, once so relevant, is no longer an adequate way in which to conceptualise and express the human condition.[96] At key points in their analyses of the Anthropocene as a disruption to our senses of space, time, and subjectivity, Morton and Clark turn to the question of our relationship with the future, offering what are, for my purposes, crucially differing responses.

Morton adopts the decision-making language of game theory in order to explain what the Anthropocene's confusion of scale means for posterity. For Morton, posterity in the Anthropocene is best framed as a 'prisoner's dilemma', a hypothetical scenario in which two accomplices are arrested and interrogated individually, with each given the option of confessing and implicating the other.[97] Game theory demonstrates that the pursuit of individual reward encouraged by utilitarianism results in harsher punishment all round, whereas coalition and cooperation enable greater payoffs in the long term; as Morton notes, this insight is given greater clarity and urgency in the Anthropocene.[98] Future

---

[95] Morton, *Hyperobjects*, pp. 1, 9; on correlationism, Morton is citing philosophers of speculative realism, such as Quentin Meillassoux, *After Finitude: An Essay on the Necessity of Contingency*, trans. Ray Brassier (London: Continuum, 2010).

[96] Clark, *Ecocriticism on the Edge*, p. 139.    [97] Morton, *Hyperobjects*, pp. 129–30.

[98] The basic version of the dilemma is a scenario in which two accomplices are arrested and interrogated individually. Each of the prisoners, who cannot communicate with the other, is given the option of defecting, that is, confessing and implicating the other. If the prisoner defects and his accomplice remains silent, the prisoner goes free and the accomplice is sentenced to twenty years; if they both defect, both receive sentences of five years each; and if both remain silent, they are awarded reduced sentences of one year. Over time, if the game is played on both prisoners simultaneously in mutual ignorance, defection results in a slightly higher payoff for the individual; if it is played sequentially, where prisoners are aware of previous behaviour, defection proves also to be the best strategy. However, on an overall basis, and if the number of games is completely randomised, the best outcome for both prisoners is mutual cooperation.

human and non-human beings may be 'strange strangers', a term Morton uses to describe the ultimate unknowability or withdrawnness possessed by all objects (and, most of all, by hyperobjects); yet, Morton insists, present humans must adopt an attitude of sincerity towards strange strangers, because no matter how strange or withdrawn, all objects are sincere inasmuch as they 'are what they are, in the sense that, no matter what we are aware of, or how, there they are, impossible to shake off'.[99] The ethical leap that Morton makes from this is to insist not only that the ideas of cooperation affirmed by the prisoners' dilemma must reach across time, but that we must replace distance with intimacy. According to Morton, the 'future self is ... unimaginably distant in one sense, and yet hyperobjects have brought her into the adjoining prison cell. She is strange yet intimate. The best course of action is to act with regard to her. This radical letting go of what constitutes self has become necessary because of hyperobjects.'[100]

Like Morton, Clark explicitly refers to spatial and temporal dislocation: 'the demand to think of human life at much broader scales of space and time ... alters significantly the way that many once familiar issues appear'.[101] Clark's concept of Anthropocene disorder is specifically what he terms a 'scale effect', emerging from the 'scalar derangement' between everyday human activity and the enormity of its future impact spatially (particularly on the species that inhabit the biosphere) and temporally: 'at a certain, indeterminate threshold, numerous human actions, insignificant in themselves (heating a house, clearing trees, flying between the continents, forest management) come together to form a new, imponderable physical event, altering the basic ecological cycles of the planet'.[102] Also like Morton, Clark has recourse to game-theoretical discussions to demonstrate how the Anthropocene challenges conventional and, particularly, utilitarian responses to the future. He invokes Garrett Hardin's oft-cited parable of the 'tragedy of the commons', which appears to show how acting in one's best interests can lead to conflict and resource depletion on an expanded communal scale.[103] Though Hardin has been criticised for not acknowledging that, historically speaking, there have existed successful commons models of resource use based on mutual responsibility and risk, Clark is at pains to point out that Hardin's concerns

[99] Morton, *The Ecological Thought* (Cambridge, MA: Harvard University Press, 2010), p. 17; *Hyperobjects*, pp. 6, 35.
[100] Morton, *Hyperobjects*, p. 123.   [101] Clark, *Ecocriticism on the Edge*, p. 13.   [102] Ibid., p. 72.
[103] Garrett Hardin, 'The Tragedy of the Commons', *Science* 162 (13 December 1968), 1243–8.

hold if the scale is enlarged beyond the communal to the global, and therefore to the impersonal.[104] Moreover, citing Stephen Gardiner, Clark shows how the effects of impersonality are further magnified when they occur across not just space but time: 'each human generation, living with the immediately surrounding effects of a cumulative environmental degradation, will very probably find itself doing only the minimum or less to reduce its own ecological impact'.[105] Unlike Morton, however, Clark offers no moral pointers, no calls to action. The Anthropocene's scale effects require a critical awareness of how we attend to scale, what Clark calls 'scale framing'; yet, Clark's analysis also suggests that it is impossible to perform this successfully: there are 'unresolved and perhaps unresolvable conflicts revealed by thinking the world of the Anthropocene at different scales'.[106] On the one hand, to reframe the distant as the immediate, as Morton recommends, is to trust that a 'human' response will resolve a problem whose scale constantly outstrips, outwits, and outdoes the human; to accept its enormity of space and time, on the other hand, is to abandon the need for a (human) response altogether. For Clark, 'neither frame of reference is adequate as a basis for a definitive ethics or for dismissing the importance of the other'; there is, then, no ethical solution to the unknowable future that would avoid either naïveté or nihilism.[107]

Morton and Clark diverge in important and, I suggest, revealing ways. Because of his underlying investment in sincerity, Morton's critique of self-interest leads him to what initially looks like its opposite: acting with 'regard', which one could restate as an ethical stance of concern or even care. Indeed, in a passage in which he considers the legacy of nuclear waste, another hyperobject, Morton explicitly invokes the language of care. Writing approvingly of the Nuclear Guardianship movement, which encourages ongoing vigilance of the containment of radioactive waste, he states: 'What must happen . . . is that we must care consciously for nuclear materials'; he notes, too: 'Guardianship, care – to *curate* is to care for.'[108] Meanwhile, Clark similarly critiques the utilitarian self-concern that leads to a tragedy of the commons, but he refuses to posit a concern for others as a viable alternative. In an argument that recalls Sandilands's radical, non-

[104] Clark, *Ecocriticism on the Edge*, pp. 84–6.
[105] Ibid., p. 86; see also Stephen Gardiner, *The Perfect Moral Storm: The Ethical Tragedy of Climate Change* (Oxford University Press, 2011).
[106] Clark, *Ecocriticism on the Edge*, pp. 73, 154.    [107] Ibid., p. 154.
[108] Morton, *Hyperobjects*, p. 121.

identitarian alternative to care ethics, he identifies such concern as itself invested in human subjectivity, or what he describes, following Wilfred Sellars, as the 'manifest image' of the self, that 'lived illusion of an intelligible and coherent world at the personal scale, centred on individual agency, its needs and projects'.[109] Unsurprisingly, Clark criticises Morton's position as 'an underdefined and mildly sentimental ethic of care arising from the knowledge of interconnection and interdependence'.[110] Certainly, Morton's recourse to the language of sincerity, notwithstanding his claim that his description of selflessness represents a 'radical letting go of what constitutes a self', seems an inexplicable return to the essentialist, subject-object ontology he attempts to discredit, and ends up allowing a re-entry of correlationism through the back door. For its part, Clark's analysis offers no normative guidance beyond a recognition of how the Anthropocene's ontological confusion is wrought by the simultaneous desirability and undesirability of a belief in a coherent human self bounded from human and non-human others.

### Art in the Anthropocene: Climate Change Fiction

An Anthropocene response that imagines a sincere and stable self reaching out to others, with that action conceptualised as a gesture of care and those others framed as familiar and cognisable fellow beings, is easily discernible as the impulse behind the rhetoric of posterity-as-parenthood. But, as we have seen, those assumptions of coherence of identity and agency are destabilised by the very distance they attempt to bridge; hence, that rhetoric is rendered suspect in the Anthropocene. Though, as I have already suggested, parental responses to posterity continue to be stated and restated in cultural discourse, it is nonetheless tempting to speculate on the potential for art in the Anthropocene to question rather than reinstate such rhetorical and ethical manoeuvres. Particularly, the potential exists for such art to posit instead radical, alternative visions of the future, of the kinds I have already provisionally outlined.

Again, the analyses of Morton and Clark offer paths into this discussion. Both consider the Anthropocene's challenge to notions of human identity as, consequently, a challenge to human expression. Clark, indeed, hints that art is impossible in the ontological impasse

---

[109] Clark, *Ecocriticism on the Edge*, p. 164; see Wilfred Sellars, 'Philosophy and the Scientific Image of Man', in Robert Colodny (ed.), *Frontiers of Science and Philosophy* (University of Pittsburgh Press, 1962), pp. 35–78.
[110] Clark, *Ecocriticism on the Edge*, p. 188.

in which we now find ourselves, for human agency constitutes both art's source and, in climate-changing times, its rightful target for subversion; for him, the Anthropocene might therefore 'form a threshold at which art and literature touch limits to the human psyche and imagination themselves'.[111] Morton, in contrast, proposes that some art – most often, the avant-garde – has the potential to shock humans out of our subject-object orientations and into a properly ecological and intergenerational worldview. Such art offers, Morton clarifies, an opportunity not to reason ourselves into action, but to immerse ourselves in an aesthetic and affective space that somehow (and it is not clear how) makes both ontological awareness and ethical motivation possible: 'Reasoning on and on is a symptom of how people are still not ready to go through an affective experience that would existentially and politically bind them to hyperobjects, to care for them. We need art that does not make people think … but rather that walks them through an inner space that is hard to traverse.'[112] Unsurprisingly, Clark finds that Morton's celebration of avant-garde art fails to convince, first, on how such art manages 'to intervene positively in prisoner dilemma/tragedy-of-the-commons type situations by bringing others nearer into a recognizably shared space', and, second, on how 'the knowledge of interconnection must somehow lead to an ethic of care'.[113] Such an interpretation forces experimental art 'too hastily into ethical and cultural agendas one would have expected it to question' – identitarian agendas that Morton purports to eschew.[114]

Concerns about art's ability to apprehend the unknowable and distant future, and particularly to do so without simply and somewhat futilely insisting on its knowability and intimacy, are especially relevant when considering the climate change novel. Where experimental forms of art might be considered likely sites of subversion or resistance of expectations of subjectivity and identity, the novel, as Clark points out, is a remarkably conventional art form, relying on and in turn reproducing those very expectations. 'Linguistic narrative in particular', writes Clark, 'seems at issue solely as that mode which … fits least well into the demands of the Anthropocene, seemingly more allied with forms of anthropocentric thinking to be overcome, or as an art of sequences of human action or attention geared to a definite significant end in some fulfilled or unfulfilled intention.'[115]

---

[111] Ibid., p. 176.    [112] Morton, *Hyperobjects*, p. 184.
[113] Clark, *Ecocriticism on the Edge*, pp. 188–9.    [114] Ibid., p. 188.    [115] Ibid., p. 187.

Clark calls, then, for the 'still-dominant conventions of plotting, characterization and setting in the novel ... to be openly acknowledged as pervaded by anthropocentric delusion', as evidence of our need for a coherent manifest image of the self – all the same, this is a need that Clark concedes, after Sellars and Ray Brassier, is vital to humans' psychological survival.[116]

An initial survey of climate change fiction suggests that it has hardly effected the kind of subversion of subjectivity Clark calls for, ostensibly confirming his somewhat sorry suggestion of literary art stumbling, as it were, at the threshold of the Anthropocene. Taken together, climate change novels certainly reveal a tendency to employ highly conventional literary strategies of world-building and character development.[117] Sylvia Mayer usefully distinguishes between climate change novels that are set in the future and those that are set in the present, the former drawing imaginative appeal from catastrophe and the latter from anticipation, both of which depend on profoundly traditional and anthropocentric expectations.[118] The first strand – futuristic climate change fiction – is indebted to the generic conventions of science fiction and its traditions of building strange, but nevertheless internally consistent, environments, which characters inhabit and into which readers enter.[119] In Darko Suvin's now-authoritative analysis, the creation of a *novum* – a new but cognitively logical and coherent setting – is a special characteristic of science fiction; in Tom Moylan's memorable description of the expectation that this generates, 'the experienced sf reader

---

[116] Ibid., p. 191; see Sellars, 'Philosophy and the Scientific Image of Man', and Ray Brassier, *Nihil Unbound: Enlightenment and Extinction* (Basingstoke: Palgrave–Macmillan, 2007).

[117] For surveys of climate change fiction, see Adam Trexler and Adeline Johns-Putra, 'Climate Change in Literature and Literary Criticism', *WIREs Climate Change* 2.1 (2011), 185–200, and Johns-Putra, 'Climate Change in Literature and Literary Studies: From Cli-Fi, Climate Change Theater and Ecopoetry to Ecocriticism and Climate Change Criticism', *WIREs Climate Change* 7 (2016), 266–82.

[118] Sylvia Mayer, 'Explorations of the Controversially Real: Risk, the Climate Change Novel, and the Narrative of Anticipation', in Mayer and Alexa Weik von Mossner (eds.), *The Anticipation of Catastrophe: Environmental Risk in North American Literature and Culture* (Heidelberg: Universitätsverlag Winter, 2014), pp. 21–37.

[119] Particularly early examples of climate change fiction appear to have taken inspiration from earlier science fiction representations, by authors such as J. G. Ballard, Brian Aldiss, Frank Herbert, and H. G. Wells, of disastrous global climatic conditions, what Trexler has labelled a 'considerable archive of climate change fiction' and Jim Clarke 'proto-climate-change' fiction; see Trexler, *Anthropocene Fictions: The Novel in a Time of Climate Change* (Charlottesville: University of Virginia Press, 2015), p. 8, and Clarke, 'Reading Climate Change in J. G. Ballard', *Critical Survey* 25 (2013) 8.

moves through a text like a traveler in a foreign culture or a detective seeking clues to unravel the mystery at hand'.[120] Many climate change novels, especially early examples appearing from the 1970s through to the first decade of the twenty-first century, are set in such futuristic worlds – which one could characterise as apocalyptic, post-apocalyptic, or dystopian, depending on just how much the future setting is premised on sudden disaster, its aftermath, or a state of decline – and into which the reader is apparently invited. The second, realist strand of climate change fiction has become increasingly more prevalent. It tends to invoke a recognisable present (or very near future) in which the threat of climate change poses an ethical, political, or economic dilemma – or, more often, a combination of these – for the individual. To some extent, this reflects a move towards 'respectability' for the climate change novel, as relatively highbrow, realist writers such as Ian McEwan and Barbara Kingsolver have taken up the task of writing about climate change.[121] At any rate, this realist impulse underlines climate change fiction's dependence on highly conventional and canonical novelistic techniques grounded in identification and empathy with characters.

This is not to say, however, that the climate change novel is resolutely devoid of innovation; indeed, some recent analyses of climate change fiction have strenuously argued for a recognition of its tendency towards the stylistically experimental and unexpected. Adam Trexler's study of the climate change novel is premised on the idea that anthropogenic climate change constitutes a formal challenge to fiction: Trexler argues that 'the underlying causes of the Anthropocene have altered the horizon of human activity, as well as the capacities of the novel'.[122] According to Trexler, the nature of climate change – its composite make-up, emergent properties, and unpredictable agency – forces the novel to abandon some of its conventional strategies, such as the reliance on dominant protagonists and character-driven plot lines; instead, he suggests, climate change fiction

---

[120] Darko Suvin, *Metamorphoses of Science Fiction: On the Poetics and History of a Literary Genre* (New Haven, CT: Yale University Press, 1979) p. 63; Tom Moylan, *Scraps of the Untainted Sky: Science Fiction, Utopia, Dystopia* (Boulder, CO: Westview, 2000), p. 7.

[121] Nonetheless, the examples of Jeanette Winterson's and Margaret Atwood's SF-inflected climate change novels show that the association between realist fiction and 'serious' authorship is hardly a firm one; see Winterson, *The Stone Gods* (first published 2007; London: Penguin, 2008) and Atwood, *Oryx and Crake* (first published 2003; London, Virago, 2004), *The Year of the Flood* (first published 2009; London: Virago, 2010), *MaddAddam* (New York: Nan A. Talese–Doubleday, 2013).

[122] Trexler, *Anthropocene Fictions*, p. 15.

favours character ensembles and tends to introduce environmental or scientific entities as key motivators in order to portray climate change as a complex phenomenon. Echoing this, Astrid Bracke contends that 'post-millennial fictions . . . participate in a reshaping of existing narratives to present new ways of imagining the natural environment in a time of climate crisis' and Antonia Mehnert foregrounds the 'representational and conceptual challenges that climate change poses' in order to focus on how 'writers come up with innovative narrative means to overcome the elusiveness of climate change'.[123] So much is this so that, even though Trexler discerns a resurgence of realism in recent climate change fiction, he maintains that 'there remain real limits to realist fiction. It cannot imagine novel technological, organizational, and political approaches to climate change. Its focus on a narrow locale and set of characters compresses distributed, global events. It struggles to understand the devastating potential of climatic disaster.'[124]

Importantly, though, Clark reminds us that the effect of the Anthropocene on the novel is not as radical as studies such as Trexler's contend. Clark's considered response to Trexler suggests that analyses such as this remain committed to notions of coherent subjectivity, to the 'intelligible and coherent world at the personal scale, centred on individual agency' that is the illusion of the manifest image. Clark astutely argues that such analyses propose that climate change fiction finds innovative ways to represent climate change as a complex phenomenon and a destabilising experience, but that, ultimately, the representation they invoke depends on conventional and anthropocentric expectations of readers' empathetic identification with characters and imaginative projection of themselves into settings.[125]

Nonetheless, rather than bemoan the apparent lack of an avant-garde climate change fiction, I hope to show, contra both Trexler and Clark, that it is worth considering the kinds of interventions that climate change novels might achieve through their seemingly retrogressive and anthropocentric evocations of reader empathy and inhabitation. I suggest that the use of familiar techniques does not automatically translate into an affirmation of narrowly human accounts of space and time, including, in this case, the conventional conceptualisation of posterity as a matter of humans' obligation to future humans. Indeed, some climate change novels deploy

---

[123] Astrid Bracke, *Climate Crisis and the Twenty-First-Century British Novel* (London: Bloomsbury, 2018), p. 6; Antonia Mehnert, *Climate Change Fictions: Representations of Global Warming in American Literature* (London: Palgrave–Macmillan, 2016), p. 16.

[124] Trexler, *Anthropocene Fictions*, p. 233.       [125] Clark, *Ecocriticism on the Edge*, pp. 179–83.

the geography and psychology of parenthood in order to destabilise these anthropocentric worlds and identities as a basis for environmental concern for the future. Some, I suggest, go further, and manage to destabilise the very idea of coherence in world and identity. In the case of the latter, the space thus evacuated allows radical non-identitarian or ecocentric versions of posterity – of the kind I have already sketched – to emerge.

## What Can the Novel Do?

That the novel exerts a complex emotional appeal on the reader, one that plays a role in the formation of an ethical position, might seem axiomatic; such appeal, indeed, is what Clark construes as highly conventional. Yet, the ties that link emotions, ethics, and literature have been too often vexed in the history of literary criticism. In his reassessment of *The Value of the Novel* (2015), Peter Boxall describes a critical shift over the course of the twentieth century from a belief in the moral worthiness of literature to a preoccupation with literature's ability to interrogate the foundations of moral value (and, indeed, to interrogate the idea of value itself). However, as Boxall argues, the mid- to late-century 'struggle between the Leavisites and the new wave of critics committed to "theory"' has, in the first decades of the new century, given way to a renewed interest in literature's ethical purpose.[126] This heralds not a return to morality as much as a recalibration of it, emerging out of 'the growing desire for a new means of articulating a set of values of our own generation'.[127] Certainly, Boxall's analysis is joined by other recent studies, such as Kenneth Asher's *Literature, Ethics, and the Emotions* (2017), that seek to understand anew the place of the novel in our moral – and, by extension, emotional – universe.[128] Yet, as Boxall rightly warns, anyone advocating a new ethical turn in literary scholarship must be wary of repeating the value judgements of earlier ideologues, that is, of mistaking literature's purchase on our moral lives for a normative statement of rights and wrongs:

> The challenge that faces those who would measure, now, the value of the arts, is how to capture and articulate the ethical force of the literary, without resurrecting a conservative, Leavisite language in which to express it; how to produce an adequately rich account of the democratic power of the literary imagination, its capacity to continually remake the world in which we live, without returning to a prior model of the critic as 'arbiter of public taste'.[129]

---

[126] Peter Boxall, *The Value of the Novel* (Cambridge University Press, 2015), p. 2.　　[127] Ibid., p. 2.
[128] Kenneth Asher, *Literature, Ethics, and the Emotions* (Cambridge University Press, 2017).
[129] Boxall, *The Value of the Novel*, p. 9.

In addition, as Boxall reminds us, such an account must apprehend literature not just as representations of moral matter but as drawing on the resources of stylistics and aesthetics, that is, it must be equally alert to form as it is to content. Additionally, it must be ready to understand the interplay between so-called form and content, for it is this interplay that continually shapes and reshapes the reader's sense of subjectivity, ontology, and, with these, ethics.

Thus, one way in which to consider 'the ethical force' of the climate change novel is to begin not from literary scholarship but from discussions about literature and ethics in moral philosophy. This has the advantage not only of avoiding some of the entrenched literary critical positions that Boxall describes but also of allowing me to undertake a stepped discussion of content and form. That is, I begin with these philosophical assumptions that emphasise novelistic content (that is, as transparent depictions of moral behaviour in plot, character, and so on), before going on to complicate these with considerations of style and form (including narrative points of view and focalisation) and to show how these encourage a critical awareness (for example, through the strategies of irony and destabilisation). Like Asher, I consider the moral philosophy of Martha Nussbaum to be a 'promising starting point' – and an oft-neglected one – for an understanding of the triangular relations among emotions, ethics, and the novel; I employ Nussbaum's ideas in order to elaborate a model of reading that takes account of these relations.[130] However, far from a Leavisite vision of the novel as an emotional tool that perpetuates or engenders moral norms (an approach which Nussbaum sometimes takes), I particularly want to argue for the climate change novel's potential to intervene in these norms and to establish a critical awareness of their power. That is, despite the novel's seemingly anthropocentric and conservative formal techniques and psychological concerns, I suggest that it also uses these to critique conventional ideas about and idealisations of the moral power of human affect – in this case, the power of parental care and love. I thus set out here a mode of reading the climate change novel that is critically aware of existing expectations and ideas about literature's ethical and emotional power, as well as showing how the novel itself formally participates in this critical awareness.

---

[130] Asher, *Literature, Ethics, and the Emotions*, p. 12.

*Ethics, Emotion, and Literature: A Eudaemonistic Framework*

Although Western moral philosophy has traditionally relied on the coordinates of reason, principle, and duty (as has already been suggested in my discussion of the emergence of parental care ethics), the work of Nussbaum and others represents an important strand of investigation into the relationship between ethics and emotion. In particular, Nussbaum has argued over the course of her career for the cognitive value of emotions; in such works as *Cultivating Humanity* (1997), *Upheavals of Thought* (2001), and *Political Emotions* (2013), she has elaborated a theory of the relationship between emotions and value judgements, a theory that offers a first (though, at this point, necessarily identitarian and anthropocentric) step towards a mode of reading climate change novels' emotional appeal as a potential ethical intervention.[131]

Nussbaum constructs a model of compassionate ethical decision-making. As she summarises it, emotions 'involve judgements about important things', judgements which comprise 'appraising an external object as salient for our own well-being'.[132] In short, emotions are 'eudaimonistic evaluations'.[133] This is, then, a neo-Stoic ethics, drawing on the Aristotelian idea of eudaemonia (that is, as we have seen, human well-being or flourishing). Nussbaum focuses on compassion as an emotion that functions in positive ways to determine what is important to one's flourishing (while disgust and shame, among other emotions, work negatively to this end). Unlike Groves's conceptualisation of the act of caring as constitutive to the flourishing of the one-caring, however, Nussbaum's work extends emotional concerns beyond direct relationships and attachments. The emotion of compassion occurs when one witnesses or otherwise becomes aware of another's distress and, in Nussbaum's account, has three cognitive requirements: 'the judgment of *size* (a serious bad event has befallen someone); the judgment of *nondesert* (this person did not bring the suffering on himself or herself); and the *eudaimonistic judgment* (this person, or creature, is a significant element in my scheme of goals and projects, an end whose good is to be promoted)'.[134] It is Nussbaum's explication of this third belief that sheds particular light on the role of compassion in ethical assessment and on the widening of what she calls 'the circle of concern'.[135] According

---

[131] Martha C. Nussbaum, *Cultivating Humanity: A Classical Defense of Reform in Liberal Education* (Cambridge, MA: Harvard University Press, 1997); *Upheavals of Thought: The Intelligence of Emotions* (Cambridge University Press, 2001); *Political Emotions: Why Love Matters for Justice* (Cambridge, MA: Belknap Press, 2013).
[132] Nussbaum, *Upheavals of Thought*, p. 19.    [133] Ibid., p. 300.
[134] Ibid., p. 321; original emphasis.    [135] Ibid., p. 319.

to Nussbaum, eudaemonistic judgement replaces Aristotle's standard requirement for compassion – the 'judgment of similar possibilities' – because, she argues, similarities and similar possibilities between the spectator and the sufferer are not in and of themselves a vital component of compassion.[136] What is important is that they bring home to the witness of suffering her shared vulnerability with the one suffering. Preventing that distress or pain, therefore, is inextricably tied to her own well-being, because it alleviates her sense of her potential for distress or pain. The eudaemonistic judgement that another's experiences, particularly painful experiences, are part of a common vulnerability, along with the compassion that results from this judgement, are at the crux of Nussbaum's ethical framework.

Before I introduce literature to this configuration of ethics and emotions, I should explain the terms I will use in this book to describe these emotions, as, over the course of the history of the philosophy of moral sentiments, some terms and descriptions have tended to overlap. First, when it comes to discussing emotions, I take 'emotions' as referring, in fairly self-explanatory fashion, to affective states, and I use 'emotion' and 'feeling' interchangeably. Robert Solomon introduces the additional terms 'sentiments' and 'sentimentality'. Solomon, like Nussbaum, is concerned with defending emotions as 'an essential part of the substance of ethics itself'; he sees sentiments as a term used in an unnecessarily pejorative way for emotions, particularly suggesting '"excessive" emotion', 'emotional self-indulgence' or '"false" or "fake" emotions', although, as he maintains, there is little that is inherently egregious about emotions.[137] Using Solomon's definition, I shall refer to sentiments and the sentimental when there is an accompanying suggestion of an 'excessive manipulation' of emotions, such as in the sentimental novel.[138] Second, in my discussion of emotional sharing, I have so far employed Nussbaum's model as a point of departure and thus shared her use of 'compassion' to refer to 'a painful emotion occasioned by the awareness of another person's undeserved misfortune'.[139] Nussbaum distinguishes this from 'empathy', which is simply 'an imaginative reconstruction of another's experience, without any particular evaluation of that experience'; that is, unlike compassion, empathy does not include any suggestion of a negative emotion, such as pain or distress, arising from the awareness of that experience.[140] As Nussbaum notes, however, her definition of compassion

---

[136] Ibid., p. 321; original emphasis.    [137] Solomon, *In Defense of Sentimentality*, pp. 8–9.
[138] Ibid., p. 8.    [139] Nussbaum, *Upheavals of Thought*, p. 301.    [140] Ibid., p. 302.

coincides with definitions of sympathy in eighteenth-century moral philosophy as well as with contemporary uses of the word. Solomon, for one, tends to discuss sympathy in this way, and, indeed, to distinguish between it and empathy on much the same grounds on which Nussbaum contrasts compassion and empathy. Thus, according to Solomon, empathy refers to 'the *sharing* of emotion (any emotion). Sympathy, by contrast, *is* an emotion, a quite particular though rather suffuse and contextually defined emotion. It is therefore sympathy that does the motivational work ... but that in turn requires empathy, the *capacity* to "read" and to some extent share other people's emotions'.[141] From this point, then, I follow, for convenience, the many commentators on narrative empathy and emotion who use 'sympathy' to mean what Nussbaum means by 'compassion'. In all cases, I treat sympathy/compassion as an evaluative emotional response to another's emotion, usually painful, and view it as the result of empathy, the ability to partake of the other's emotion. Both sympathy/compassion and empathy, in this model of emotion and ethics, are important components of ethical judgement. Identification, meanwhile, is a term I shall sometimes use to describe literature's encouragement of the reader to assume a similarity with a character, which invokes patterns of empathy and sympathy. It is to literature that I now turn.

Literature enters this formulation of emotion and ethics because it seems to allow the witnessing of the experiences of unknown others, widening the circle of concern. As Nussbaum puts it, 'If distant people and abstract principles are to get a grip on our emotions' and create 'a sense of "our" life in which these people and events matter as parts of our "us", our own flourishing', then 'symbols and poetry are crucial'.[142] Novels, in particular, with their constructions of fictional situations and experiences create cognitive opportunities for compassion: 'Narrative art', writes Nussbaum, 'has the power to make us see the lives of the different with more than a casual tourist's interest – with involvement and sympathetic understanding, with anger at our society's refusals of visibility.'[143] Such an account of the effect of literature chimes, as Suzanne Keen suggests, with popular perceptions of novel reading and, indeed, with responses of actual readers, who 'report feeling both empathy with and sympathy for fictional characters. They believe that novel reading opens

---

[141] Solomon, *In Defense of Sentimentality*, p. 69; original emphasis.
[142] Nussbaum, *Political Emotions*, p. 11.
[143] Nussbaum, *Cultivating Humanity*, p. 88; see also Nussbaum's early work on Henry James in two chapters of *Love's Knowledge: Essays on Philosophy and Literature* (Oxford University Press, 1990), pp. 125–67.

their minds to experiences, dilemmas, time periods, places, and situations that would otherwise be closed to them.'[144] For Nussbaum, such reader empathy and sympathy enable a moral recalibration; though she concedes that 'Literature does not transform society single-handed', she argues nonetheless that 'the artistic form makes its spectator perceive, for a time, the invisible people of their world – at least a beginning of social justice.'[145] This model of reading, which I term eudaemonistic, emphasises the reader's imaginative identification with fictional characters and their conditions, as well as the immersive experience of novelistic worlds, as conducive to the development of sympathetic acknowledgment of shared vulnerability with others and of a eudaemonistic desire to address that common vulnerability and promote a common flourishing.[146]

## *Reading Climate Change Fiction: A Critical Eudaemonistic Framework*

As persuasive and seemingly commonsensical as such a model of literature might be, a eudaemonistic framework requires a number of important qualifications if it is to be related to the experience and effect of reading the climate change novel. For one thing, there is no easy translation of the reader's emotional response to ethical action. Keen cautions against being too quick to assign ethical power to literature, without taking full account of the differing contexts and conditions in which empathetic reading takes place, and without allowing that readers' ethical actions might arise from other factors, including an existing predisposition to empathetic insight and sympathetic conduct.[147] She also warns that the very otherness of the novelistic world from the 'real' world might even mitigate against the

---

[144] Suzanne Keen, *Empathy and the Novel* (Oxford University Press, 2007), p. ix.

[145] Nussbaum, *Cultivating Humanity*, p. 94.

[146] Eudaemonistic reading chimes with very recent ecocritical studies that emphasise the immersive and experiential aspect of narratives and that show how this engenders compassionate responses to social and environmental injustice. See, for example, Erin James's theory and praxis of econarratology, which 'studies the storyworlds that readers simulate and transport themselves to when reading narratives, the correlations between such textual, imaginative worlds and the physical, extratextual world, and the potential for the reading process to foster awareness and understanding for different environmental imaginations and experiences', *The Storyworld Accord: Econarratology and Postcolonial Narratives* (Lincoln: University of Nebraska Press, 2015), p. xv. See also Alexa Weik von Mossner's study of readers' responses to environmental issues in literature and film as 'embodied cognition', that is, as a cognitive response that is both physical and emotional, since it forces comparisons and conflations between the reader's material, or 'real' world with fictional or filmic worlds, as well as ethical since it promotes empathetic engagement, *Affective Ecologies: Empathy, Emotion, and Environmental Narrative* (Columbus: Ohio State University Press, 2017), pp. 1–13.

[147] Keen, *Empathy and the Novel*, pp. xiv–xv.

exercise of political or social conscience: 'the contract of fictionality offers a no-strings-attached opportunity for emotional transactions of great intensity. A novel-reader may enjoy empathy freely without paying back society with altruism.'[148] Also relevant here is Wayne Booth's reminder, in his still-influential study of literature and ethics, *The Company We Keep* (1988), of the two kinds of experience that readers seek with any work. Booth adopts Louise Rosenblatt's distinction between aesthetic and efferent readerly transactions, readers focused in the former on 'what happens *during* the actual reading event' and in the latter on 'the concepts, solutions, to be "carried away" from their reading'; Booth argues not that aesthetic reading fails to produce ethical outcomes, but that very different ethical consequences follow from each kind of reading.[149] In other words, a critical eye needs to be kept on the very complex nature of ethical reflection that accompanies reader identification, empathy, and sympathy, a complexity not reducible to simple altruistic attitudes and actions such as environmental awareness and environmentally sensitive behaviour.

Along with a critical consideration of the causal relationship between sympathy and action, attention needs to be paid to the political contours of eudaemonistic reading. Nussbaum tends to press reading into the service of a progressive and liberal democratic politics of tolerance: literature fulfils 'a vital role in educating citizens of the world'.[150] Yet, as studies of novelistic sympathy show, the emotional power wielded by the novel is not necessarily ideologically benign. Elizabeth Barnes's exploration of the American novel in the wake of independence highlights its role in constructing a coherent democratic identity for the new union. As Barnes shows, the depictions of family in a range of post-Revolutionary and antebellum novels function to invite readers not just to view but to participate in sympathetic ties, which become on the one hand the ideal expression of private conduct and on the other an ethical model for a fledgling democratic citizenry: 'familial feeling proves the foundation for sympathy, and sympathy the foundation of democracy.'[151] Thus, the novels in Barnes's analysis exemplify the eudaemonistic dynamics that Nussbaum propounds, but, at the same time, Barnes shows how such dynamics are far

---

[148] Ibid., p. 168.

[149] Louise M. Rosenblatt, *The Reader, the Text, the Poem: The Transactional Theory of the Literary Work* (Carbondale, IL: Southern Illinois University Press, 1978); Wayne Booth, *The Company We Keep: An Ethics of Fiction* (Berkeley: University of California Press, 1988), pp. 13–14.

[150] Nussbaum, *Cultivating Humanity*, p. 88.

[151] Elizabeth Barnes, *States of Sympathy: Seduction and Democracy in the American Novel* (New York: Columbia University Press, 1997), p. 2.

from innocent. Eudaemonistic reading is readily available, I would therefore argue, to a range of uses, and any critical account of it must attend to the political hues of the sympathy – or, perhaps more accurately here, sympathies – called forth by the novel. These sympathies are not always, after all, transparently or straightforwardly beneficial to the kinds of reflections and behaviours demanded by the Anthropocene.

Specifically, and not wholly surprisingly, an uncritically eudaemonistic account of reading risks reiterating the kind of identitarian position critiqued by Sandilands and dismissed as woefully inadequate by Clark, for whom it represents 'our normal entrapment in the delusory and potentially destructive projections of the personal scale'.[152] It would appear that Nussbaum's eudaemonistic reader, who immerses herself in fictional situations and identifies with, relates to, and feels sorry for the characters therein, is understandable as an unproblematically stable subject, developing reliably consistent feelings of compassion and applying these systematically to the world around her. While it must be pointed out that Nussbaum does not construct her ethical reader in entirely naïve identitarian terms – her moral framework is alive to fluctuations in identity and recognises that emotional, eudaemonistic evaluations are part of becoming, to some extent, 'a different person' – her conceptualisation of emotions' role in identity shifts and transformations does not provide the kind of insight into the slipperiness of identity propounded by thinkers as different as Parfit, Sandilands, and Clark.[153] For example, as I have already suggested, Sandilands's Arendtian understanding of identity emphasises it as an 'intra-social' event, formed in moments of social and political coalition and action but existing in an ongoing state of incompleteness.[154] Thus, where, for Nussbaum, identity is something of a work-in-progress, I would argue that identity is better comprehended as always already a collection of parts (and that it will never be a *sum* of these parts is what causes the Lacanian trauma of subjectivity, as Sandilands suggests). To understand identity as contingent is to value moments of empathy and sympathy as coalitional interactions that make political and ethical action practicable and identity momentarily possible, rather than to view them as tools employed by a singular, developing identity in the first place. To understand identity as contingent is also to remain alert to the (mis)assumptions of stability of identity that may be operative in a eudaemonistic reading.

---

[152] Clark, *Ecocriticism on the Edge*, p. 191–2.    [153] Nussbaum, *Upheavals of Thought*, p. 83.
[154] Sandilands, *Good-Natured Feminist*, p. 84.

In particular, the eudaemonistic account of reading as a process of identification seems to reinforce the myth of a stable identity for the reader. Nussbaum's version of reading, imbricated with empathy and sympathy, assumes that the reader's sense of identity and, with it, morality will be both activated by reading and enhanced by it: the reader encounters a manifest image of the self (to invoke Clark's use of Sellars) and employs this as a basis for ethical action. It is no accident, after all, that, historically speaking, novels have played a central role in establishing the modern category of the individual, particularly doing so by purporting to demonstrate the ethical coherence and power of the self; in some studies, the novel has been shown, indeed, to be no less than the discursive consolidation of the concept of individualism, that discourse dependent on the flow of reader empathy and sympathy. For example, analyses by Nancy Armstrong and Gillian Brown have explained how eighteenth- and nineteenth-century British and American novels construct the middle-class woman as the embodiment of moral agency, thanks to her supposed capacity for sympathy, which her readers were invited to emulate.[155] A non-identitarian critic would do well to keep in mind the novel's discursive power in consolidating the myth of identity's coherence and completeness, as well as the novel's potential to reveal the impossibility of that myth. This requires, then, a critical awareness of the identitarian assumptions that underpin novelistic techniques of empathy and sympathy, along with a vigilance in demonstrating when and how novelistic irony might work to undermine these assumptions.

Moreover, the identificatory processes of novel reading, in a eudaemonistic account, are liable to replay the conservative identity politics at the heart of parental care ethics (certainly, Armstrong's and Brown's historical accounts of the discursive construction of morally superior domestic womanhood by British and American sentimental novels bear this out). The sympathy provoked in the eudaemonistic reader is that of concern for those whose plight is shared not just with the reader but with those for whom she cares – the reader's children or children she might imagine having. As Nussbaum notes in discussing Aristotle's judgement of moral similarity, 'the similarity should be not to my own possibilities alone, but to those of my loved ones as well'; Nussbaum's eudaemonistic version of this judgement extends shared vulnerability rather than simply moral

[155] Nancy Armstrong, *Desire and Domestic Fiction: A Political History of the Novel* (New York: Oxford University Press, 1987); Gillian Brown, *Domestic Individualism: Imagining Self in Nineteenth-Century America* (Berkeley: University of California Press, 1990).

similarity to loved ones, including children, and their futures.[156] On this view, the novel would set up what Keen calls 'situational empathy', inviting the reader to step into a familial relationship (or circle of concern) within the novel, and to care *for*, rather than *with*, child characters.[157] Where that circle of concern repeats traditional nuclear family dynamics and invites the reader to inhabit idealised stereotypes built on heavily gendered norms, the reader is, as it were, interpellated as parent into suspiciously heterosexist or patriarchal ideological expectations.

All this echoes Edelman's concerns with the disingenuous use of the figure of the child and Seymour's particular identification of this pattern in environmentalist discourse. Of course, the novel has a long history of utilising images of childhood to reflect adult desires and quests for identity. Building on Philippe Ariès's grand account of the construction of childhood as a social category in the modern age, Susan Honeyman has shown how the twentieth-century novel's idea of the child is more the projection of adult interests than any authentic notion of children.[158] Meanwhile, Karen Sánchez-Eppler's exhaustive study of nineteenth-century American writing about children shows how they were discursively employed as – among other things – 'social actors', capable of exerting power on the reader through 'affective ties'.[159] Sánchez-Eppler suggests that children's vulnerability and victimhood were exercised in the service of agendas as varied as temperance and abolition, with readers called on to display the moral decency or active concern expected of parents. As such examples show, where the eudaemonistic reading relies on a sentimental use of the figure of the child, a critical awareness is required to identify and interrogate the parental care ethics that underpin it.

Here, it is worth noting, if briefly, the differences and similarities between parental care ethics and philosophical treatments of emotion and ethics such as Nussbaum's. Whereas care ethics emerged as an alternative to the dominant emphasis on reason, justice, and rights in Western moral philosophy and thus tended to promote care as a non-cognitive ethical response, philosophers such as Nussbaum and Solomon have been keen to describe both emotions and judgement as forming equal parts of a

---

[156] Nussbaum, *Upheavals of Thought*, p. 316.   [157] Keen, *Empathy and the Novel*, p. 13.

[158] Philippe Ariès, *Centuries of Childhood: A Social History of Family Life*, trans. Robert Baldick (New York: Vintage, 1962); Susan Honeyman, *Elusive Childhood: Impossible Representations of Childhood in Modern Fiction* (Columbus: Ohio University Press, 2006).

[159] Karen Sánchez-Eppler, *Dependent States: The Child's Part in Nineteenth-Century American Culture* (University of Chicago Press, 2005), p. xxii.

cognitive ethical appraisal.[160] Moreover, Solomon, in particular, is aware of the shortcomings of an uncritical reliance on parental care as a political model, approaching as it does the dangers of parochialism (and thus echoing Tronto): 'To care for is also to be prepared to fight for, and against the sweet image of women caring for the world in the way mothers have always cared for their children should be juxtaposed the not-so-sweet image of a mother defending her children against the dangers of the outside world.'[161] Nussbaum voices similar concerns in relation to compassion (though here, and elsewhere, she never explicitly compares her ethical model to care ethics): 'Compassion for our own children can so easily slip into a desire to promote the well-being of our children at the expense of other people's children. Similarly, compassion for our fellow Americans can all too easily slip over into a desire to make America come out *on top* and to subordinate other nations.'[162] Nonetheless, Nussbaum's characterisation of the eudaemonistic reader has important points of similarity with the moral agent called forth by parental care ethics. I argue, therefore, that a critical deployment of a model of eudaemonistic reading must acknowledge any replication – however unwitting – of some of the key political risks, such as parochialism and paternalism, raised by parental care ethics.

Finally, in reading the climate change novel, critical caution must be taken to ensure that a eudaemonistic version of reading does not remain an anthropocentric exercise. To be fair, Nussbaum's circle of concern is capable of crossing species boundaries. Rather like O'Neill, who contends that non-human flourishing is constitutive of human flourishing, Nussbaum considers that humans often recognise non-human animals as possessing a 'common vulnerability' on the basis of 'pain, hunger, and other types of suffering'; indeed, it is possible, she notes, to feel sympathy for 'precisely those aspects of an animal's suffering that are unlike our own – for example, their lack of legal rights, their lack of power to shape the laws that affect their lives, or (in some cases) their lack of understanding of what is happening to them. . . . We think, how horrible it would be to suffer pain in that way, and without hope of changing it.'[163] As laudable as it might be,

---

[160] For the position in care ethics, see Noddings, *Caring*, pp. 22–7, and Held, *The Ethics of Care*, pp. 12–13.

[161] Solomon, *In Defense of Sentimentality*, p. 57.

[162] Martha C. Nussbaum, 'Compassion and Terror', *Daedalus* 132.1 (2003), 13; original emphasis. Though Nussbaum does not compare her work with ethics of care, Tronto notes that Nussbaum's 'capabilities approach – which, building on the work of Amartya Sen, focuses on meeting others' capabilities to achieve *eudaemonia* – is akin to an ethic of care; see Tronto, *Moral Boundaries*, p. 140.

[163] O'Neill, *Ecology, Policy and Politics*; Nussbaum, *Upheavals of Thought*, p. 319.

however, a reading that encourages sympathy with non-human animals on these grounds risks simply constructing the non-human in insistently human terms, assigning to non-human nature a 'voice', as Sandilands puts it, that might easily speak to the human. More productive for an ecocentric reading is Nussbaum's description of the extension of moral considerability on the non-eudaemonistic grounds of 'wonder', which aligns with Cuomo's ethics of flourishing.[164] That is, the non-human is valued not because its flourishing is a component of human flourishing but because of its inherent complexity: writes Nussbaum, 'when I see with compassion the beating of an animal, a wonder at the complex living thing itself is likely to be mixed with my compassion, and to support it'.[165] Such a conception of wonder points the way to an ecocentric eudaemonistic reading that, first, is alert to examples of non-human flourishing without claiming these as simple extensions of or services to human eudaemonia, and, second, remains equally alert to stark omissions of non-human wonder and its possibilities.

## *The Critical Method and Structure of This Book*

What all this calls for in dealing with the climate change novel is a critical understanding of eudaemonistic reading. This is not simply about being critically aware of identificatory practices that disclose the political limitations of parental care ethics, display the arrogance of human exceptionalism, or conform to identitarian assumptions of human subjectivity and agency. It requires, too, a consideration of how the processes of readerly eudaemonistic sympathy play out in climate change novels, and an identification of where these novels interrupt these processes to point to more radical possibilities.

Specifically, I redeploy a key concept of Nussbaum's model of reading: tragic spectatorship. A concept implicit in much of her writing, tragic spectatorship is defined by Nussbaum in a 2003 essay, 'Compassion and Terror', and elaborated on in *Political Emotions*. In its initial iteration, tragic spectatorship clearly fits into Nussbaum's eudaemonistic ethical framework. Noting how Athenian tragedy concerns itself with the possession and subsequent loss of 'attachments that seem essentially reasonable', such as children, health, and freedom, Nussbaum goes on to state: 'the tragic dramas encourage us to understand the depth of such loss and, with the protagonists, to fear it. In exercising compassion, the audience is learning its own possibilities and vulnerabilities – what Aristotle called

---

[164] Nussbaum, *Upheavals of Thought*, p. 321.     [165] Ibid., pp. 321–2.

"things such as might happen".[166] In her later work, Nussbaum readily resumes such a definition, but also refers to the progress of the tragic drama as a factor in the effect of tragic spectatorship, namely that the spectator proceeds from a position of unconcern and even disgust for the protagonist to one of compassion; that is, sympathy is awakened. Thus, what Nussbaum calls the expectation of 'segmentation' is breached: tragedy reminds the relatively privileged just how much they are like the tragic and deprived protagonist: 'terrible plights are the common lot of all, even the most privileged'.[167] Tragic spectatorship involves, then, not just the witnessing of tragic events but a process from unconcern to concern, as a shared exposure to those events is gradually revealed.

What this means, first, is an ecocentric understanding of the potential in tragic narrative for the undoing of species segmentation in particular. Tragic spectatorship challenges 'anthropodenial', a term that Nussbaum borrows from primatologist Frans de Waal to refer not just to our denial of all things of the 'body' and our desire to transcend the 'animality' of our existence, but to our idea of ourselves as 'truly human', as inhabiting a highly individualised and invulnerable state of transcendence, unity, and omnipotence.[168] The spectator's assumption of immunity from distress, so rudely disrupted by tragic narrative, includes the notion that the *human* spectator is exempt from the kind of deprivations that non-humans might undergo. But what is also made possible is an ecocentric recognition that the deprivation of non-human flourishing is of concern in and of itself.

Furthermore, to emphasise tragic spectatorship is to be mindful of the progress undertaken by readers of fiction. This is particularly relevant to a critical awareness of the political and ideological biases of reader sympathy, for an attention to the stages by which reader sympathy is developed allows some of the norms that underpin that sympathy to be questioned. What this requires is critique that sheds light on the invitations issued to the reader at key points in the novel. That is, while I do not conduct a blow-by-blow account of reader response, I do attend to moments in which identification and eudaemonistic sympathy, whether with characters or situations or, more often, a combination of these, are called forth, and I am mindful of how plot and character development (or, perhaps, lack thereof) allows these moments to make or unmake eudaemonistic sense. I also pay heed to endings, not just closing pages but points of plot resolution and dénouement that might occur in earlier sections of the novel; I will take up,

---

[166] Nussbaum, 'Compassion and Terror', pp. 25–6.    [167] Nussbaum, *Political Emotions*, p. 265.
[168] Ibid., p. 184.

for example, false endings, open endings, or tragic conclusions, and their effects, where relevant.

The reading I propose here therefore involves a focus on the sympathetic – one might say, sentimental – journey undertaken by the reader in empathy with narrators or protagonists, as well as a readiness to read that sympathy as destabilised by such elements as unreliable narrators or focalisers. It also enables the questioning of the sympathetic (or, indeed, caring) dispositions and actions of those protagonists or narrators in their parental roles, and thus the active interrogation of care that they display. Then, it highlights the importance of endings, particularly where those endings involve the destabilisation of the emotional investments made by the reader. I realise that some might ask why a novel would invite sympathy from a reader only to undercut it. I contend that, in some cases, the novel enacts emotions – and even asks for an enactment of emotional identification on the part of the reader – so as to critique those emotions all the more powerfully. That is, if the eudaemonistic rug is to be pulled out from under the reader's feet, the reader has to be standing on that rug in the first place.

Moreover, the potential for destabilisation applies not only to the sympathetic investment made by the reader but to the larger framework of identity from which such sympathy is supposed to originate. That is, more radical possibilities exist for the reader to be invited to identify with protagonists or narrators whose own identities come into question. The process of identification becomes a means for self-reflexively querying that process, recalling Sandilands's strategy of 'ironic' essentialism, whereby coherent identity is assumed in full knowledge of its impossibility, as well as Clark's almost offhand comment, via Sellars, that the manifest image is an important coping mechanism for the human psyche.[169]

In the first half of this book, I read novels that encourage a relatively uncritical eudaemonistic response, but do so in order to invite the reader to inhabit a parental care ethics and subsequently to critique these ethical stances. This critique tends to take the form of the positioning of readers as critical tragic spectators, destabilising the emotions of care and identifications with parenthood that lead them to tragic compassion, and inviting critical reflection on those parental emotions and perspectives. Thus, in chapter 2, I read Cormac McCarthy's *The Road* (2006) and Maggie Gee's *The Ice People* (1998) for the ways in which they shed light on the power dynamics of parental care ethics when it serves as a model for intergenerational action, specifically, the merging of attitudes of parochialism and

---

[169] Sandilands, *Good-Natured Feminist*, p. 114; Clark, *Ecocriticism on the Edge*, p. 164.

paternalism into a narrow genetic or biological survivalism, and the exclusionary gender politics that underwrites this.[170] Chapter 3 takes up the thread of the gendered norms of parental care ethics, reading the risks of expanding motherhood environmentalism into an intergenerational ethics in Edan Lepucki's *California* (2014) and Liz Jensen's *The Rapture* (2009).[171] These novels particularly juxtapose maternalised care ethics and their emphasis on the moral power of procreation and parenting against the threat of overpopulation in the Anthropocene.

As I show in the second half of this book, however, some novels do more than critique; they enable radical ethical alternatives to emerge. Specifically, they question the basic assumptions of human interest and identification on which eudaemonistic readings rest. In chapter 4, I employ reconceptualisations of political identity as contingent and coalitional to read Jeanette Winterson's *The Stone Gods* (2007) for its insights into the hybrid nature of identity and its critical awareness of how nostalgic desire for the past informs our ethical relationship with the future, and Sarah Hall's *The Carhullan Army* (2007) as a demonstration of the process by which identity is made and unmade, and the opportunities and hazards this creates for a future-oriented ethical agency.[172] Finally, chapter 5 compares two heroic treatments of science's ability to save the future. It contrasts Kim Stanley Robinson's 'Science in the Future' trilogy (2004, 2005, 2007), reliant as it is on an anthropocentric account of science, with Barbara Kingsolver's *Flight Behaviour* (2012), which enables an ecocentric awareness by way of a surprising ending.[173] In particular, I argue that Kingsolver employs the kind of widening of the circle of concern that is only hinted at by Nussbaum's concept of wonder but more fully developed in Cuomo's ethics of flourishing.

Throughout, this book argues that climate change fiction builds worlds in which readers might be immersed and creates characters with whom we might identify in order not merely to evoke emotional response but to provoke ethical reflection. This is the case across the full range of climate change fiction's generic inflections, from the parental dilemmas brought on by the apocalyptic and post-apocalyptic

---

[170] Cormac McCarthy, *The Road* (first published 2006; London: Picador, 2007); Maggie Gee, *The Ice People* (first published 1998; London: Telegram, 2008).

[171] Edan Lepucki, *California* (first published 2014; London: Abacus, 2015); Liz Jensen, *The Rapture* (London: Bloomsbury, 2009).

[172] Winterson, *The Stone Gods*; Sarah Hall, *The Carhullan Army* (London: Faber, 2007).

[173] Kim Stanley Robinson, *Forty Signs of Rain* (first published 2004; London: HarperCollins, 2005), *Fifty Degrees Below* (first published 2005; London: HarperCollins, 2006), *Sixty Days and Counting* (London: HarperCollins, 2007); Barbara Kingsolver, *Flight Behaviour* (London: Faber, 2012).

scenarios of chapters 2 and 3 (in *The Road, The Ice People, California,* and *The Rapture*), to the science fiction dystopias of chapter 4, from which dystopian outsider-protagonists strive to make a radical break from their communities (in *The Stone Gods* and *The Carhullan Army*), to the realist settings and political/personal dilemmas of chapter 5 (whether the comic, utopian narrative of 'Science in the Capital' or the *Bildungsroman* of *Flight Behaviour*). Ultimately, I argue, the parental figures, familial ties, and interpersonal crises we encounter in these climate change novels take us beyond simple sentiment towards a critical awareness and active interrogation of the affective, anthropocentric foundations to the anxieties of the Anthropocene.

# CHAPTER 2

# The Limits of Parental Care Ethics: Cormac McCarthy's *The Road* and Maggie Gee's *The Ice People*

> Often, because people who care become enmeshed in the caring process, the great moral task for them is not to become involved with others (the problem of moral motivation, a fundamental problem in contemporary moral theory), but to be able to stand back from ongoing processes of care and ask, 'What is going on here?' It requires honesty, and a non-idealized knowledge of selves and others.
>
> Joan C. Tronto, *Moral Boundaries: A Political Argument for an Ethic of Care*

> My job is to take care of you. I was appointed to do that by God. I will kill anyone who touches you.
>
> Cormac McCarthy, *The Road*

To scale up the many interpersonal attitudes and acts that mark the parent–child relationship into a rationale for intergenerational justice is to reveal the limits of parental care as an ethical position. For this scaling up risks exacerbating such dangers as parochialism and paternalism, allowing, for example, one generation's obligation to future generations to be simplified as one's obligation to one's own lineage, and thus allowing intergenerational justice to be expressed as nothing more than biological survivalism. It also risks eliding the gender dynamics that underpin parental care as a private set of activities and dispositions under the territorial and exceptionalist logic of identity politics.

Such are the concerns explored in this chapter. The limitations of parental care as intergenerational ethics are revealed by two contemporary novels, *The Road* (2006) by Cormac McCarthy and *The Ice People* (1998) by Maggie Gee, the one popularly read as a global warming parable despite its apparent reticence on that matter and the other an early novelistic engagement with climate change that precedes the twenty-first-century fanfare around climate change fiction.[1] Strikingly, the reception of *The Road* shows the traction that parental care ethics has gained in the Anthropocene, and this parentally inflected reception provides the context for my reading. Gee's less celebrated but no less important novel, as I go on to show, develops the kind of critique of parental care ethics that is only implicit in McCarthy's novel and that would seem to be entirely missed by those who would hail *The Road* for its moral power.

Yet, this chapter also asks, what would happen if the future could talk back? What would be the point of view from a posterity in receipt of a parental ethics of care, an ethics compromised by its historical location within exclusionary identity politics and its potential narrowness of vision to the intimate and the immediate? The climate change novel allows not only an identification with the moral agent (or, as Nel Noddings would have it, the 'one-caring'),[2] but is capable, as I suggest in this chapter, of rupturing that identification, inserting in the spaces of rupture a response from the one 'cared-for', and mounting, via that response, a critique of the power games and conflicts that potentially mark and mar parental care ethics.

### Parochialism, Paternalism, and Genetic Survivalism

Embedded within care ethics is a set of political and ethical risks, closely connected to care's origins in private and immediate attachments, as I have already suggested in chapter 1. Joan Tronto argues, in a detailed account of the ethics of care and its potential as a political position, that care ethics is too often concerned 'with relationships of care that are now considered personal or private', when what is instead required is 'an assessment of needs in a social and political, as well as a personal, context'.[3] Tronto proposes a configuration of care not simply emanating from a private disposition in a domestic space, as in Noddings's pioneering account of it, but as a broad worldview expressed in concrete practices.[4] This is, for Tronto, not just about the important difference between 'caring about' and 'caring for'; it is also about recognising the need to widen the concept of

---

[1] Cormac McCarthy, *The Road* (first published 2006; London: Picador, 2007); Maggie Gee, *The Ice People* (first published 1998; London: Telegram, 2008). Subsequent page references to these texts are in parentheses.

[2] Nel Noddings, *Caring: A Relational Approach to Ethics and Moral Education*, updated edn. (first published 1984; Berkeley: University of California Press, 2013), p. 24.

[3] Joan C. Tronto, *Moral Boundaries: A Political Argument for an Ethic of Care* (New York: Routledge, 1993), p. 137.

[4] Noddings, *Caring*.

care beyond a narrow definition of identity and activity, so that it might be applied to a range of issues, responsibilities, and potential conflicts, while contextualising it sufficiently to account for diverse kinds of actions, concerns, and demands. Drawing on a framework that she first developed with Berenice Fisher, Tronto defines care as 'a species activity that includes everything we do to maintain, continue, and repair our "world" so that we can live in it as well as possible'.[5] This definition has been criticised by care ethicists such as Virginia Held and Christopher Groves for being too broad, but it is intentionally so, in order that care might be turned into a politically useful stance.[6] Tronto goes on to show how care so defined would inform different phases of caring: 'caring about' (that is, recognising the need to care); 'taking care of' (assuming the responsibility of meeting that need); 'care-giving' (directly meeting that need); and 'care-receiving' (perceiving and assessing whether the need has been met).[7] These relate to four components of an ethics of care: 'attentiveness, responsibility, competence, and responsiveness'.[8] Tronto, then, is careful to understand caring responsibilities and activities in terms applicable to public conduct, rather than to model these on immediate attachments and particular standpoints.

In a related move, Tronto shows how the focus on intimate and dyadic relationships of care gives rise to moral dilemmas, which an uncritical celebration of care risks ignoring and therefore replicating. Most strikingly, as Tronto suggests, 'paternalism, or maternalism' and 'parochialism' emerge as problems for a political model of care.[9] The risks of inappropriate types and amounts of care are enfolded, as it were, in its origins as a sentiment arising out of relations and attachments. Care in its particular and private expressions leads, for example, to problems in assessing 'proper levels of care, of anger and gratitude', as well as the danger of giving 'smothering care as opposed to care that leads to autonomy'.[10] Tronto warns of paternalism: 'We can well imagine that those who are care-givers, as well as those who have decided to take care of a particular need, will come to accept their own account of what is necessary to meet the caring need as definitive.' That is, the one-caring may indulge in unintentionally self-serving kinds of care, such as over-protectiveness and possessiveness.[11]

---

[5] Tronto, *Moral Boundaries*, p. 103, original emphasis; Tronto and Berenice Fisher, 'Towards a Feminist Theory of Caring', in Emily K. Abel and Margaret K. Nelson (eds.), *Circles of Care: Work and Identity in Women's Lives* (Albany: State University of New York Press, 1990), p. 40.

[6] Tronto, *Moral Boundaries*, p. 104; Virginia Held, *The Ethics of Care: Personal, Political, and Global* (Oxford University Press, 2005), p. 31; Christopher Groves, *Care, Uncertainty, and Intergenerational Ethics* (Basingstoke: Palgrave–Macmillan, 2014), p. 107.

[7] Tronto, *Moral Boundaries*, pp. 106–8.     [8] Ibid., p. 127.     [9] Ibid., p. 170.     [10] Ibid., p. 141.

[11] Ibid., p. 145.

And of parochialism, Tronto asks: 'How are we to guarantee that people, who are enmeshed in their daily rounds of care-giving and care-receiving, will be able to address broader needs and concerns for care? If mothers care for their own children, why should they not take the needs of their own children more seriously than the needs of distant children?'[12] Robert Solomon voices a related concern with the territorialising aspects of care: 'caring about anyone or anything sets up a zone of dangers and threats that promote aggressive defensiveness and hostility'.[13] In other words, the tightness of the emotional focus of the caring dyad or group has its limits, for it easily translates into a lack of compassion for and even violence towards others.

Parochialism and paternalism are united in the tendency towards self-gratification and self-interest, a selfishness that becomes more apparent when parental care is idealised as a disposition towards posterity. When the intimate connections of care serve as a model for obligation and action towards the future, they allow the kind of delusory self-importance that Timothy Clark cautions against in assuming that the non-human dimensions of the Anthropocene crisis require solutions at the human scale.[14] They potentially limit the view of that unknowable future to a version of the knowable present, at just the point at which an ethical position should be expansive rather than restrictive. The absence and thus powerlessness of future generations in moral decision-making risk a situation in which decisions are based on the values and interests of the present. At the same time, it is tempting to restrict moral considerability to present interests too, for example, to lineage (as John Rawls suggests in his brief reflection on the rationale of intergenerational justice, in which the decision-makers of his idealised 'original position' are imagined as heads of 'family lines') or community (as Avner de-Shalit proposes in his vision of a 'transgenerational community').[15]

In other words, parental care ethics is translatable into a limited position of concern that, interestingly, resembles the biological argument for posterity – that is, the perpetuation of genes. When expressed as a paternalistic attitude to the future as a version of the needs of the present and as a parochial concern with the future as lineage, parental care ethics

---

[12] Ibid., p. 142.

[13] Robert C. Solomon, *In Defense of Sentimentality* (Oxford University Press, 2004), p. 57.

[14] Timothy Clark, *Ecocriticism on the Edge: The Anthropocene as a Threshold Concept* (London: Bloomsbury, 2015), p. 164.

[15] John Rawls, *A Theory of Justice* (Harvard University Press, 1971), p. 255; Avner de-Shalit, *Why Posterity Matters: Environmental Policies and Future Generations* (London: Routledge, 1995), p. 13.

approximates genetic survivalism. Certainly, care construed in this way is hardly a model for an altruistic attitude to the planet as a whole and the continuation of its many species. Indeed, even in biological terms, simple, lineal, genetic preservation constitutes the most basic of evolutionary imperatives when compared with more advanced strategies such as kin selection and group or reciprocal altruism. One could say that it reveals, to borrow Richard Dawkins's controversial description, the genes at their most selfish.[16]

In the readings that follow, I argue that McCarthy's *The Road*, the reception of which, as a climate change novel, depends almost solely on its searing depiction of parental care in a damaged world, concludes, on close reading, with a critique of the narrow biological survivalism associated with an ethics of care. I then show how Gee's *The Ice People* holds these problems up to scrutiny throughout, and, moreover, brings into fuller view the gendered norms of care, which McCarthy's novel only hints at and never quite recognises. My analyses depend on a recognition of the reader's own journey of sympathy for characters; that is, I note the processes involved in a eudaemonistic reading, which become the grounds for a critical eudaemonistic interpretation. For one thing, each novel relies on the reader's identification with its protagonist and on the calling forth of empathy, sympathy, and, indeed, care for those within the protagonist's circle of concern (that is, with the exercise of sympathy not just for the protagonist but in tune with his own sympathetic and caring attitude and actions to his child). Yet, the protagonists' capacity for care is limited and, thus, their apparently unswerving commitment to care is unreliable. In this way, and ultimately revealing the boundaries of care, or the limits of what Martha Nussbaum calls 'the circle of concern', the novels bring the reader to an acknowledgement of those boundaries and a reconsideration of parental care.[17] For another thing, each novel grants access, at key points, to the perspectives of characters other than the focalising or narrating protagonist; most importantly, these include the child who serves as the object of care in each novel. These identificatory disruptions not only represent critical interventions in the reader's sympathetic development; they also gift the reader with alternative points of view, which, crucially, look beyond the survivalist dimensions of parental care ethics.

[16] Richard Dawkins, *The Selfish Gene*, new edn. (first published 1976; Oxford University Press, 1989).
[17] Martha Nussbaum, *Upheavals of Thought: The Intelligence of Emotions* (Cambridge University Press, 2001), p. 319.

## The Road

A simple conceptualisation of parental care underpins the reception of McCarthy's *The Road* as a climate change novel, though the novel itself, as my reading suggests, is careful to reveal the cracks in such a monolithic ideal. McCarthy is known for works – such as *Blood Meridian* (1985), the Border trilogy (*All the Pretty Horses*, 1992, *The Crossing*, 1994, and *Cities of the Plain*, 1998), and *No Country for Old Men* (2005) – in which heroes, usually male, undertake physical and psychological journeys and endure violence and isolation; McCarthy usually presents these traits as unavoidable, if extreme, aspects of human experience. In this respect, *The Road*, an account of an unnamed man and his son travelling south in an unimaginably devastated and dangerous landscape, takes up typical McCarthyian concerns, focalising the reader's empathy and sympathy on the man and his experiences in protecting himself and his son. However, it differs in other, crucial respects. For one thing, the setting's geographical uncertainty and the anonymity of the two characters lend the narrative a deeper fabular tenor than McCarthy's other novels. It casts a starker spotlight on the man as a representative of humanity and conjures up the possibility that the world in which he travels is a version of our – that is, the reader's – future, which in turn hints at the possibility of a moral to the story. For another thing, the pair's deep and abiding bond serves not only to offset the brutality and barrenness of the journey but, by the novel's end, to introduce, in the child's point of view, an alternative perspective to that of the everyman who apparently dominates the novel and the reader's purview.

The novel's mythical contours have played a pivotal role in its reception as a climate change parable. The British paperback edition of *The Road* carries one of the most oft-quoted endorsements of the novel, that it is the 'first great masterpiece of the globally warmed generation', a statement attributed to the author Andrew O'Hagan on BBC Radio 4.[18] In a comparable statement, the British writer and activist, George Monbiot, praised the novel for offering an object lesson in environmental awareness in his regular column in the broadsheet *The Guardian*, in October 2007:

> A few weeks ago, I read what I believe is the most important environmental book ever written. It is not *Silent Spring, Small is Beautiful* or even *Walden*. It contains no graphs, no tables, no facts, figures, warnings, predictions or

---

[18] McCarthy, *The Road*, back cover.

even arguments. It is a novel, first published a year ago, and it will change the way you see the world.[19]

This reading of *The Road* as an expression of human experience in a time of climate change has occurred in spite of McCarthy's silence on the topic as well as the novel's refusal to register the cause of such destruction. Some scholars have pursued the task of identifying possible causes, scouring plot and setting for clues; whatever the hypotheses turned up – an asteroid strike, nuclear attack, divine apocalypse – it is fair to say that climate change never definitively figures among the events that so transform the world of *The Road*.[20] However, the temptation to link the novel to climate change is strong, and O'Hagan's and Monbiot's claims are part of a growing exegesis of the novel as a document of and for a world in the midst of environmental crisis.[21] In the analysis that follows, I show how the reader might be led towards such a 'globally warmed' interpretation, but I also suggest that this in turn enables a further reading, with very different ethical implications.

The first reading is facilitated in large part by the stripped-down setting and style, for the absence of any sense of place, combined with the distillation of plot and character into the single-minded quest of the man and the boy, results in an unflinching focus on the relationship between father and son. These terms are accomplished early in the novel; indeed, its opening establishes what one critic has called a particular set of 'survivalist semiotics'.[22] From the first page onwards, the reader's attention is with the man's, from his awakening into darkness to the grey landscape that is

---

[19] George Monbiot, 'Civilisation Ends with a Shutdown of Human Concern: Are We There Already?', *The Guardian* (30 October 2007).

[20] Lydia Cooper suggests that McCarthy identifies the disaster as 'a meteor strike' in 'Cormac McCarthy's *The Road* as Apocalyptic Grail Narrative', *Studies in the Novel* 43 (2011), 218; Carl Grindley discusses a 'supernatural cause' in 'The Setting of McCarthy's *The Road*', *Explicator* 67 (2008), 12; and Francisco Collado-Rodríguez and Tim Blackmore suggest nuclear disaster in Collado-Rodríguez, 'Trauma and Storytelling in Cormac McCarthy's *No Country for Old Men* and *The Road*', *Papers on Language and Literature* 48 (2012), 45, and Blackmore, 'Life of War, Death of the Rest: The Shining Path of Cormac McCarthy's Thermonuclear America', *Bulletin of Science, Technology and Society* 29 (2009), 18–36.

[21] Ben De Bruyn, 'Borrowed Time, Borrowed World and Borrowed Eyes: Care, Ruin and Vision in McCarthy's *The Road* and Harrison's *Ecocriticism*', *English Studies* 91 (2010), 776–81; Susan Kollin, '"Barren, Silent, Godless": Ecodisaster and the Post-Abundant Landscape in *The Road*', in Sara L. Spurgeon (ed.), *Cormac McCarthy: All the Pretty Horses, No Country for Old Men, The Road* (New York: Continuum, 2011), pp. 157–71; Andrew Keller Estes, *Cormac McCarthy and the Writing of American Spaces* (Amsterdam: Rodopi, 2013), pp. 189–216.

[22] Donovan Gwinner, '"Everything Uncoupled from Its Shoring": Quandaries of Epistemology and Ethics in *The Road*', in Sara L. Spurgeon (ed.), *Cormac McCarthy: All the Pretty Horses, No Country for Old Men, The Road* (New York: Continuum, 2011), p. 139.

gradually revealed in the daylight, before coming to a realisation, with the boy's awakening, that the man is not alone, and thence to the prospect of another day on the road. All this sets up the narrative's most important contrast: the juxtaposition of what lies without (a world of environmental devastation and human cruelty) with what lies within (the bond between man and boy: a sanctuary of care). In the first few pages, the reader encounters the shocking emptiness of the 'Barren, silent, godless' (2) landscape, but more significant are the terms of the journey through that landscape (to head south) and the yoking of these with the father's unabated care and concern for the boy. Their first conversation carries all the unspoken affection of a typical parent–child exchange:

> The boy turned in the blankets. Then he opened his eyes. Hi, Papa, he said.
>     I'm right here.
>     I know. (3)

In addition, and strikingly, this dialogue is an interpellative moment for the reader as parent; in Philip Snyder's Levinasian reading, it is an ethical '*me voici*' or 'here I am!' moment, presenting the son as an ethical other and giving to him a face to which not just father but reader might respond.[23] Both the warmth of the short exchange and the father's sense of responsibility contrast with the assertion of the lines immediately preceding: 'This was not a safe place. They could be seen from the road now it was day' (3). The dangers of the world beyond give urgency to the father's obligations to protect his child on their journey, and to the reader's apprehension of these.

As the novel progresses, the world which the reader of *The Road* enters seems, more and more, to be designed not just to contrast the devastation in the landscape on the one hand with the care and love between man and boy on the other, but also to establish the very special import of that care and love. To begin with, the bare landscape through which the pair walk is not merely bare, but haunted by loss; the novel's tenor, in short, is elegiac. Much has been made of the lyrical emptiness of the novel's setting: the 'cauterized terrain' (13), the 'ashen scabland' (14), 'a colorless world of wire and crepe' (123), and the 'coastal plain rivers in leaden serpentine across the wasted farmland' (214); Rune Graulund asserts, for example, that it is 'a desert that never ends nor begins, a landscape as devoid of difference as it is

---

[23] Phillip A. Snyder, 'Hospitality in Cormac McCarthy's *The Road*', *Cormac McCarthy Journal* 6 (2008), 74–5.

of life'.[24] But, as Linda Gruber Godfrey notes, 'the old geography of the lost, greener world is revered and mourned in the novel'.[25] The significance of this emptiness is that it creates a vacuum which remnants of the past rush to fill, whether such material vestiges as the last bottle of Coke or the telephone on which the man 'dialed the number of his father's house in that long ago' (5), such verbalised reminders as the bits of information the man gives his son of the world as it used to be, or such psychic spectres as memory and dream. But these remnants can give no comfort to the man and, by extension, the reader. What makes the loss so keenly felt is that what is lost can only return incompletely, as traces. Because the past is spoken of, thought of, remembered, only in order to know it is not there, loss becomes an ongoing state of being in the novel. That is, the traces of the pastoral past – dream, memories, remnants, stories, bits and pieces – constantly establish and re-establish the incompleteness of the present. So, for example, in a feverish dream, the man finds 'the vanished world returned' (199); on other nights, he dreams of his long-dead wife and other elements of the long-gone world that emphasise the deathliness of the world to which he awakes: 'Rich dreams now which he was loathe to wake from. Things no longer known in the world' (139). The last material residue of this lost world has much the same effect: he remembers 'Chile, corn, stew, soup, spaghetti sauce. The richness of a vanished world' (147). Even the marvellous plenitude of the bunker upon which the man and boy miraculously stumble underlines the emptiness of the world outside.

These traces of what is lost possess a double vulnerability, being not merely impartial, but also at risk of disappearing altogether. Over and over, the reader is exposed, through the man's encounters, not just to the old world's extinction but the process of its extinguishing. Its objects are rotting and useless: the telephone the man dials calls nowhere, and the once vital contents of his billfold – 'credit cards', 'driver's license' (52) – are now of so little import that he decides to leave them on the road. The man's memories, the reader learns, are being forgotten: 'Like the dying world the newly blind inhabit, all of it slowly fading from memory' (17). His memories of language, too, fade, so that language itself ceases to exist: 'The names of things slowly following those things into oblivion' (93). The man's stories make little sense when they are of

---

[24] Rune Graulund, 'Fulcrums and Borderlands: A Desert Reading of Cormac McCarthy's *The Road*', *Orbis Litterarum* 65 (2010), 61.

[25] Laura Gruber Godfrey, '"The World He'd Lost": Geography and "Green" Memory in Cormac McCarthy's *The Road*', *Critique* 52 (2011), 171.

a world the boy cannot know, 'that for him was not even a memory' (55).[26]

The novel emphasises its elegy by embodying it in the man's experiences, and conveys it all the more powerfully by placing the reader in the man's shoes. More than once, memories explicitly situate the father and son in the footsteps of others in the long-lost pastoral, the boy standing beside the man 'Where he'd stood once with his own father in a winter long ago' (33–34). The same may be said of the man's countless memories of different views from different times in the same place, of how, for example, 'In the long ago somewhere very near this place he'd watched a falcon fall down the long blue wall of the mountain' (19). The reader looks upon and experiences, with the man, not just the world but the loss of that world.

As the journey proceeds, the novel clarifies exactly what has been lost, or, more precisely, what kind of loss the man must constantly face. The man and the boy are not humans in a dead world as such; they are humans in an inhuman world. The man's realisation that 'On this road there are no godspoke men', that 'They are gone and I am left and they have taken with them the world' (32), is a realisation that *he* constitutes a remnant of moral worth. This worth is figured in the characteristically McCarthyian compound of 'godspoke', the medieval quaintness of the word bringing an element of the mythical and biblical to the text.[27] That the world itself has disappeared with the 'godspoke men' underscores how the quality of being humane – rather than merely human – is what defined the now-extinct world. If humanity, in both senses of the word, is the hallmark of the lost pastoral past in *The Road*, then not simply a lack of life, but a lack of humanity even where there is life, brings about the novel's present nightmare.

At the heart of such morality, it seems, is the father's bond with the boy. The novel's early pages establish the father's awareness that the boy is 'his warrant' (3), suggesting that the man's love for his son is his justification for and guarantee of life, a warrant in both senses of the word. This idea is

[26] For more on the tenuousness not just of objects but of memory and, with it, language, see De Bruyn, 'Borrowed Time', 781–5; Tim Edwards, 'The End of the Road: Pastoralism and the Post-Apocalyptic Waste Land of Cormac McCarthy's *The Road*', *Cormac McCarthy Journal* 6 (2008), 58; Godfrey, '"The World He'd Lost"', 169–70; Louise Squire, 'Death and the Anthropocene: Cormac McCarthy's World of Unliving', *Oxford Literary Review* 34.2 (2012), 211–18; and Linda Woodson, 'Mapping *The Road* in Post-Postmodernism', *Cormac McCarthy Journal* 8 (2010), 91–3.

[27] Benjamin Mangrum discusses the prayer-like quality of the word 'godspoke' in 'Accounting for *The Road*: Tragedy, Courage, and Cavell's Acknowledgement', *Philosophy and Literature* 37 (2013), 277.

underlined later in the novel by a remembered statement of his wife's, a memory brought on by the boy's fragility: 'He held the boy close to him. So thin. My heart, he said. My heart. But he knew that if he were a good father still it might well be as she said. That the boy was all that stood between him and death' (29). The boy's pitiful thinness is, at once, a source of anxiety and a reminder of parental duty for both the man and the reader, thanks to the vividness and tactility of the description of the boy. Here, the phrase, 'My heart', offers itself as an expression not just of painful concern ('oh, my heart!') but of identification ('my son *is* my heart'), which subliminally echoes the empathy and sympathy between reader and man as caring parents, even as it demonstrates the centrality of parental love to the man's humanity, that is, his humanness and humaneness.

If such humanity has as its lodestone the love of the man for his child, it is also because, in the inhuman world beyond, there exists the utter absence of such love. In this world, children are raped (as the boy's mother fears he will be) and killed; worst of all, they are eaten. Paedophagy, the most dramatic and visceral opposite of parental care, lies at the heart of the nightmarish world of *The Road*. It is the unspeakable subtext of the man's instructions to the boy to kill himself with the revolver or his anxiety about having to 'crush that beloved skull with a rock' (120) to save him from their near encounter with cannibals. More explicit and more shocking are the remains of a baby they chance upon in the forest – 'a charred human infant headless and gutted and blackening on the spit' (212); yet, this is still, within the novel, unspeakable, for the man wonders if the boy (or, perhaps, he means himself) would 'ever speak again' (212) after this. Strikingly, the horror is most fully expressed when the reader is explicitly invited to place herself, alongside the man, in a 'world . . . largely populated by men who would eat your children in front of your eyes' (192). As Arielle Zibrak notes of the novel's evocation of 'these extreme poles' of the treatment of children, it means that 'upholding the sacred role of parent is no less than the preservation of one's humanity'.[28] Unsurprisingly, this grotesque juxtaposition of cruelty and love informs the repeated expression of the father-and-son bond, their shared refrains not just that they are 'carrying the fire' (87) but that they are 'the good guys' (81). The dialogue that passes between father and son after their escape from the cannibals' house with its cellar prison establishes explicitly that 'We wouldnt ever eat anybody' because 'we're the good guys' and 'we're carrying the fire' (136). In other

[28] Arielle Zibrak, 'Intolerance, A Survival Guide: Heteronormative Culture Formation in Cormac McCarthy's *The Road*', *Arizona Quarterly* 68 (2012), 111.

words, their bond – 'the fire' – is one of the world's last vestiges, according to the novel, of unconditional parental love and the shelter it brings.

The reading I have put forward here depends, so far, on the reader's sympathetic identification with the man, an identification grounded on the value of parenthood and particularly provoked by the emotional intensity of the tests of his parental responsibilities – the preservation not just of the well-being but the very survival of his son. Such sympathies underlie, for example, Michael Chabon's assessment of the novel. In an eloquent review that first appeared in the *New York Review of Books*, Chabon describes it as 'a testament to the abyss of a parent's greatest fears', and, in doing so, gives voice to his sympathies for the man.[29]

The eudaemonistic reader might further extend this sympathy to consider parental care as constituting a humane and ethical position, and, indeed, to find that it is just this kind of ethical position that is required in the face of environmental devastation. Such a conclusion is made by Monbiot's evaluation of the novel as 'the most important environmental book you will ever read'. It must be said that such a 'globally warmed' reading of the novel attributes environmental damage to carelessness or inhumanity and identifies environmental rescue with care and humanity, even though the novel makes no such connection. Aligning the death of the non-human world with the rise of inhuman humans, the novel enables – but never actually performs – an alignment of environmental disaster with the loss of (parental) care. The novel's stark contrast between the human and inhuman is not a contrast, after all, between the human and *non*-human. It is odd, then, that readers such as Graulund should concede that this is 'a novel that is squarely anthropocentric', but also find that 'the second and contradictory desert lesson to be learned from *The Road* is that without nature . . ., there can be no humanity either'.[30] For *The Road* is not as interested in the non-human environment as it seems, requiring instead a relentless anthropocentrism for its logic; hence, a reading of the novel in the context of climate change must proceed by a kind of thought association, placing parental care in proximity with – and, from there, in contrast to – virtually wholesale biospheric devastation (except for humans, one or two dogs, and, surprisingly, a handful of mushrooms). All this invites an easy correlation of uncaring with ecocide and an

---

[29] Michael Chabon, 'Dark Adventure: On Cormac McCarthy's *The Road*', *Maps and Legends: Reading and Writing along the Borderlands* (San Francisco: McSweeney's, 2008), p. 120.
[30] Graulund, 'Fulcrums and Borderlands', 74–5.

equally easy identification of uncaring as one of the direst losses that humans will suffer if we continue with ecocide.

However, a more informed reading of the novel's eco-credentials must take account of the boy's role in this dynamic of parental care. Importantly, the boy is the bearer of his own ethics (quite aside from his enigmatic quality, inviting readings of him as a messianic figure).[31] Crucially, this ethics is very different from the parental position held by his father, and thus very different from the sympathetic anxieties called forth in the reader. The reader would do well to recall that the boy attempts to return the care his father extends to him, insisting in one instance that they share a can of Coca Cola and chiding his father on another occasion for foregoing cocoa for his sake. The boy's language, importantly, turns parental care back on itself: 'You promised not to do that ... I have to watch you all the time' (35).[32] Later, when his father proclaims, paternalistically and self-righteously, that he is 'the one who has to worry about everything', the boy's response is 'I am the one' (277). The curious absolutism of the phrase 'the one' construes the boy's capacity to care not as equally valid as the man's but as valid in a way that the man's paternalistic authority is not. That is, it challenges the foundations of the man's power to make caring decisions for the boy.

The man's brand of parental care belies what Donovan Gwinner describes as 'survivalist insularity'; that is, it exercises the parochial impulse, identified by critics of parental care ethics, of saving one's offspring at the expense of others.[33] Protecting the boy requires harming or killing others who pose a threat to the boy. Here, of course, Lee Edelman's forthright condemnation of 'reproductive futurism' is worth considering.[34] The figure of the child – which dominates the man's and thus the reader's frame of reference – is associated by Edelman with adults' false and ultimately narcissistic attempts at realising their own desires for the future. The child is, according to Edelman, 'the site of a projective identification of

---

[31] For remarks on the boy's 'messianic' qualities, see Grindley, 'The Setting of McCarthy's *The Road*', 11–13; Allen Josephs, 'What's at the End of *The Road?*', *South Atlantic Review* 74 (2009), 23–9; Ashley Kunsa, '"Maps of the World in Its Becoming": Post-Apocalyptic Naming in Cormac McCarthy's *The Road*', *Journal of Modern Literature* 33 (2009), 65–7.

[32] Gwinner, 'Everything Uncoupled from Its Shoring', p. 147; however, in an otherwise compelling reading of the way in which this clash of ethical codes plays out in the novel, Gwinner glosses this statement as an early example of the pair's 'shared precepts' and misses the son's appropriation of moral authority here.

[33] Ibid., p. 153.

[34] Lee Edelman, *No Future: Queer Theory and the Death Drive* (Durham, NC: Duke University Press, 2004), p. 2.

an always impossible future'.[35] For Zibrak, the man's survivalism 'can be precisely described within Edelman's model' and is, in her analysis, 'unfounded in any real hope for the boy's future'.[36] It is possible to read, in other words, the man's blinkered, desperate care for his son as also a brutal inability to care for anyone else, coming increasingly to resemble a selfish and stubborn mission to save something of himself – to preserve *his* "warrant" (3), *his* "heart" (29).

At the same time, an awareness of an alternative ethics casts attention onto the actions of the boy's mother. That is, the boy's perspective reminds the reader of other marginalised perspectives and, with them, other ethical positions.[37] Having committed suicide before the action of the novel, the mother is focalised for the reader through the man. Thus framed by his memory and his interactions with her, her suicidal thoughts are, strikingly, recalled by him as her metaphorical description of death-wish as infidelity: she expresses her desire to kill both herself and the boy not only as 'the right thing to do' (58), but also as akin to 'a faithless slut' (58) with 'a whorish heart' (59) taking on 'a new lover'. Yet, while the mention of faithlessness might initially suggest a betrayal of the man and even, perhaps, the boy, the mother's words do not simply disavow parental care; they also raise the possibility of a version of parental love to rival the man's. His survivalist ethics holds onto a binary understanding of life versus death – he insists: 'We're survivors' (57). Her response complicates this with an alternative description of their life – 'We're not survivors. We're the walking dead in a horror film' (57) – and a wistful invocation of death as 'eternal nothing-ness' (58). The woman's advice to anyone who might find himself alone in such a world chillingly fits with the man's treatment of the child in the novel from the very first pages. She states: 'A person who had no one would be well advised to cobble together some passable ghost. Breathe it into being and coax it along with words of love' (59); in contrast, her solution presents, tantalisingly, as a release. Unfortunately, her death silences her and the very different scenario she wishes for the boy.

Importantly, it is the child who talks back. From the first instance in the narrative of the man's survivalist inflection of parental care ethics, the boy raises questions about its tenability. Having shot a potential assailant, the father washes the boy free of blood and gore, musing: 'This is my child . . . . I wash a dead man's brains out of his hair. This is my job' (77). This job is

[35] Ibid., p. 31.      [36] Zibrak, 'Intolerance, A Survival Guide', 109.

[37] Indeed, in Squire's reading, the mother, father, and boy illustrate three different responses to the existential challenge presented by death as an unavoidable aspect of the human condition, a challenge brought into focus by the Anthropocene; Squire, 'Death and the Anthropocene', 211–28.

clarified to the boy: 'My job is to take care of you. I was appointed to do that by God. I will kill anyone who touches you' (80). Such a wrenching example of parental care invites the unwary reader into sympathetic accord with the man, and indeed, aided by divine invocation, gives any eudae-monistic reading an additional sense of ethical uprightness. Yet, tellingly, the child's response – 'Are we still the good guys?' (80) – questions the code of exclusionary survivalism that underwrites the father-and-son bond. For the reader, the boy's alternative approach is crystallised much later in the narrative, in the incident with the old man who calls himself Ely. The encounter is initiated by the boy's desire to help, feed, and protect others, which runs counter to the man's assumptions. It is remarkable for, first, showing explicitly that ethical agency can originate from that half of the bond too easily constructed as the passive 'cared-for' and, second, for its identification of a third-party recipient outside the confines of the dyadic, parochial bond of care. In other words, it introduces an alternative, democratically inclined ethical action.

The boy's democratic ethos is further defined against the father's in their conversations about 'good guys' and 'bad guys', a motif that, as I have already noted, carries much of the import of the father's love for the boy. Often in the novel, the man acknowledges only in the abstract the presence of 'other good guys' (196). But, in noting that a mutual fear of danger conceals 'good guys' from each other, he renders their presence as good as absence (or, to turn the man's own query onto himself: 'How does the never to be differ from the never was?' (32)). In contrast, the boy constantly proffers the hope of the existence of other good guys: of tracks in the road, he suggests, 'They could be good guys. Couldnt they?' (108), and, of whomever constructed the bunker, he asks, 'They were the good guys?' (148). But another such question from the boy, 'What if some good guys came?' is met by: 'Well, I dont think we're likely to meet any good guys on the road' (160). Similarly, when the boy thinks of writing in the sand 'a letter to the good guys', this is countered by his father's question, 'What if the bad guys saw it?' (261). As Gwinner puts it, 'there is no model for "good guys" besides the protagonists themselves.'[38] Other good guys do not exist in the man's ethical universe.

The bearded veteran who saves the boy puts the lie to this denial of other good guys, revealing the man to be an unreliable and somewhat undeser-ving focaliser of the reader's sympathies. Crucially, the veteran's attitude is in keeping with the boy's ethos of open compassion and in contrast with

[38] Gwinner, 'Everything Uncoupled from Its Shoring', p. 148.

the father's code of fiercely guarded, filial protection. The decision to come after the pair, over which the veteran admits there was 'some discussion' (303), suggests an interest in the welfare of others beyond the immediate attachments of care ethics. The father's relentless care for his son at this point seems emblematised by their single-minded focus on the road, for the veteran's advice to 'keep out of the road' (303) provocatively suggests an alternative code of behaviour and, possibly, ethics. Importantly, this advice suggests a mode of survivalism – indeed, a set of ethics – that is rather more enlarged than the father's. After all, the boy is not just a trace of the past and the world as it was; he is also one of the rightful inheritors of this dead past. On the 'intestate earth' (138), such inheritors are in danger of being mere traces of the past, of themselves being made extinct, if they do not procreate; thus, the survival of the boy and such other children as the boy and girl of the family who save him is paramount to a wider survivalism – the survival of the human species.

As I have suggested, a globally warmed reading of the novel would equate a lack of humanity towards children with a lack of humanity towards the non-human world. For some, this may appear to be consolidated by the novel's quixotic conclusion. The vivid description of brook trout that ends the book, apparently *a propos* of nothing, is a paean to non-human ecology that seems to offer relief and even eulogy after the devastation of the novel. Critics have pointed out how it echoes the man's memory of trout earlier in the novel.[39] What has not been noted in their commentaries, however, is how the coda's evocative reminiscence of the beauty of the world – 'A thing not to be put back. Not to be put right again' (307) – repeats a moment in the narrative when the man 'bent to see into the boy's face under the blanket hood [and] very much feared that something was gone that could not be put right again' (143–4). This occurs after their discovery of the prison cellar of human prey and the child's awareness of the existence of cannibalism. In echoing this moment in the enigmatic conclusion, the novel seems to correlate the irrevocable violence done to the child's innocence with the irreversibility of environmental damage, and hence to reaffirm a parental care ethics for the good of posterity.

Nonetheless, the boy's covert presence in this ending should also alert the reader to the significance of his ethical conduct and to the value of his perspective. It is one thing to associate the inhuman traumas visited on the

[39] See, for example, De Bruyn, 'Borrowed Time', 785; Edwards, 'The End of the Road', 58; Godfrey, '"The World He'd Lost"', 172; Josephs, 'What's at the End of *The Road*?', 29; and Hannah Stark, '"All These Things He Saw and Did Not See": Witnessing the End of the World in Cormac McCarthy's *The Road*', *Critical Survey* 25.2 (2013), 81.

child with the utter devastation of non-human nature, but it is quite another to suggest that the man is able to safeguard against or reverse such atrocities – to 'put [things] right again'. That is, the novel might, in the final analysis, be making a tentative alignment of the ecological destruction and our obligations to future generations, but it also hints at the need to consider a different kind of ethos for the sake of both. Once we attend to the boy's motivations, we find that the plot's conclusion refines definitions of what it is to care for and about children, and of what kinds of care allow them to survive and thrive in an inhuman world. A *critical* eudaemonistic reading of *The Road* reveals an ethical attitude to children, inasmuch as they stand for the generations of the future, that requires more than the naïve parochialism that would care about and for them alone. It requires a reaching out to others – to other children and, indeed, other humans.

## Re-Gendering Care

As much as it might problematise the blinkered and exceptionalist view of parental care ethics, *The Road* disregards – and, indeed, reinforces – the glaring issue of its gender politics and power games. The brief appearances of the mother in the narrative marginalise her: she serves in the man's memories and the reader's identification with these to point to the lost world of (male) fulfilment and pastoral, and becomes, in short, another vestige of the past. Because, in Zibrak's words, the mother's character 'comes in and out of narrative focus in brief flickers', the novel effectively screens female presence out of 'a tale of abounding natalism in an almost exclusively male environment'.[40] What is noteworthy is not that the novel neglects the conventional feminisation of parental care ethics – itself, notes Zibrak, a problematic 'construction of motherhood as the ultimate source of female fulfillment' – but that it passes up the opportunity to interrogate and scrutinise these gender norms.[41] Moreover, the novel re-inscribes such norms by situating parental obligation within behaviours heavily coded as masculine – gunmanship, threats, physical violence; it would seem the man is not so different from other McCarthyian heroes, after all. Yet, in the popular reception of the novel, this machismo surrounds an enactment of parenthood for an ungendered reader (presumably, the reader of 'the globally warmed generation' whose sympathies stem from 'a parent's greatest fears').

[40] Zibrak, 'Intolerance, A Survival Guide', III.     [41] Ibid., III.

The novel's masculinised version of parental care is a reminder that we should not be too ready to assume that images of fatherly care might help neutralise the gender norms and power dynamics of parenthood. Indeed, the risks are apparent in the rise of the 'new fatherhood' in late-twentieth-century cultural discourse in the West. Cultural critics and sociologists have noted the increasing prevalence of images of fathers sharing in primary caregiving duties and displaying the kind of emotional involvement traditionally associated with the mother;[42] some have suggested that this coincides with genderless or gender-balanced references in parenting discourses, such as parental advice literature.[43] However, quite aside from the question of just how new the new father really is (Ralph LaRossa shows how such expectations around fatherhood first appeared in the 1920s and 1930s), the imagery of new fatherhood has not magically resolved the gender politics of parenthood.[44] In some cases, the subtext of the new father narrative holds stubbornly onto antifeminist and heterosexist expectations of women's care as primary and men's as part-time and secondary, so that one must ask to what extent traditional stereotypes linger in this apparently progressive agenda.[45] In others, it is recast within patterns of masculinist power, as, for example, in the disturbing phenomenon of the neoconservative appropriation of new fatherhood discourse to shore up narratives of patriarchal control over the nuclear family.[46] In other words, though the new father as a source of an equally important brand of care as the mother may be an admirable aspiration for many families, even – or, indeed, particularly – where these are not conventionally nuclear, he is not always immune from the exclusionary logic of parental care's identity

---

[42] Deborah Lupton and Lesley Barclay, *Constructing Fatherhood: Discourses and Experiences* (London: Sage, 1997); Janice Kelly and Laura Tropp, 'Introduction: Changing Conceptions of the Good Dad in Popular Culture', in Tropp and Kelly (eds.), *Deconstructing Dads: Changing Images of Fathers in Popular Culture* (Lanham, MD: Lexington, 2016), pp. xi–xx; Glenda Wall and Stephanie Arnold, 'How Involved Is Involved Fathering?' *Gender and Society* 21.4 (2007), 508–27.

[43] Jane Sunderland, '"Parenting" or "Mothering"? The Case of Modern Childcare Magazines', *Discourse and Society* 17.4 (2006), 503–27.

[44] Ralph LaRossa, *The Modernization of Fatherhood: A Social and Political History* (University of Chicago Press, 1997); LaRossa, 'The Culture of Fatherhood and the Late-Twentieth-Century New Fatherhood Movement: An Interpretive Perspective', in Laura Tropp and Janice Kelly (eds.), *Deconstructing Dads: Changing Images of Fathers in Popular Culture* (Lanham, MD: Lexington, 2016), pp. 3–30.

[45] For example, television and print advertisements overwhelmingly show fathers indulging children in desserts, fast food outings, and breakfast, and mothers cooking meals, administering medicine, and doing domestic chores; see Wall and Arnold, 'How Involved Is Involved Fathering?', and Gayle Kaufman, 'The Portrayal of Men's Family Roles in Television Commercials', *Sex Roles* 41 (1999), 439–58.

[46] Robert L. Griswold, *Fatherhood in America: A History* (New York: Basic Books, 1993), pp. 244–6.

politics. That is, if, as I suggested in chapter 1, the 'solidification of identity results in politics of exclusion', and parental care ethics sets apart and even empowers the parental identity group, such an ethics might also enable the emergence of competing identities of care within the group in ways that are ultimately inimical to caring itself.[47] Thus, though it may seem churlish not to laud representations of caring fatherhood for helping to dismiss the stereotypes and norms of 'motherhood environmentalism' explored and discussed in chapter 1, it is also incumbent on any critical examination of discourses of paternal care to interrogate any gender norms that persist, rather than to reaffirm these through silence.[48]

### The Ice People

Gee's *The Ice People* enables just such a critical excavation of the gendered history of parental care ethics, while pointing to the vulnerability of parental care to traditional gender power dynamics.[49] By alternating between reader identification with its male narrator on the one hand and moments of ironic distance and insight into its female protagonist on the other, the novel allows two gendered worldviews – encompassing parental care and environmental awareness – to unfold. Each is subject to critique, and together these critiques lead to an understanding of the limitations that gendered identity politics impose on parental care ethics.

Gee's first novel, *Dying, in Other Words*, appeared in 1981. Critically acclaimed from the outset, Gee nevertheless remained relatively underrated until the 2002 publication of *The White Family*, a searching narrative about racial prejudice in contemporary England. Described by one scholar as a 'compassionate humanist feminist' and by another as a revivalist of the mid-Victorian 'condition-of-England novel', Gee displays in her work an interest in the tenuousness of middle-class life, investigating the impact on individuals – usually networks of family and friends – when what is taken for granted is somehow lost.[50] Disaster is often enacted stylistically and

---

[47] Catriona Sandilands, *The Good-Natured Feminist: Ecofeminism and the Quest for Democracy* (Minneapolis: University of Minnesota Press, 1999), p. 47.

[48] Ibid., p. xiii.

[49] Rather than interpret the novel – as Susan Watkins does – as a celebration of the 'maternal imaginary', my reading of Gee's novel emphasises its trenchant critique of maternal care as environmental solution; see Watkins, 'Future Shock: Rewriting the Apocalypse in Contemporary Women's Fiction', *LIT: Literature Interpretation Theory* 23 (2012), 119.

[50] John Sears, '"Making Sorrow Speak": Maggie Gee's Novels', in Emma Parker (ed.), *Contemporary British Women Writers* (Cambridge: D. S. Brewer, 2004), p. 55; Mine Özyurt Kılıç, *Maggie Gee: Writing the Condition-of-England Novel* (London: Bloomsbury, 2013), p. 5.

structurally too: catastrophes occur as interruptions to Gee's normally realist style, for example, in the black pages and bird-shaped visual poetry that represent nuclear holocaust in *The Burning Book* (1983) and in the montage of disconnected paragraphs after London is deluged in *The Flood* (2004).[51]

*The Ice People* is characteristic of Gee's fiction in its exploration of apparently average life devastated by environmental, social, or political change, and its use of such upheavals to critique that appearance of normality. Like her more recent novel, *The Flood*, *The Ice People* is set in a recognisably futuristic world. Also like this novel, it treats of environmental crisis by demonstrating its impact on a single family. In Gee's own words, she aims for her environmental novels to achieve their power not by being 'message-y' but by enabling the reader 'to live other lives and become other people' and, in so doing, to 'feel fear while it is still useful'.[52] Also in keeping with Gee's *œuvre* generally, the novel is characterised by its interrogations of gender inequity, particularly in questioning conventional equations of oppressor and oppressed. In 1995, around the time of writing *The Ice People*, Gee remarked on the 'black and white' tendency of 'women's fiction': 'I think it's too obvious to be a woman, and a feminist woman, writing about nice women and horrid men, which is a lot of what's going on, isn't it?'[53] Gee's novels, indeed, tend to expose gender biases by scrutinising their impact on both men and women, and inviting reader sympathy on all sides.

*The Ice People* effectively describes two climate change events. It is set in the middle of the twenty-first century, when global warming suddenly experiences a rapid reversal: the world enters an Ice Age, and anthropogenic climate change is countered by an apparently 'natural' climate phenomenon. While the novel's present-day setting shows the effects of rapid glaciation, its past, conveyed in flashback by the male narrator Saul, details first a warmed world and then the drastic process of cooling. In the first few pages of the novel, Saul despatches a description of the globally warming world in which he grew up. Born in London in 2005, at the start of what would become known as 'the Tropical Time' (16), climate change

---

[51] For commentary on these novels' stylistic devices, see Magdalena Maczynska, 'This Monstrous City: Urban Visionary Satire in the Fiction of Martin Amis, Will Self, China Miéville, and Maggie Gee', *Contemporary Literature* 51 (2010), 48–9; and Sarah Dillon, 'Imagining Apocalypse: Maggie Gee's *The Flood*', *Contemporary Literature* 48 (2007), 374–97.

[52] Diana McCaulay, Michael Mendis, and Maggie Gee, 'The Untold Story: The Environment in Fiction', Hay Festival, 29 May 2014.

[53] Margaret McKay, 'An Interview with Maggie Gee', *Studia Neophilologica* 69.2 (1997), 216.

has reached its height by his teens and twenties. Along with climate change, the world has also experienced dramatic social breakdown: epidemics of diseases such as Ebola and mutant HIVs have just about shut down entire governments, including Britain's. The biosphere has been irretrievably damaged, medical tinkering in the form of antibiotics has produced resistant strains of killer diseases, and unrestrained profit motive only further encourages social, political, and environmental dysfunction. But this is a time during which young men and women – feeling all the invincibility of youth – revel in, rather than worry about, climatic conditions. Saul's response, like that of others in the developed West, is to use the hot weather and many technological advances to his advantage and enjoyment.

Initially, the reader is invited to empathise and sympathise with Saul, who seems intelligent and likeable. This sympathy is further encouraged by Saul's position as a dystopian outsider, which sees him negotiating and attempting to retain his perspective in something of a brave new world. The twentieth-century battle of the sexes has given way to mutual antagonism and a trend for gender segregation, or 'segging' (23), in which young men and women simply avoid each other; yet, Saul describes himself as 'a man who wanted women. . . . It seemed so natural, like having children' (24). He further rebels when he falls in love with the apparently likeminded Sarah, and settles down in what he describes as an 'old-fashioned', 'twentieth century' kind of way (28). If the reader still empathises with Saul at this point, it is by inhabiting an insistently heteronormative parental attitude, framed as a desire for pastoral bliss: 'We imagined raising a family by the sea, with forests, fields, clean bright water. The children were running, shouting, towards us' (35). All this, crucially, is described by Saul as overwhelmingly normal, Sarah's *womanly* characteristics complementing his wish to be 'manly' and resulting in an 'absolute feeling of rightness together' (32; original emphasis). That is, as Sarah Dillon's perceptive analysis suggests, Saul is the ideological mouthpiece for the kind of 'reproductive futurism' that Edelman describes: Saul's desire for conventional family life is expressed as a love for the child, even while that desire betrays, in Lacanian terms, a self-directed wish for wholeness.[54]

For the attentive and sympathetic reader, discomfort with Saul's self-serving heterosexist outlook sets in early. In particular, Saul's response to segging is telling; his inability to understand it and offer a coherent

---

[54] Sarah Dillon, 'Literary Equivocation: Reproductive Futurism and *The Ice People*', in Sarah Dillon and Caroline Edwards (eds.), *Maggie Gee: Critical Essays* (Canterbury: Gylphi, 2015), p. 113.

rationale for it allows Sarah's perspective – half-expressed and focalised through Saul – to come into play. Saul fails to see that segging is motivated by women, as a backlash against what they perceive to be the gender inequalities that still predominate in twenty-first-century life; thus, Sarah provides an alternative insight. Employed as part of a state initiative to combat segging and to improve falling fertility rates, she teaches teenagers how to fall in love and finds that, while boys are receptive enough to the idea of 'having women to love and support them', girls are 'not all that excited about developing their nurturing sides' (36). The girls' concerns centre on the inequality that informs caring expectations, with the burden of care assigned to women rather than to men: 'I want to look after kids . . . But why should I want to look after a man? They're not babies' (36). Sarah's attempts to explain the girls' perspective to Saul actually produce an example of such imbalance: her suggestion that 'they have a point about housework, too' provokes Saul's response that 'you enjoy it . . . . I mean, you turn that side of things into pure pleasure. I wish those girls could see what you do' (37). In this context, Sarah's growing indecision over whether to marry and have children with Saul, reflecting her increasing detachment from their attempt to revive traditional gender norms, is unsurprising. Her experience points to segging as the outcome of women's dissatisfaction with the conventional gendering and marginalisation of the role of the one-caring. What follows for the reader is an empathetic split, initially between Saul and Sarah. Saul's narrative point of view continues to dominate, but his angry outbursts over Sarah's actions, framing her as irrational and cruel, tend not to strengthen reader sympathy for him. Instead, Saul's irrationality creates an ironic distance between him and the reader, creating space for a competing sympathy with Sarah.

The birth of their son, Luke, heralds the first of many separations for Saul and Sarah, as well as coinciding with the start of the world's descent into an Ice Age. The parental conflicts over Luke are mirrored by humanity's inability to safeguard the planet, thus aligning parental care – inadequate as it is shown to be – with environmental stewardship. Luke becomes, not unproblematically, a symbol for the future of the planet. Moreover, as the narrative turns into a chronicle of arguments, separations, and reunions between Saul and Sarah, the reader is invited to consider their argument in the context of a gendered conflict between two different approaches to both parental and planetary care.

The first approach is discernible in a catalogue of environmental failings construable as masculine. Certainly, Saul's initial description not just of the crisis of global warming but of his disregard for it betrays a casual arrogance: 'I felt on the brink of owning the world. I was a man, and human beings ran the planet. There were eight billion of us, though numbers were shrinking, but few other animals were left to compete. . . . I was tall, and strong, and a techie, which qualified me for a lifetime's good money' (24). Once the reader becomes attentive to Saul's unreliability as a narrator, it is possible to read this as a mutually reinforcing mix of masculinist, technological, and anthropocentric power, and to recognise the novel's context for runaway climate change as unmistakably gendered. In this respect, the domestic robots called Doves represent an extreme masculinist appropriation of apparently organic or 'natural' processes, for they replicate the physical actions of human and non-human animals not just in thinking, talking, and moving but in reproducing and evolving, abilities made possible, crucially, by nanotechnologists like Saul. Indeed, he decides that 'as a techie, I was full of admiration for the basic Dove design' (95). It is no surprise that Saul's companions at the all-male club called The Gay Scientists – not just a pun on Nietzsche's *Die fröhliche Wissenschaft* but an indicator of the rise of masculinist scientism – vote to purchase 'a fleet of halfadozen [Doves] for us to play with' (95).

The second – and opposing – attitude is expressed by the collective that Sarah joins; it represents, like segging, women's backlash against androcentric power. Yet, the novel's account of the group is no straightforward celebration of feminism's environmentalist potential against male oppression. Indeed, the rise of the women's collective replays for the reader some of the vexed history of ecofeminism, particularly its investment in motherhood environmentalism. First, it particularly queries the motivations behind the feminist appropriation of a maternal ethics of care, given that such an appropriation replays the associations of women and care that are often criticised as reductive and problematic in the first place (as, for example, in the rise of segging described in the novel). Second, it highlights the problems that arise when applying care ethics to a political mode. In other words, the feminist celebration of parental care ethics is shown to be founded on the need to gain and maintain control, a need that is unhelpful to the putative 'cared-for', whether that designates children or the future of the planet. The women's collective, begun as a Children's Commune, evolves into a political movement called Wicca. The original commune is one of many such communities that develop as segging progresses, with women 'drawing up the battlelines around the scarce, precious children' and in which 'the childless ones found a kind of fulfilment' (68). While this description – Saul's – couches such groups in threatening terms, it nonetheless reveals them to be just as much about meeting adults' needs as it is about caring about and for children. Unsurprisingly, Wicca is overtly formulated along lines reminiscent of motherhood environmentalism. In Saul's sarcastic description, it is founded on 'a wacky female nature worship, centring on "the Hidden Goddess", who apparently "gave suck" to us all' (117), and he and his male friends respond with derision to Wicca's promotional film, whose 'voice-over spoke of "revaluing nature", "nurturing the future"; "the future is green"' (137). More importantly, Wicca represents an attempt to politicise a maternal ethics of care, winning the national election on the promise of a 'caring revolution' (137), with the tagline 'Vote for Wicca. Wicca Cares' (138). Most importantly of all, Wicca fails because its care ethics stems from a maternalistic belief in the superiority of its brand of care over others. When the effects of glaciation become impossible to ignore, Wicca's anti-male stance means that it refuses to incorporate the 'techfixes' (147) suggested by scientists and neglects to meet the challenge of securing international cooperation and funding in order to launch a concerted environmental effort.

In this way, the novel peels back the layers of the gender norms and conflicts that underpin parental care ethics. It shows both positions to be about the assertion of identity and maintenance of control. Unsurprisingly, then, in the closing events of the plot, Saul's efforts at parental care are part of a masculine backlash against the ecofeminist backlash. As the world enters the Ice Age in earnest and European society begins to come apart, Saul, helped by a newly formed men's collective called Manguard, abducts Luke from the Wicca commune to take him to the relative warmth and safety of Africa. In doing so, he institutes a particularly violent, survivalist kind of care, executed along masculinised codes of behaviour. He invokes the Old Testament's hyper-patriarchal mythology to describe his role: 'I was a *man*, Esau, Moses, leading my tribe to the promised land' (220; original emphasis). Saul and Luke travel with Briony, the sympathetic Wicca weapons officer who befriends them, but Saul disregards her munition skills and advice, a sexist arrogance which eventually leads to her death. Yet, Saul sees this as a sacrifice for his son: 'I told myself it was all for him. I had even sacrificed Briony – I held on to the thought it was somehow heroic' (272). Here, as in *The Road*, parental – specifically, paternal – care has become genetic survivalism. However, the older, wiser Saul of the present comes to understand this for what it is, and allows a critique of its efficacy as an ethical stance: 'I see I wasn't a hero, or a villain, or any of the things they say in stories – but merely one tiny unit of biology, stopping at nothing to save his genes' (273).

Towards the novel's end, Luke makes an important intervention into both parents' attempts to assert care and control over him. Certainly, Luke's emergence as the moral recipient of a future-oriented care ethics would be problematic if it remained unquestioned, for this would simply re-establish, for the reader, a eudaemonistic position of caring for the child as posterity. Crucially, however, Luke's perspective is a wholesale rejection of care, and, moreover, is correlated with the experience of others of his generation. One should note that the novel has already opened up a space in which the reader might identify and sympathise with Luke; as the reader oscillates, via Saul's and Sarah's constant negotiations throughout the narrative, between two conflicting viewpoints, he is placed, uncomfortably, in the position of the child at the centre of parental dispute. Thus, when Luke runs away to join a band of 'salvajes' (283) in Spain, the reader glimpses an alternative future for the child, away from the paternalistic and parochial constraints of care.

The novel ends in a distant future, with the dominance of such 'wild boys and girls' (172) and with Luke becoming something of a 'leader among the wild children' (309). At the novel's conclusion, the reader is able to piece together the moments from Saul's present that punctuate his narrative, and to realise that Saul and other survivors of the older generation are eventually forced to live with just such wild children and to adopt a life marked by primitive competition for food and sex, but seemingly free from emotional conditions and demands. A question asked by Saul earlier in the narrative now makes sense: 'How can I explain it to these crazy kids, who live for food, and fire, and sex? How love was so important to us. How tiny shades of wants and wishes made us fight, and sob, and part' (63). That is, implicated in love are behaviours that result in the alienation of those who are loved; contained in parental care are attitudes, such as paternalism and parochialism, that work to the detriment of those cared for.

According to these novels, so proximal is parental care to positions of control that, when expanded into an ethics of posterity, it slips easily into the expression of power and self-interest: the preservation of lineage, the shoring up of one's own interests against others', and the rehearsal of gendered behaviours in order to retain control. This is the futural ethics that McCarthy's novel discloses and that Gee's novel actively critiques. Such insights are achieved through a process of reader empathy; thus, while the ethical bases of care are interrogated, the solidity and stability of identity are never in any real doubt. In the following chapter, my consideration of motherhood environmentalism continues these concerns with gendered identity politics and ethics, and attempts a more thoroughgoing critique of the processes by which (female) identity feeds into parental care ethics.

# CHAPTER 3

# Overpopulation and Motherhood Environmentalism: Edan Lepucki's *California* and Liz Jensen's *The Rapture*

Pregnancies and child-bearing ... are a woman's link to the natural world and the hunted animals that are part of that world.

Andrée Collard with Joyce Contrucci, *Rape of the Wild*

Clearly, an individual's reproductive choices can have a dramatic effect on the total carbon emissions ultimately attributable to his or her genetic lineage ... ignoring the consequences of reproduction can lead to serious under-estimation of an individual's long-term impact on the global environment.

Paul Murtaugh and Michael Schlax, 'Reproduction and the Carbon Legacies of Individuals'

Parental care ethics is intertwined with a set of gender assumptions that, following Catriona Sandilands, I shall term 'motherhood environment-alism'.[1] Like Sandilands, I am referring here to a reductive construction of women as mothers and the subsequent identification of maternity with the non-human environment under either the biologically deter-ministic signs of fertility and nurture or the standpoints of oppression and exploitation. In the wide-ranging discourse of motherhood envir-onmentalism, 'nature' and 'woman' share everything from caring responsibilities for all species now and in the future to the status of victimhood at the hands of masculinist ideologies. Often, its shorthand is the automatic equivalence of motherhood with an attitude of envir-onmental concern.

In the previous chapter, I showed how Maggie Gee's *The Ice People* enables some of this discourse to be critiqued. In two more recent climate change novels, this catchall designation of motherhood is further dis-mantled. Both Edan Lepucki's *California* (2014) and Liz Jensen's *The Rapture* (2009) invite, to differing extents, readers' identification with

---

[1] Catriona Sandilands, *The Good-Natured Feminist: Ecofeminism and the Quest for Democracy* (Minneapolis: University of Minnesota Press, 1999), p. 4.

characters' maternal desires.[2] They critique the idea of maternal identity as a self-evident ecological ethos by juxtaposing it with the problem of over-population in an under-resourced world. They thus contrast the desire for children in the immediate and relational sense that is favoured by care ethics with a concern for children in the figurative sense – the generations of the distant future – invoked by rhetorical constructions of posterity as parenthood. However, before I read each novel, and its manipulation of reader sympathy with maternal desire in an overpopulated world, as a commentary on the sentimental contours of motherhood environmental-ism, I first outline the development of motherhood environmentalism in the context of ecofeminism and then explore the issue of human over-population and its implications for the idealisation of posterity ethics as parenthood – here, specifically, motherhood.

### Ecofeminism and Motherhood Environmentalism

The assumption at the heart of motherhood environmentalism is that core characteristics of womanhood parallel the core characteristics of 'nature'; this assumption is itself a long-standing tenet of ecofeminism. In the logic of ecofeminism, as Sandilands describes it, 'the fact of being a woman is understood to lie at the base of one's experience of ecological degradation; of one's interests in ecological protection, preservation, and reconstruc-tion; and of one's "special" ecological consciousness'.[3] The history of ecofeminism, in Sandilands's detailed account, is a chronicle of variations on the theme of the affinity between 'woman' and 'nature', both construed monolithically. From the invention of the term *ecoféminisme* by Françoise d'Eaubonne in 1974 to Sherry Ortner's provocative question in the title of a paper published that same year, 'Is Female to Male as Nature is to Culture?', ecofeminism has grappled with how to treat of the link between woman and the non-human world.[4] While d'Eaubonne affirms the affinity between these, declaring that 'the planet in the feminine gender would become green again for all', Ortner subjects that conventional link to heavy

---

[2] Edan Lepucki, *California* (first published 2014; London: Abacus, 2015); Liz Jensen, *The Rapture* (London: Bloomsbury, 2009). Subsequent page references to these texts are in parentheses.
[3] Sandilands, *Good-Natured Feminist*, p. 5
[4] Françoise d'Eaubonne, *Féminisme ou la Mort* (Paris: Femme et Mouvement, 1974); Barbara T. Gates, 'A Root of Ecofeminism: *Ecoféminisme*', in Greta Gaard and Patrick D. Murphy (eds.), *Ecofeminist Literary Criticism: Theory, Interpretation, Pedagogy* (Urbana: University of Illinois Press, 1998), pp. 15–22; Sherry B. Ortner, 'Is Female to Male as Nature is to Culture?' in Michelle Zimbalist Rosaldo and Louise Lamphere (eds.), *Woman, Culture, and Society* (Stanford University Press, 1974), pp. 67–87.

critique, answering her question by postulating that the 'universal devaluation' of woman derives from the universal identification of woman with nature, and the consequent devaluation of both.[5]

This split between celebration and critique of the idea of an essential connection between women and non-human nature has played out in subsequent expressions of ecofeminism. In some of ecofeminism's early manifestos, women are exhorted to regale in a special relationship with nature, a relationship framed as the stuff of early matriarchal religions, to be revived and reinstated. So, for example, Mary Daly's *Gyn/Ecology* (1978) argues that patriarchal power, which she describes in quasi-religious terms, has polluted both the non-human world and women: 'Phallic myth and language generate, legitimate, and mask the material pollution that threatens to terminate all sentient life on this planet.'[6] Meanwhile, Susan Griffin's *Woman and Nature: The Roaring inside Her* (1979) laments how men have become deaf to the voice of nature, a voice inherent in women. In some of these 'spiritual' ecofeminist statements, the common ground between women and nature is distilled to an essential characteristic of care; that is, women, it is implied, possess an innate connection with the non-human based on their shared capacity for connectedness, whereby women's supposedly inherent empathy for others is construed as a version of ecological interdependence.[7] And, certainly, such care is explicitly maternalised. Andrée Collard, for example, writes of early matriarchal societies, 'women's skills developed beyond her famed endurance and purveyance of care and wellbeing. She learned the ways of plants. She learned the ways of other creatures of the land, air and sea. She learned them in a spirit of recognition and respect. And with a similar spirit, she partook of them'.[8] For Collard, then: 'Pregnancies and child-bearing . . . are a woman's link to the natural world and the hunted animals that are part of that world.'[9]

At the same time, and in contrast, ecofeminism has also consisted of careful historicist work, building on Ortner's concerns, that has characterised the alignment of women with nature as a symptom of patriarchal oppression and been wary of making any immanent or

[5] Eaubonne, *Féminisme ou la Mort*, p. 67; Ortner, 'Is Female to Male as Nature Is to Culture?', pp. 71–2.

[6] Mary Daly, *Gyn/Ecology: The Metaethics of Radical Feminism* (London: Women's Press, 1978), p. 9.

[7] Susan Griffin, *Woman and Nature: The Roaring inside Her* (New York: Harper and Row, 1979).

[8] Andrée Collard with Joyce Contrucci, *Rape of the Wild: Man's Violence against Animals and the Earth* (London: Women's Press, 1988), p. 11.

[9] Ibid., pp. 14–15.

inherent link between them. Most famously, Carolyn Merchant's *The Death of Nature* (1980) traces the history of 'the formation of a worldview and a science that sanctioned the domination of both nature and women'.[10] Val Plumwood's *Feminism and the Mastery of Nature* (1993) similarly critiques masculinist thought as based not just on the equations 'women = nature' and 'men = reason', but on assumptions about the inferiority of the first pair and the superiority of the second.[11] Building on these insights, much ecofeminist discussion in the 1980s and 1990s tended to be couched not in spiritual terms but in the language of standpoints, figuring women and the non-human as structurally historical victims of patriarchal systems of exploitation. As Mary Mellor argues, 'the two are linked' but the 'linkage is not seen as stemming from some essentialist female identification with nature, for which some early ecofeminists were criticised, but from women's position in society, particularly in relation to masculine-dominated economic systems'.[12]

Even so, standpoint ecofeminism is not immune to the problem of essentialising the identities of both women and nature, and, in doing so, it reifies care as defining female experience and as the grounds for women's connections with the non-human. For example, Merchant argues that, as women meet social and cultural expectations that place them in caring positions, they become qualified to practise 'earthcare'; Merchant uses the word to unite a collection of her essays from the 1980s and 1990s.[13] Through these decades, ecofeminism tended to theorise the sociological connection between women and nature in the language of object-relations psychoanalysis, having recourse to the care ethics initiated (as discussed in chapter 1) by Carol Gilligan as an explanation for how women's experiences condition them to be both more caring and how such caring places them in closer connection with nature.[14] The position argued by Ariel Salleh is representative; Salleh posits that 'the actuality of caring for the concrete needs of others gives rise to a morality of relatedness among ordinary women, and this sense of kinship seems to extend to

[10] Carolyn Merchant, *The Death of Nature: Women, Ecology, and the Scientific Revolution* (first published 1980; San Francisco: Harper Collins, 1990), p. xxi.

[11] Val Plumwood, *Feminism and the Mastery of Nature* (London: Routledge, 1993).

[12] Mary Mellor, 'Ecofeminist Political Economy and the Politics of Money', in Ariel Salleh (ed.), *Eco-Sufficiency and Global Justice: Women Write Political Ecology* (London: Pluto, 2009), p. 251.

[13] Carolyn Merchant, *Earthcare: Women and the Environment* (London: Routledge, 1995)

[14] Sandilands, *Good-Natured Feminist*, p. 21; Carol Gilligan, *In a Different Voice: Psychological Theory and Women's Development* (Cambridge, MA: Harvard University Press, 1982).

the natural world'.[15] Mellor goes further, insisting that women, socialised into undertaking caring responsibilities, are then unavoidably brought into a biological connection with nature: 'Ecological impacts and consequences are experienced through human bodies, in ill health, early death, congenital damage and impeded childhood development. Women disproportionately bear the consequences of those impacts within their own bodies (dioxin residues in breast milk, failed pregnancies) and in their work as nurturers and carers.'[16] Such positions, seemingly concerned with sociological explanations of structure, nonetheless reconnect women to a reductive maternal identity. As Sandilands reminds us, 'social construction and essentialism are not necessarily opposed concepts'.[17]

In addition to being a particularly reductionist account of female identity, this political discourse of ecofeminism, perversely, restricts the range of political responses to patriarchal and environmental violence available to both women and men. By following spiritual ecofeminism in aligning violations against women's maternalised bodies with degrading practices against non-human species and ecosystems, this discourse turns reclamations of either female empowerment or ecological protection into a defence of maternal rights and activities. That is, motherhood is not just the explanation for women's closer connection with nature; it also provides ongoing motivation and method for maintaining this connection for all humans. Sherilyn MacGregor describes this conglomeration of 'socio-material and experiential' arguments for connecting women and nature as the 'rhetoric of "ecomaternalism"', and exposes its logic: 'Because it is women (as mothers) who do the nurturing work that sustains human life, and that mediates the connection between humans and nature, women care about (assume a sense of compassion, responsibility, and connection towards) their environments, and this, in turn, leads them to take action to preserve and repair them.'[18] In short, 'for these ecofeminists, women are seen to hold the key to an ethical approach to socio-ecological as well as to social relationships that can solve the ecological crisis'.[19] That is, women's caring disposition as mothers enhances their awareness of the

---

[15] Ariel Salleh, 'Class, Race, and Gender Discourse in the Ecofeminism/Deep Ecology Debate', in Max Oelschlaeger (ed.), *Postmodern Environmental Ethics* (Albany: State University of New York Press, 1995), p. 82.

[16] Mary Mellor, *Feminism and Ecology* (London: Polity Press, 1997), p. 2.

[17] Sandilands, *Good-Natured Feminist*, p. 71.

[18] Sherilyn MacGregor, *Beyond Mothering Earth: Ecological Citizenship and the Politics of Care* (Vancouver: University of British Columbia Press, 2006), pp. 4, 59.

[19] Ibid., p. 59.

interconnections among and between humans and non-humans, while their caring activities, in bringing them into proximity with biological processes, means that they are emotionally and practically affected by environmental damage: both the attitude and act of caring subsequently offer the means for women to take ecological action. Such action, then, necessarily confuses female autonomy with environmental concerns, and, further, collapses both into the need to preserve women's role as mothers.

It must be noted that more recent iterations of ecofeminism have actively problematised this reliance on a connection between woman and nature on the grounds of maternal care. Studies, such as those by Sandilands, MacGregor, and Chris Cuomo, have questioned the essentialist bases of the women-nature affinity.[20] Such insights enable important alternatives to maternalised understandings of women's ecological action and activism; I consider some of this critique in the second half of this chapter, and more fully in chapter 4. At this point in this chapter, however, I remain concerned with a particular ecofeminist configuration of maternity as a guarantor of ecological conscience, as I turn to the ways in which this problematises, and is problematised by, the re-emergence of population debates in the Anthropocene.

## Procreation: Human Overpopulation and Reproductive Rights

To what extent is procreation compatible with the well-being of future generations? Obviously, the simple *generation* of a species depends on the continued reproduction of that species, but, in a world of limited resources, uncontrolled procreation just as easily heralds extinction. Certainly, the idea that humans will continue to survive – with adaptation and natural selection taking care of any Malthusian worries about population growth – is an overconfident one. Even Darwinian principles allow that, though individuals will strive for survival, they may do so at the expense of their species, a phenomenon first considered by the evolutionary biologist J. B. S. Haldane, who wrote in 1932 of situations in which members of a species 'inevitably begin to compete with one another', the results of which 'may be biologically advantageous for the individual, but ultimately disastrous for the species'.[21] A similar narrative of biological survival instincts leading inexorably to unregulated competition and

---

[20] Sandilands, *Good-Natured Feminist;* MacGregor, *Beyond Mothering Earth;* Chris J. Cuomo, *Feminism and Ecological Communities: An Ethics of Flourishing* (London: Routledge, 1998).

[21] J. B. S. Haldane, *The Causes of Evolution* (London: Longmans, Green and Co., 1932), pp. 119–20.

thence to resource depletion is told by Garrett Hardin's parable of the tragedy of the commons.[22] This is the parochial danger of biological survivalism, discussed in the previous chapter, writ large. The ultimate act of genetic survival that is reproduction is, perversely, also a threat to the species.

The Anthropocene puts such a threat in the spotlight. As Timothy Clark points out, if overpopulation refers to a 'situation in which the population of a species exceeds the long-term carrying capacity of its ecological context', then the current ecological crisis, in which that species is 'humanity' and the context is 'the Earth as a whole', places the problem of human overpopulation on the environmentalist agenda.[23] In some ways, this is not new: concerns about overpopulation raged in the 1960s and 1970s, expressed not just by Hardin but by Paul and Anne Ehrlich and the Club of Rome.[24] However, the apparent panic about overcrowding, starvation, and famine that marked this discourse made it vulnerable, sometimes justifiably, to accusations of global North antagonism towards the global South, and particularly to what Diana Coole calls 'population-shaming' rhetoric, which sometimes serves as 'a subterfuge for pursuing heinous ulterior motives'.[25] But the question has returned with urgency in the twenty-first century amid additional concerns over resource sustainability on the one hand and carbon emissions on the other. The most recent report of the Intergovernmental Panel on Climate Change, which Clark cites, states, for example, that 'economic and population growth continue to be the most important drivers of increases in $CO_2$ emissions from fossil fuel combustion'.[26]

Yet, the contemporary overpopulation debate is a particularly controversial and, in Clark's words, 'politically and culturally toxic' topic.[27] For Clark, the lack of political will to address overpopulation has to do with scale effects, namely, the disparity between the vast intergenerational and interspecies concerns demanded by environmental crisis and the

---

[22] Garrett Hardin, 'The Tragedy of the Commons', *Science* 162 (13 December 1968): 1243–8.

[23] Timothy Clark. *Ecocriticism on the Edge: The Anthropocene as a Threshold Concept* (London: Bloomsbury, 2015), p. 80.

[24] Paul R. Ehrlich, *The Population Bomb* (first published 1968; London: Pan, 1971); Donella H. Meadows, Dennis L. Meadows, Jorgen Randers, and William W. Behrens, *The Limits to Growth: A Report on the Club of Rome's Project for the Predicament of Mankind* (New York: Universe Books, 1972).

[25] Diana Coole, 'Too Many Bodies? The Return and Disavowal of the Population Question', *Environmental Politics* 22.2 (2013), 199; see also Ursula K. Heise, *Sense of Place and Sense of Planet: The Environmental Imagination of the Global* (New York: Oxford University Press, 2008), pp. 68–9.

[26] Clark, *Ecocriticism on the Edge*, p. 80.     [27] Ibid., p. 81.

individualistic frame through which much political and cultural discourse flows. This is evident not just in the recourse to the language of equalising global wealth distribution, which Clark describes as 'evasive and anthropocentric' and which Coole traces to the desire to avoid population-shaming.[28] More to the point, concerns about overpopulation abut directly onto cultural valorisations of parenthood, based on, among other things, the association of parental care as ethical good. In its starkest terms, the overpopulation debate asks whether parenthood itself is an act of wilful environmental degradation. In an influential and much-debated paper that appeared in 2009, a statistician and an atmospheric physicist from Oregon State University presented their calculations of present humans' 'carbon legacies'.[29] In it, Paul Murtaugh and Michael Schlax suggest that the average environmentally conscious American woman might save 486 tons of $CO_2$ in a year but, if she had two children, she would eventually contribute forty times that amount to Earth's atmosphere. While they concede that it is important to understand 'the ways that an individual's daily activities influence emissions and explain the huge disparities in per capita emissions among countries', they argue that 'ignoring the consequences of reproduction can lead to serious under-estimation of an individual's long-term impact on the global environment'.[30] Other scientists have since concurred with their conclusions.[31] A debate published in a 2014 issue of *The New Internationalist* that responds, in part, to Murtaugh and Schlax's study is representative of the framing of such concerns as a battle of environmental 'care' against parental 'care', its central question being: 'If you care about climate change, should you have children?'[32]

The scalar schism between the intergenerational threat of overpopulation and the immediate concerns of parenthood are a challenge not merely to notions of the ethical good attached to parental care but to the idea that parenthood is an essential aspect of identity. Arguments about overpopulation strike at the heart of deep-seated cultural expectations that the right to have children is a matter of an individual's civil liberties, enshrined by no

---

[28] Ibid., p. 81; Coole, 'Too Many Bodies?', 198.

[29] Paul A. Murtaugh and Michael Schlax, 'Reproduction and the Carbon Legacies of Individuals', *Global Environmental Change* 19.1 (2009), 14–20; see also Sam Wong, 'Baby Emissions Fuel Global Warming', *The Guardian* (5 August 2009).

[30] Murtaugh and Schlax, 'Reproduction and the Carbon Legacies of Individuals', 18.

[31] Brian C. O'Neill, Michael Dalton, Regina Fuchs, *et al.*, 'Global Demographic Trends and Future Carbon Emissions', *PNAS* 107 (2012), 17521–6.

[32] Anne Hendrixson and Erica Gies, 'If You Care about Climate Change, Should You Have Children?', *New Internationalist* 480 (March 2015). http://newint.org/sections/argument/2015/03/01/climate-change-children

less than the United Nations Universal Declaration on Human Rights (at which Hardin took aim so many years ago, describing any criticism of it as 'taboo').[33] The Declaration states that 'men and women of full age, without limitation due to race, nationality or religion, have the right to marry and found a family', a statement further clarified by then General Secretary U Thant to mean that 'any choice and decision with regard to the size of the family must irrevocably rest with the family itself, and cannot be made by anyone else'.[34] But, as Coole puts it, the distillation of the population debate to private 'matters of reproductive health and individual welfare entitlements', 'eminently worthy' as they are, has 'had the effect of displacing population growth as a global environmental issue', and – one should note – as a question of ethical obligation to future human and non-human well-being.[35]

It therefore becomes evident how Anthropocene concerns over overpopulation run counter to the assumptions of motherhood environmentalism. As we have seen, by the logic of motherhood environmentalism, maternity and, with it, the exercise of maternal care, are a matter of autonomy and identity. This is not to say, of course, that the population debate is to be always decoupled from questions of gender. There are certainly instances in which it is important to keep the two within the same frame. For example, the notion of reproductive rights underpins worthy campaigns around the world that would defend the entitlement of girls and women to decide for themselves whether to bear or not to bear children, in contexts as diverse as abortion information and rights, the prevention of child marriage, and access to fertility treatment, which are, as Clark concedes, 'obvious goods'.[36] Indeed, one could elaborate on what Coole calls population-shaming, with Rachel Stein's identification of a tendency towards 'Negative associations of women of color with overpopulation', a tendency that has historically enabled a catalogue of crimes and violations, such as 'the coercive use of birth control, forced sterilization, and ... possible eugenics misuses of genetic research or biogenetic manipulation of environmentally stricken populations'.[37] Yet, equally, one must remain vigilant against removing specific – and admittedly grave –

[33] Hardin, 'The Tragedy of the Commons', 1246.
[34] United Nations General Assembly, *Universal Declaration of Human Rights* (New York: United Nations, 1967); U Thant, Statement at Presentation of Declaration on Population Growth (10 December 1967), www.un.org/en/development/desa/population/theme/rights.
[35] Coole, 'Too Many Bodies?', 209.    [36] Clark, *Ecocriticism on the Edge*, p. 82.
[37] Rachel Stein, Introduction, in Stein (ed.), *New Perspectives on Environmental Justice: Gender, Sexuality, and Activism* (New Brunswick, NJ: Rutgers University Press, 2004), p. 6.

cases of gendered and raced exploitation from their particular contexts to shore up, in more general terms, the argument that maternal identity is an absolute good. Coole argues for the need for a franker discussion of 'demographic policies' and their relevance to environmental issues, based on an awareness not just of how these are 'susceptible to entanglement in broader geopolitical struggles', but also that the tendency to connect population, race, and gender is 'a contingent one embedded in particular histories'.[38] Or, as Noël Sturgeon reminds us in proposing 'a *global feminist environmental justice analysis*', which she defines as 'an intersectional approach (seeing at all times an interactive relationship among inequalities of gender, race, sexuality, class, and nation)', one must attend to historical context and contingency, highlighting the intersections that might arise in particular cases, and avoiding simple dualisms.[39]

In this respect, *The New Internationalist*'s debate is interesting for demonstrating how contexts might be conveniently elided in the population argument. The 'no children' stance of journalist Erica Gies is focused, via the findings of Murtaugh and Schlax, on the carbon footprint of 'children and their descendants', while the argument *for* children, mounted by population studies professor Anne Hendrixson, aligns ethical responsibility to the planet initially with the ethical efficacy of parental care in and of itself, and then with the need to preserve reproductive rights as a matter of individual liberty.[40] Hendrixson contends: first, that corporations and the military are greater culprits for carbon emission and environmental damage generally; second, that change can be brought about in part by the ethical guidance of parents (Hendrixson advises, 'If you want to address climate change, you and your children should challenge the excesses of the military-industrial complex', and 'Hold these powerful companies accountable for their actions and teach your children to do likewise'); and, third and most importantly, that parental rights in the domestic sphere are sacrosanct against wider environmental concerns: 'Ultimately, people should be able to choose to have children or not.'[41] Strikingly, Hendrixson's argument implies these parental rights to be maternal rights. She cites the work of ARROW (the Asian-Pacific Resource and Research Centre for Women, a not-for-profit group that campaigns for sexual and

---

[38] Coole, 'Too Many Bodies?', 200, 202.

[39] Noël Sturgeon, *Environmentalism in Popular Culture: Gender, Race, Sexuality, and the Politics of the Natural* (Tuscon: University of Arizona Press, 2009), p. 6; original emphasis.

[40] Anne Hendrixson and Erica Gies, 'If You Care about Climate Change, Should You Have Children?'.

[41] Ibid.

reproductive rights for women in the developing world) in order to insist, in general terms, on the need to 'safeguard sexual and reproductive health and rights – including having kids – even as we hold the worst carbon emitters accountable'; she moves almost indiscernibly from a particular context of securing reproductive rights for disempowered women to a universal standpoint of parenthood. She thus ends her argument on the issue of preserving women's maternal rights as an absolute good and returns to her earlier association of this with the ability to initiate environmental action through parental activism. In other words, the possibility of parenthood as an environmentally compromised act is countered by an insistence on the inviolability of its rights and the power of its ethical, educational potential.[42]

The tendency to invoke a universalised position of motherhood as grounds, motive, and means by which the environment might be saved, even in the face of the questions posed by overpopulation, is replayed in two climate change novels (where such a universal standpoint is also, conveniently, represented by white, heterosexual, socio-economically privileged subjects). Lepucki's *California* and Jensen's *The Rapture* contextualise the need to fulfil individual reproductive rights within a scenario of overpopulation threat. Where Lepucki's narrative, with its unsympathetic female protagonist, tends towards a simplification of this into a story of motherhood as selfishness, Jensen's use not just of overpopulation discourse but of reader identification with her female character prioritises environmental and maternal concerns equally, bringing the two into conflict. Jensen, I shall argue, ultimately demonstrates the contradictions that inhere in motherhood environmentalism. However, rather than staging this, like Lepucki, as an exposé of motherhood environmentalism, she enables an understanding of the complexity of female identity, an understanding worth reading through the lens of recent ecofeminist investigations into women and their bodily experiences.

## California

Lepucki's *California* imagines a resource-scarce environment in which arguments rage over the environmental justice of having children, and depicts, in the final analysis, the extent to which any decision to have children is a potentially self-interested choice. The novel, the first by Lepucki, a graduate of the distinguished Iowa Writers' Workshop, came

---

[42] Ibid.

to national attention in something of a lucky break. Published by Hachette at the height of its controversial dispute with online bookseller Amazon over e-book prices, Lepucki saw her work promoted, by chance, by television personality and fellow Hachette author Stephen Colbert; seeking not just to publicise an Amazon boycott but to make the case that Amazon's actions were most damaging to first-time authors, Colbert urged viewers to buy books such as Lepucki's.[43] *California* subsequently entered the *New York Times* bestseller list at number three.[44] This unconventional and unexpected publicity may account for the gap between the novel's reputation and its lack of polish. While a promising first novel, its plot and characters remain underdeveloped, a thinness in characterisation that contributes to its simplistic critique of parental – particularly, maternal – care ethics.

The novel is set in California in the mid-twenty-first century, when environmental and political disasters – 'Overpopulation, pollution, drought, disease, oil, terrorism' (57) – have virtually torn apart the country's economic and social fabric. Extreme weather events have devastated the national infrastructure: in addition to earthquakes in California, there have been 'wildfires in Colorado and Utah', 'snowstorms across the Midwest and the East Coast, and 'rainstorms north of here' (46). While the wealthy reside in gated enclaves known as Communities, those less fortunate survive in rundown cities or outposts in the wild, vulnerable to marauding bandits. The novel begins with two such survivors, young husband and wife, Cal and Frida, who eke out an existence on their own in a shack in woodland outside Los Angeles until they discover a mysterious settlement nearby, a place called the Land. The conjunction of the two names – Cal and Frida – punningly identifies them with the name of the state, and aligns their struggle for survival, along with the lessons they learn about procreation and posterity, with the sacrifices to be made by a once-affluent society in a climate-changed future. Moreover, Frida's discovery at the start of the novel that she is pregnant means that the narrative is focused throughout on the couple's concerns for their unborn child, since the plot's duration exactly covers that of Frida's pregnancy.

The narrative splits the reader's attention between the two protagonists. It systematically switches between their points of view, proceeding as tightly focalised passages that alternate between Frida's and Cal's free,

---

[43] Brookes Barnes, 'Winner in the Amazon War', *New York Times* (3 July 2014).
[44] Carolyn Kellogg, 'Edan Lepucki Thanks Colbert Nation for Making *California* a Hit', *Los Angeles Times* (22 July 2014).

indirect discourses. This has several effects. First, flashbacks reveal their very different backgrounds and outlooks. The reader learns, for example, of Frida's privileged Hollywood upbringing by a film-maker father and a glamorous mother, which contrasts with Cal's rural Midwestern childhood, particularly the influence of his farming father and his experience at a nontraditional, all-male college called Plank (modelled on Deep Springs College in northern California, where the education philosophy combines small-group teaching with agricultural labour and student governance). The urban and urbane Frida wants to live in a community, while Cal wishes to live a primitive and isolated life on the land. Indeed, the couple's departure from a ravaged Los Angeles had been at Cal's behest but delayed by Frida's desire to stay in the city. This creates a sense of distance between the characters, and splits reader empathy and identification between the two.

The alternating focalisations and interior monologues also function to highlight the secretiveness that marks Cal and Frida's relationship: each repeatedly keeps information – important or trivial – from the other. This includes Cal's early discovery of the Land, which he tries to withhold from Frida, and Frida's hidden stash of 'artefacts' (2) from her previous life. The reader is made privy to the secrets that the couple keep from each other – for example, Frida's announcement of her pregnancy, out loud and to herself, means that the reader learns of it before Cal. These secrets emphasise the alignment of Frida with civilisation and Cal with wilderness: for example, Frida's cache of keepsakes – an abacus, a shower cap, a perfume bottle, and a turkey baster that she particularly cherishes for being both brand new and utterly useless – represent her tendency to cling to a past life of trivial and now defunct material goods, along with the holidays and rituals they represent. Meanwhile, Cal keeps his knowledge of the Land's existence a secret from Frida so that they can maintain their self-sufficiency in the forest. The novel, then, is a series of alternating ironic insights into Frida and Cal that underline their differences.

These differences are also emphasised by the apparent necessity of traditional gender norms in a devastated environment of scarce resources. The couple 'rely on an antiquated division of labor' (64), in which, for example, Frida performs the chores of washing their clothes at a nearby creek and preparing their meals while Cal digs animal traps. The connection between gender norms and a successful life in the wild is further suggested by their neighbours, the Miller family, whose self-sufficiency is managed by the adoption of a gendered hunter-gatherer lifestyle: the father Bo hunts, while the mother Sandy forages and cooks. Not only do the

Millers pass on this gendered knowledge to Cal and Frida, the younger couple find themselves surprisingly well-suited to their allotted tasks. Already aligned with the domestic sphere through her love of and expertise at baking, Frida becomes such 'an expert at foraging' that Cal concedes that 'foraging was women's work ... maybe Bo was right' (58). Frida, meanwhile, sees the Millers' life as a lesson in working with the land: 'with Bo and Sandy, ... the earth was to be respected. Only then would it collaborate with you, tell you what it needed and what it was willing to give. And it was willing to give you a lot, if you knew how to ask' (24–25). This correlates the Millers' gendered knowledge with a kind of 'natural' understanding of the world, a yielding to the environment's differing physical demands on men and women that, in addition, masculinises predatory activity and feminises nurture.

Connected to this is the existence of an embodied and feminised knowledge around reproduction and maternity. While the men discuss 'how to handle larger predators' (25), Sandy teaches Frida how to chart her menstrual cycle by 'the phases of the moon' (26). That Frida is ignorant in this respect is a result of her past reliance on the contraceptive pill. Sandy's teachings represent, it would seem, the handing down of an exclusively 'natural' female expertise, replacing Frida's previous abnegation of that responsibility to the 'artificial' apparatus of medical knowledge. Moreover, Sandy explicitly connects this information to reproductive power, specifically advising Frida that she could, and should, use it to have children. At this point, Frida's prior reluctance to become a mother – for 'Who wanted to bring children into this world?' (26) – undergoes a transformation: 'Frida felt her perspective shifting, tilting the world, blurring the colors, brightening them' (28). It is immediately after this that Frida refuses to practise the withdrawal method when having sex with Cal. What she acquires, then, is a reproductive power explicitly tied to Sandy's feminised wisdom and her highly gendered relationship with the land: that is, Frida engages in a version of motherhood environmentalism.

Yet, this is no simple delineation of Cal as protector and Frida as nurturer. Cal's focalised narrative details his dedication to a conventional and masculinised responsibility of looking after his wife and child, but Frida's traces her gradual reluctance to assume the feminised role set out for her by the Millers. While Cal finds that 'they'd learned a lot' from the Millers and 'were getting the hang of things' (66), Frida comes to resist the gender norms they have enforced – she laments how 'No one cared about voting rights and equal pay because everyone was too busy lighting fires to stay warm and looking for food to stay alive', and complains that 'It's like the only thing that matters anymore is upper-body strength' (65). What she eventually resists, it would seem, is the motherhood environmentalism that the Millers represent.

As Cal and Frida enter the Land (which – in a complicated subplot – is led by Frida's supposedly long-dead brother, Micah), the narrative focuses further on the couple's differences, particularly in their attitudes towards their unborn child. As the decision to allow Cal and Frida to stay in the community is put to a general vote, the impending birth is kept secret. Thus, a further layer of insulation is added to each character in the already highly divided narrative; focalised thus far on each protagonist's secretive thoughts about the other, the narrative is now more intensely concerned with their private concerns over the impending birth, which they cannot share with others in the community and are loath to share with each other. While Cal's actions become focused on discovering the complex mechanisms by which the Land is run, including its striking lack of children, Frida's uncertain relationship with motherhood comes under scrutiny.

Motherhood, for Frida, is far from being an innate and inherent part of her identity, and certainly very far from an expression of a connection with 'nature'. Frida experiences maternity in somewhat second-hand terms, basing her responses on received ideas; remembering her mother's descriptions of 'a peculiar peace that descended upon her with each pregnancy' (106), she tries to imagine feeling the same way. The child also becomes a means to an end, an opportunity to be accepted onto the Land; feeling optimistic that the birth of her child will be welcomed by the community and will bring her acceptance into the Land, she finds herself 'channeling Sandy Miller, she realised, triumphant before her chart of menstrual cycles, glory be to the gift of children . . . . Because that's what moms did, right? They chose to believe the future was good' (343–4). However, when she starts to worry that her pregnancy will lead to exile from the Land, she contemplates terminating it, wondering, 'if she could see it as something inhuman, then she might be able to rid herself of it' (217). Indeed, the reader might consider the absurd motif of the turkey baster as a metaphor for Frida's superficial relationship to her child and her wish to use it to gain access to the Land. Not only is the baster an object to which she is sentimentally attached, she – secretly, of course, and inexplicably – intends to proffer it as a gift to the community. Moreover, if the turkey baster is indeed an objective correlative of Frida's maternity, this hints at a sense of artificiality: turkey basters are, after all, associated in the popular imagination with artificial methods of impregnation (as a synonym for do-it-yourself insemination), and the baster functions in the narrative as a memento for Frida and a sign of her nostalgia for her consumerist, materialist past. Frida, it would seem, is no earth mother, and her child represents a way to secure material comforts for herself.

That Frida's maternal desires are a projection of her desires for herself becomes even more evident when these maternal wishes are pitted against the wishes of the community. The Land is unable to sustain children. As Micah explains of his arrival at and eventual leadership of the community:

> The Land was a mess when we first got here. There were children, but they were underweight. . . . Almost all of them were still too young to contribute anything, and the adults spent a lot of time looking after them, and they couldn't get as much work done, couldn't make preparations for their own survival. That endangered the whole community. Plus, the older ones would be teenagers in a few years, and who knows what would happen then? They might not follow rules or do their jobs. (320)

The Land practises a policy of 'containment' (211), out of concern about the energy demands of parenting, children's use of resources without contribution to labour in return, the health risks of parturition to both mothers and babies, and the difficulty of both keeping older children safe and ensuring that they adhere to its strict social order. The Land has settled for a future life without children in order to ensure a life in the present: 'Kids had been removed from the future' (312). To be clear, this puts the lie not just to Frida's self-absorbed version of maternity but also to the celebratory motherhood environmentalism expressed by Sandy. In the resource-stricken future imagined by *California*, children represent a luxury. The Millers' dreams of a pastoral future ensured by children – 'Their children would mark the beginning of a new and better species, start the world over' (15) – appear just as irresponsible as Frida's desire for a child in order to secure a better life for herself. Motherhood, even motherhood environmentalism, emerges here as a manifestation of self-interest.

The novel's conclusion grants Frida a happy ending but ironically underlines what it suggests is her self-centredness. Because Frida cannot comprehend that the child is inimical to the sustainability of the Land, she impulsively announces her pregnancy before the vote, which results in the couple's violent ejection. Micah, who is revealed to be secretly trading with the wealthy Communities, saves Frida and Cal by transferring them to one such enclave, where the novel ends. The artificiality of the Community – its cheap, tailored clothes and synthetic foods – underlines the deception of their new life, and its relative wealth, derived from the exploitation of outposts such as the Land, highlights the luxury that is parenthood in the context of limited resources. Settled into the Community, Frida 'knew she was thinking only of her own family, that she had begun to see them as special: separate from the rest of the world with all its attendant suffering and corruption. Maybe it was wrong but it was the choice she had made' (391–2). Thus, the conclusion, focalised through Frida, brings her to only a passing awareness of the shallowness of her actions and of the dilemmas that parenthood poses to an environmentally challenged society, but there is little suggestion that she will act on this awareness. Importantly, the reader is brought to the same insights through a persistent ironic awareness of Frida's motives and desires. Thus, the novel foregoes the potential usefulness of sympathy with and for Frida and, with it, the possibility of either a eudaemonistic interest in the elements of her ethical world or a critical awareness as both character and reader reassess the concerns that comprise that ethical world. Instead, Frida and her self-interested appropriation of motherhood become the object of criticism rather than the chance for a deeper critique of (female) identity formation.

### Motherhood, Materiality, and Female Identity

What *California* misses is the opportunity to understand female identity as a composite of several discourses. Such an approach would acknowledge and accept, rather than expose and condemn, the ways in which, for many women, maternal desire is one of a number of discursive forces (or, more precisely, forces in which the discursive is combined with material phenomena and bodily experiences) that participate in the ongoing and slippery process of self-construction.

Two important trends in ecofeminism help to shed light on this idea. The first is the range of insights represented by Donna Haraway's cyborg feminism, in which the figure of the cyborg expresses the shifts in subject positions that might offer a more productive political environmental strategy for women. 'A cyborg world', suggests Haraway, 'might be about lived social and bodily realities in which people are not afraid of their joint kinship with animals and machines, not afraid of permanently partial identities and contradictory standpoints'.[45] Haraway's arguments about the hybrid nature of identity have been further enhanced by Sandilands's work, drawing on the philosophies of Hannah Arendt, on

---

[45] Donna J. Haraway, 'A Cyborg Manifesto: Science, Technology, and Socialist-Feminism in the Late Twentieth Century', *Simians, Cyborgs and Women: The Reinvention of Nature* (London: Free Association Books, 1991), p. 154.

identity as an 'intra-social' event, formed in moments of social and political coalition and action, and always an ongoing process.[46] Second, some more recent developments in ecofeminism, specifically, new materialism, have begun to re-emphasise the importance of materiality in considering human and non-human relations. Instead of returning the discussion of women and nature to biological determinism or essentialism, however, new materialism emphasises the way in which the discursive and material are interlinked, 'since various aspects of materiality contribute to the development and transformation of discourses'.[47]

Together, these developments urge an awareness of how material-discursive practices impact on women's understandings of both female identity and their relationship with the non-human world. Of especial relevance is Karen Barad's argument that identity and agency are dynamic processes.[48] Because the 'primary epistemological unit' is not a stable object or entity but *'phenomena'*, that is, a constellation of entities acting on, in, with, or through each other, it is not inter-action between objects that matters in establishing identity and agency, but 'intra-action', the process by which objects become – momentarily and locally – separate and thereby knowable.[49] What is especially significant is the dynamic quality Barad imparts to ontology and agency, reminding us that apprehension and identification of the other occurs not in static opposition but in a coming together and enactment of separability – what Barad calls the *'agential cut'*.[50] What is of further significance is that the phenomena comprise not simply human and non-human others, but 'material-discursive practices'.[51] That is, identity is an encounter between things materially and discursively fabricated.

In *The Rapture*, the female protagonist's idea of herself is dominated by maternal desire, a domination made all the more obvious in her defence of its ideals and ethics in opposition to the discourse of overpopulation. In the final analysis, however, motherhood – its idealisation, physical manifestation, and psychological dimensions – is shown to be one of several material-discursive intra-actions that inform female identity, that is, it is

---

[46] Sandilands, *Good-Natured Feminist*, p. 84.

[47] Stacy Alaimo and Susan Hekman, 'Introduction: Emerging Models of Materiality in Feminist Theory', in Alaimo and Hekman (eds.), *Material Feminisms* (Bloomington: Indiana University Press, 2008), p. 4.

[48] Karen Barad, 'Posthumanist Performativity: Toward an Understanding of How Matter Comes to Matter', *Signs* 28.2 (2003), 801–31.

[49] Ibid., 815; original emphasis.    [50] Ibid.; original emphasis.    [51] Ibid., 818.

a conglomerate of ideas and experiences, or combinations of thoughts, speech, bodies, and things.

## The Rapture

British novelist Jensen has attracted critical acclaim over her career with innovative and intelligent novels that nonetheless have tended to be 'ignored by scholars'.[52] Though her novels range from the comic to the dystopian, they are all classifiable as thrillers of a sort, each beginning with a puzzling premise and then driving the plot towards an answer to this puzzle. In addition, these mysteries tend towards paranormal phenomena – or, at the very least, to ideas that are scientifically implausible – such as animal-human hybridity and psychic powers. Significantly, most also display a preoccupation with parenthood, from Jensen's first novel, *Egg Dancing* (1995), about a woman who suspects her perfect baby is the result of a eugenic experiment by her embryologist husband, to one of her best-known works, *The Ninth Life of Louis Drax* (2004), whose eponymous protagonist is a problem child in a coma that, we learn, is the result of an attempted murder by his long-suffering mother. A recent novel explicitly locates parenthood within the context of longer-term obligations to future generations: *The Uninvited* (2012) imagines a global phenomenon of juvenile homicides, which is revealed in a supernatural twist to be the revenge by future generations on the present for the environmental devastation visited upon them.

The themes of posterity and parenthood are also combined with environmental concerns in Jensen's seventh novel, *The Rapture*, and particularly framed through maternity. *The Rapture* is set in a near-future Britain, in which the extreme weather events of climate change are virtually an everyday occurrence. Its narrator and protagonist, Gabrielle Fox, is a child psychologist recovering from a traumatic car accident. Attempting to restart her life as a paraplegic, she takes on a challenging posting at a secure hospital for criminally insane adolescents. There she treats Bethany Krall, who has savagely killed her mother and seems, moreover, to have the ability to predict the global disasters now taking place. As Bethany's predictions become ever more vivid and accurate, Gabrielle – and the reader – must decide whether or not the teenager is in possession of paranormal powers and, if so, whether these are part of

---

[52] Barbara L. Estrin, 'Mutating Literary Form and Literalizing Scientific Theory in Liz Jensen's *Ark Baby*', *Critique* 47 (2005), 41.

the onset of some kind of supernaturally ordained final event. When Bethany foresees a cataclysmic event large enough to wipe out most of Europe and North America, Gabrielle, along with the scientist with whom she falls in love, strives to alert the world to the possibility of impending doom.[53] Shaped as what Eric Otto calls 'an ecothriller', the engine of the novel is suspense, driving purposefully towards a catastrophic climax. Aiding the overwhelming sense of apocalypse is the predominance of a religious end-times narrative. Bethany's family is part of an evangelical Christian community, the 'Faith Wave', that has embraced climate change as 'a sign we're on the brink of doomsday' (88), believing that they are living through the end of days and that the ascent to heaven – the Rapture – is nigh.

At the same time, the novel establishes a conflict to do with procreation and parenthood; it raises the spectre of overpopulation as a contributing factor to environmental crisis and pits this against individual desires for parenthood. The other 'cult' that dominates this future Britain is the Planetarians, an environmentalist, zero-population-growth movement, who welcome the many climatic catastrophes as a form of 'human cull' (36). Their spiritual leader Harish Modak explicitly frames the argument as a conflict between the immediate wish to have children and the long-term view of overpopulation, writing in a newspaper article: 'In times past, children and grandchildren were seen as a blessing, a sign of faith in the future of the gene-pool. Now, it would seem that the kindest thing to do for our grandchildren is to refrain from generating them' (37). Harish is 'a geologist and one-time colleague' of the environmentalist James Lovelock, who is described in the novel as having come up 'with the notion of Gaia, the planet as a self-regulating system with its own "geophysiology"' (36). The Planetarians are therefore associated with some of the real Lovelock's bleaker assertions that Earth's self-regulation could and perhaps should include human extinction.[54] Their argument against overpopulation, then, goes against the twin emphases of parental care ethics, that is, its interest in immediate attachments and its concern with human lives.

The novel juxtaposes the Planetarians' ecocentric position on posterity, with its visions of a virtually childless and possibly non-human future, with

---

[53] Eric C. Otto, '"From a Certain Angle": Ecothriller Reading and Science Fiction Reading *The Swarm* and *The Rapture*', *Ecozon@* 3 (2012), 106–21.

[54] Lovelock states, for example, 'like an old lady who has to share her house with a growing and destructive group of teenagers, Gaia grows angry, and if they do not mend their ways she will evict them'; James Lovelock, *The Revenge of Gaia: Why the Earth Is Fighting Back—and How We Can Still Save Humanity* (first published 2006; London: Penguin, 2007), p. 60.

Gabrielle's profound parental desires. Through a series of flashbacks and reported conversations, the reader learns gradually of Gabrielle's terrible accident and is drawn into sympathy with its psychological and physical repercussions. The reader discovers clues and hints that build towards a picture of devastation: made aware at the outset of Gabrielle's paraplegia, the reader then learns of the death of her lover, Alex, and the fact that he was married. Then comes knowledge of Gabrielle's state of advanced pregnancy at the time of the accident, and, finally, the discovery that the accident caused the loss of her unborn child and her inability, with her physical disability, to have any more children. The accident turns her, in her words, into 'a non-woman pretending to be a real one' (65). Specifically, she is 'a woman with no man, no baby, no feeling below the waist, no imaginable future' (109), a self-description which collapses various conventional idealisations of female identity into one, all imbricated in the physical (motherhood, (hetero)sexual desirability and desire) and all deemed necessary to a life worth living (an 'imaginable future'). The first-person narrative, with its vivid handling of the practical aspects of paraplegia (for example, Gabrielle's experiences of managing a wheelchair, negotiating able-bodied prejudices, and having sex), invites the reader to inhabit Gabrielle's body and sympathise with her physical state. But the revelations of Gabrielle's accident culminate in the story of the loss of her child and what is, for her, a rare concession to tears: 'If I allow myself to cry, I will never stop' (141); this works to reduce her disability to the question of childlessness, and then to turn this into the most tragic aspect of the erosion of her sense of self. It also focuses reader sympathy on the question of Gabrielle's unfulfilled maternity.

Gabrielle's desire for motherhood hints at Bethany's position as a surrogate daughter. Bethany may seem an unlikely – and initially unlikeable – candidate for the role of moral patient in a maternal care ethics, given that her crime is matricide and her mental fragility manifests itself in threatening and violent behaviour towards others, including Gabrielle. Yet, it is precisely the void left by Bethany's abusive parents that creates a space for Gabrielle's treatment of her to be constructed in affectionate and even caring terms. Gabrielle – and the reader – find themselves inexplicably drawn to Bethany. Initially, this concern is professional: after getting hurt as a result of Bethany's assault of another patient, Gabrielle muses that 'a part of me that's still professional cares' (103) about Bethany being punished with isolation, even while she feels anger at the extent of the injury. But the professional extends to maternal when Bethany finally talks to Gabrielle about the abuse that drove her to murder her mother. Gabrielle's response replaces that maternal neglect with a new source of parental – even parochial – protection: she tells Gabrielle, 'Your mother's job was to protect you. That's what parents are supposed to do', before realising that if Bethany's mother 'were standing in front of me now, perhaps I'd want to kill her myself' (275) and promising to Bethany, 'I won't leave you' (276). Then, towards the novel's climax, as Gabrielle and her new partner Frazer seek safety with Bethany from the impending disaster, they pretend to be Bethany's parents in order to avoid suspicion (Bethany having been removed from secure psychiatric confinement), and thus pose as a makeshift nuclear family.

More strikingly, Gabrielle's care towards Bethany is aligned with a concern for the planet. It is not simply that Gabrielle strives to keep Bethany safe even as she works with Frazer and his scientific colleagues to warn the public of the upcoming disaster and to save as many human lives as possible. It is also that Bethany is in tune with the extreme events occurring around the globe. In Gabrielle's assessment, Bethany's pain is 'planet-shaped and planet-sized' (36) and she is a 'raging electric Gaia' (62). This turns out to be more than a figurative description, for Frazer concludes that Bethany's predictive powers come from her hypersensitivity to changes in meteorological and geological pressure, as evidenced by the way electroconvulsive therapy refines her predictions and by the drawings in her notebooks. Furthermore, Bethany, like the planet, is troped as violated. Bethany accurately predicts the final, climactic catastrophe (which is not in itself the outcome of climate change, but is, rather, a manmade trigger for abrupt climate change – a colossal earthquake brought about by suboceanic methane drilling in the North Sea, which will create a tsunami that will submerge Northern Europe and the American East Coast and release enough methane to bring about 'runaway global warming on the scale that's beyond anyone's worst nightmare' (228)). Bethany's predictive drawings present this in sexualised terms, at least in Gabrielle's estimation – the vertical line into a devastated landscape is interpreted by Gabrielle as 'a violent invasion' and taken as evidence that Bethany has 'been sexually abused' (133). When the reader realises what the drawings really represent, Gabrielle's misinterpretation in reading the representation of methane drilling as an expression of sexual abuse only serves to bring the prospect of the girl's and the planet's violation into the same frame.

As the narrative pushes to its catastrophic climax, Gabrielle, defined by her maternal desire and care for Bethany, and positioned as a potential saviour of the planet's human beings, comes into direct conflict with the anti-procreation – and, indeed, anti-children – discourse of the

Planetarians. When Gabrielle, Frazer, and his fellow scientists attempt to recruit the Planetarians to their cause of warning the public, they must first convince Harish Modak of the ethical good of doing so. Importantly, it is Gabrielle who debates the issue with Harish and wins. She does so by psychologising Harish's responses and framing the debate in insistently immediate and familial tones. Harish notes that the childless 'are often called selfish for making what is essentially an altruistic choice' (249); Gabrielle, it seems, calls him just that. On the one hand, she uses the memory of his dead wife's desire for children 'for the sake of some kind of future' (256) to insist that parenthood is, indeed, an investment in posterity; on the other hand, she argues that a lack of concern for the survival of present humans is both selfish and murderous: 'Whatever you feel about the Great Cycle and Gaia and the futility of the species is irrelevant, Harish! The issue is about the people who are alive now, who will die if you don't help us warn them! . . . If we fail to act now, none of us is any better than any war criminal on trial in The Hague' (256). Conveniently, Harish's argument simply melts away here, in line with the reader's conditioning, by identification and sympathy with Gabrielle, to believe in the ethical power of parenthood.

All this sets the scene for a climax filled with apocalyptic spectacle, as well as for a conclusion that underlines Gabrielle's parental care ethics and the reader's eudaemonistic share in it. On the brink of disaster, as the earthquake and tsunami threaten, Bethany, Gabrielle, and Frazer head to the Olympic stadium in East London, where the other scientists have arranged for a helicopter to fly them out of the imminent flood. The three are saved just in time, being lifted out of the stadium moments before the methane tsunami flows into it and ignites:

> The fire spreads greedily as though devouring pure oil, yellow flames bursting from the crest of the liquid swell, triggering star-burst gas explosions above. With a deep-throated bellow the wave gushes across the landscape, turning buildings and trees to matchwood in an upward rush of spume. As the force catapults us upward, the scene shrinks to brutal eloquence: a vast carpet of glass unrolling, incandescent, with powdery plumes of rubble shooting from its edges, part solid, part liquid, and part gas – a monstrous concoction of elements from the pit of the Earth's stomach. (339)

The apocalyptic ending also coincides with a final prediction by Bethany, and the quasi-religious, cosmological description of this spectacular catastrophe helps to give the prediction a messianic quality. As the helicopter lifts above the ruin, Bethany senses that Gabrielle is pregnant by Frazer, something unknown to either of the couple, and informs Gabrielle before hurling herself from the helicopter. The conjunction of Bethany's seemingly superhuman powers, her martyr-like death, and the near-miracle of a child for paralysed Gabrielle casts the new birth as redemptive. Indeed, among the last words of the novel is the suggestion that this birth will coincide with the rebirth of the world – 'the birthday of a new world' (341). What is hinted at here, in purely figurative terms, is the power of maternal desire and the fulfilment of that desire to regenerate the planet.

Nonetheless, there is yet room in the novel for a sense of scepticism about the possibility of rebirth – that is, environmental salvation – through parenthood. However, this requires a critical re-evaluation by both Gabrielle and the reader of the ethical dimensions of the mother's wish for a child in a devastated world. Indeed, Gabrielle's intense focus on parenthood is ripe for reassessment by the end of the novel. At Bethany's news of the long-wished-for fulfilment of motherhood, Gabrielle's response is one of devastation, not celebration: she lets out 'a great wail, ... a cry that will echo across the rest of my life' (341). The newly born world, Gabrielle realises, is not a world for her child:

> I look out on to the birthday of a new world. A world a child must enter.
> A world I want no part of.
> A world not ours. (341)

The new world in which Gabrielle and Frazer will raise their child is a testament to humanity's failed legacy to future generations; crucially, this is framed as a failure of parenthood, for, after the manmade disaster of the tsunami, there will 'be no safe place for a child to play' (341). This world is also a monument to humanity's mistaken emphasis on immediate and artificial gratification at the expense of the future of the biosphere; it is made of 'the ruins of all we have created and invented, the busted remains of the marvels and commonplaces we have dreamed and built, strived for and held dear: food, shelter, myth, beauty, art, knowledge, material comfort, stories, gods, music, ideas, ideals, shelter' (341).[55] What the novel's end reveals, for both Gabrielle and the reader, is that selfishness might equally lie on the side of parenthood and its emphasis on the here and now, as on the refusal to have children for the sake of posterity.

[55] The repetition of 'shelter' in this list, though probably a purely typographical error, serves to emphasise the need for basic care for a child.

Nonetheless, the sympathy that the reader might have extended to Gabrielle over the course of the novel is not simply to be withdrawn. If the novel has been successful up to this point, it will have brought the reader along a journey of sympathy, and asked her to undertake and, possibly, replicate Gabrielle's emotional and eudaemonistic investments. In the reading I have proposed here, it is possible also for the novel to effect a critical awakening for both protagonist and reader, which requires that the sympathy remains even as errors in sympathetic judgement are acknowledged. What emerges, then, is the chance for the reader to understand the cultural power of the norms of motherhood, combined as they are with ideals to do with bodily vigour and sex appeal, in shaping female identity; these ideas, of course, are not just discursive phenomena but occur in interaction with different material and physical circumstances and experiences. What might also emerge is a sympathetic and critical acknowledgement, rather than condemnation, of the extent of that power and its appeal in shaping identity.

Set in worlds marked by scarce resources, both novels explode assumptions of maternity as an automatic good by juxtaposing these against the urgent fears wrought by population pressures. Yet, whereas Lepucki's underdeveloped and unsympathetic protagonists sketch motherhood environmentalism as selfishness, Jensen's use of reader empathy and sympathy allows the reader both to engage in eudaemonistic identification and to develop insights into the potency of the myths that underlie such identification. Posterity-as-parenthood rhetoric wields considerable power over our emotional and ethical lives, and both novels – Jensen's especially – help demonstrate the depth of its purchase. *The Rapture* does not, however, go as far as it could in disclosing the contingency of (parental) identity, nor does it question the anthropocentric assumptions that underpin it. In the next chapter, I show how two climate change novels unmask the process of identity-making, and how one of these in particular – Jeanette Winterson's *The Stone Gods* – shows this to be, at the same time, a process of human–non-human boundary-making.

# CHAPTER 4

# Identity, Ethical Agency, and Radical Posterity: Jeanette Winterson's *The Stone Gods* and Sarah Hall's *The Carhullan Army*

With word and deed we insert ourselves into the human world, and this insertion is like a second birth, in which we confirm and take upon ourselves the naked fact of our original physical appearance. This insertion is not forced upon us by necessity, like labor, and it is not prompted by utility, like work. It may be stimulated by the presence of others whose company we may wish to join, but it is never conditioned by them. . .

Hannah Arendt, *The Human Condition*

A quantum universe – neither random nor determined. A universe of potentialities, waiting for an intervention to affect the outcome.

Love is an intervention.

Why do we not choose it?

Jeanette Winterson, *The Stone Gods*

In parental care ethics frameworks, moral agency tends to be construed as emanating from a reliable and coherent standpoint – parenthood (or, in ecofeminist inflections, motherhood, as discussed in chapter 3). Placed on the seemingly stable ground of parental obligation (for, it would seem, what could be more fundamental?), the ethical agent responds to those in the circle of concern with something like parental affection; even where that circle is widened eudaemonistically, moral considerability hinges on the resemblance of the moral patient to the child in need of protection and of the moral agent to, first and foremost, a parental protector. The moral compass of parental care ethics depends, then, on an ethical agent who surveys all from the perspective of parenthood.

Identity, nonetheless, is a mobile and fluid phenomenon: to say parenthood is not a fixed identity is to acknowledge that, where parenthood occurs as an aspect of identity, it is one of many aspects of experience, and it is also necessarily itself (if it can indeed be isolated) fluid from moment to moment. Thus, as has been noted in the introduction, Derek Parfit defines personal identity as 'nothing more than the occurrence of an interrelated series of mental and physical events', while Catriona Sandilands finds that identity occurs as the coming together of such events – memories, perceptions, experiences – at a nodal point at which these make themselves available to be interpreted as a coherent self.[1] As I suggested in chapter 3, Sandilands's framing of identity as 'intra-social' echoes Donna Haraway's concept of female identity as cyborgian, that is, as a hybrid of partial identities, and has affinities with Karen Barad's new materialist account of identity and agency as 'intractive', that is, as constructed in encounters between 'phenomena', or constellations of material and discursive units, as well as material-discursive composites – cultural norms, genres, social codes, rhetorics, along with the human and non-human things that give them material expression.[2] Yet, as I have also indicated, it is Sandilands's account of identity formation in the processes of political action that gives especial insight into how identity-making actually has ethical potential, for identity thus understood (that is, in terms of seeming flux and mutability) does not automatically presuppose a lack of any foundation from which to act.

In what follows, I read two climate change novels for the way in which they destabilise ideas of identity, a destabilisation accompanied by the possibility of an alternative and radical ethical agency for posterity. In both cases, this radical ethics is contrasted with a parental care ethics invested in stable meanings of identity. In Jeanette Winterson's *The Stone Gods* (2007) and Sarah Hall's *The Carhullan Army* (2007), identities are shown to be in flux, capable of being made, unmade, and remade; in this context, ethical agency arises out of interaction with others.[3] In Winterson's novel, a cyborgian identity based on openness towards and desire for difference, such as that theorised by Haraway, becomes the basis for a radical kind of ethics. In Hall's novel, the process by which identity and ethical agency are shaped in coalition and in dialogue with others

---

[1] Derek Parfit, *Reasons and Persons* (Oxford University Press, 1986), p. 341; Catriona Sandilands, *The Good-Natured Feminist: Ecofeminism and the Quest for Democracy* (Minneapolis: University of Minnesota Press, 1999), p. 84.

[2] Sandilands, *Good-Natured Feminist*, p. 84; Donna J. Haraway, 'A Cyborg Manifesto: Science, Technology, and Socialist-Feminism in the Late Twentieth Century', *Simians, Cyborgs and Women: The Reinvention of Nature* (London: Free Association Books, 1991), pp. 149–81; Karen Barad, 'Posthumanist Performativity: Toward an Understanding of How Matter Comes to Matter', *Signs* 28.2 (2003), 801–31.

[3] Jeanette Winterson, *The Stone Gods* (first published 2007; London: Penguin, 2008); Sarah Hall, *The Carhullan Army* (London: Faber, 2007). Subsequent page references to texts are in parentheses.

is set out, in a way that reveals not just the ethical potential but the risks of which to beware in identity-making.

## Identity, Coalition, and the Real

As we have seen in chapter 1, Sandilands's identitarian critique draws in part on Hannah Arendt's conceptualisation of the human condition as the *vita activa*, that is, consisting of labour (the practices required to maintain the biological or 'natural' processes of life), work (those practices that shape and transform the 'natural' to create an artificial world of things), and action (political and public practices).[4] It is this third category of action, in its demand for public collaboration and interaction, that defines the human condition; it is 'the only activity that goes on directly between men', and it 'corresponds to the human condition of plurality, to the fact that men, not Man, live on the earth and inhabit the world'.[5] As Sandilands paraphrases Arendt, the individual 'reveals her unique personal identity in relation to the common world. Moving away from what they are, individuals appearing in public reveal who they are, thus constituting themselves as individuals in relation to the shared world of public life.'[6] The key component of Arendt's philosophy of public life and Sandilands's subsequent theorisation of it, then, is social interaction: Sandilands's invocation of the 'common world' and 'shared world' echoes Arendt's emphasis on how the 'revelatory quality of speech and action comes to the fore' in moments of 'sheer human togetherness'.[7] If identity exists at all, it exists as an outcome of action on these terms: it is in saying and doing in exchange with others that we both form a sense of identity and are capable of generating political or moral change. Ethical agency – the ability to affect the lives of others for either good or ill – is thus enfolded into the Arendtian notion of identity.

The contrast between an ethic of care and this radical ethics of action and coalition thus becomes clear. Where an ethic of care such as that put forward by Christopher Groves treats the uncertainty of identity-making postulated by Arendt as something to be resolved by the individual exercise of parental care and its putative ethical power, Sandilands proposes that such uncertainty provides the context in which individuals come together in an ongoing, never completely fulfilled desire for affinity – in doing so,

---

[4] Hannah Arendt, *The Human Condition*, 2nd edn. (first published 1958; Chicago University Press, 1998), pp. 7–8.
[5] Ibid., p. 7.    [6] Sandilands, *Good-Natured Feminist*, p. 159.
[7] Arendt, *The Human Condition*, p. 180.

they make and share statements, positions, and ideas, and practise an openness and coalition that are politically or ethically productive.[8] Whereas in an ethic of care concerns for the future are predicated on standpoints such as the identity conferred by motherhood or parenthood, in the kind of radical ethics of posterity sketched here, there occurs not only an acknowledgement of the conditionality of identity but an insistence, on this basis, on the importance of interaction and conversation to create identity and the potential for moral agency.

More complexly, such an ethics is based on a reconceptualisation of identity as contingent and coalitional not just in the present but in the future; specifically, it necessitates an embrace of the future as fundamentally unknowable. Turning to Lacanian theory, Sandilands posits an 'ethics of the Real', an ethics that recognises the impossibility of wholeness and acknowledges the trauma associated with this impossibility.[9] The Real, in this account, is 'the gap between reality and representation' and 'the unreachable horizon of universality'.[10] In Sandilands's analysis of ecofeminism and environmental activism, this refers to the fantasy of the recovery of a lost affinity between woman and nature. In an ethics of posterity, this could be construed – in more straightforwardly Lacanian terms, one might suggest – as the constant and unfulfillable quest to know the future; after all, we desire to know it in the same way we believe we know the past. This is what lies behind the face of the child and prompts its ubiquitous use as a marker of parental care and future desire, as identified by Lee Edelman's Lacanian critique of the figure of the child: we desire a future over which (we think) we have control, the control of care.[11] But, as Sandilands would have it, 'while the Real is always with us but never apprehended, an ethical relation to it demands that we pay attention to its leftovers, its traces, its scars'.[12] What this implies, for this analysis, is the need to attend to how the doomed desire for the future to be knowable is also a desire for the future to resemble the past. An ethical relation towards posterity involves not just accepting the unknowability of the future, but accepting that our desire to know it derives from an attempt to recover the irrecoverable past. If, in Sandilands's analysis of an ecofeminist ethics of the Real, the answer lies in the exercise of ironic gestures, such as the parodying

---

[8] Christopher Groves, *Care, Uncertainty, and Intergenerational Ethics* (Basingstoke: Palgrave–Macmillan, 2014); Sandilands, *Good-Natured Feminist*, pp. 99–104.
[9] Sandilands, *Good-Natured Feminist*, p. 181.    [10] Ibid., p. 180.
[11] Lee Edelman, *No Future: Queer Theory and the Death Drive* (Durham, NC: Duke University Press, 2004).
[12] Sandilands, *Good-Natured Feminist*, p. 189.

of identity, or an acceptance of incompleteness, such as the foregrounding of representations of partial identity (or, indeed, partial representations of identity), then it may be that such a critical ethics of posterity must similarly ironise, parody, or otherwise shed light on the need to render the future familiar, and on the origins of this need in a nostalgic desire for the past.[13] Such critical reflection, as this chapter suggests, is enacted and enabled by the narrative processes (that is, mirrored in both plot and form) of *The Stone Gods*. Such reflection also recalls Arendt's model – outlined in chapter 1 – in which it is the 'activity of thought' that allows us to 'settl[e] into the gap between past and future', and to treat that gap not as a 'battleground' but as a 'home'; one ceases situating that home elsewhere, and ceases striving towards it.[14]

## The Stone Gods

Winterson's *The Stone Gods* maps hybridised identities and queer desire onto an ethical openness towards others, in a move that entails not just a coalitional and contingent view of identity but a specifically cyborgian one, after Haraway. This is offset, however, by the experience of maternal love, and, by implication, the ethical efficacy of parental care. Yet, the novel ultimately points to the reductive and recursive dimensions of parental care ethics. Specifically, it reveals how parental care engenders a nostalgic desire to recreate the future in the image of the past and it uses this revelation to make even more evident the need for a radical, future-oriented ethics of posterity.

The novel is Winterson's tenth for adults – eleventh, if one considers her early graphic novel, *Boating for Beginners* (1985) – and is part of a considerable *œuvre* that began with the immediate critical and popular success of *Oranges Are Not the Only Fruit* (1985). Follow-up novels such as *The Passion* (1987) and *Sexing the Cherry* (1989) cemented Winterson's reputation as a writer of experimental, queer narrative. Despite her own dislike of such labels, she has become something of an 'institution of queer postmodernism' and her writing has long been placed in 'the boxes labelled "lesbian fiction" or "postmodern fiction"'.[15] In Winterson's work, indeed, non-linear narration and non-heterosexual modes of desire

---

[13] Ibid., p. 78, p. 186.
[14] Arendt, *Between Past and Future: Eight Exercises in Political Thought* (first published 1954; Harmondsworth: Penguin, 1977), p. 13.
[15] Jago Morrison, '"Who Cares about Gender at a Time like This?" Love, Sex and the Problem of Jeanette Winterson', *Journal of Gender Studies* 15 (2006), 171; Lyn Pykett, 'A New Way with Words?

are often imbricated with each other; that is, her novels express alternative modes of desire both *in* and *as* avant-garde style, especially
experimental points of view and non-sequential temporality. At the
same time, Winterson's more recent work has tended to frame its
multiple, shifting perspectives and untraditional modes of desire
within an ethos that might best be described as the search for a higher
truth. Jago Morrison charts an important shift in Winterson's recent
work towards 'a highly essentialising commitment to the discovery of
Love in the agapeic mould'.[16] In later novels, from *The Powerbook* (2000)
and *Lighthousekeeping* (2004) onwards, queer desire is combined with
what Morrison calls a 'Christian sensibility' of love as metaphysical, an
emphasis on 'an ideal, transcendent love – one that is not only distinct
from the problematic of sexuality, but that involves a sacrificial shedding
of the erotic body itself'.[17]

 *The Stone Gods*, then, privileges a queer erotics of open-endedness, but
does so as a means to establishing an overriding ethos that makes sense of
love and life. The novel begins on a note of openness, troping spiritual and
sexual development as a journey in which new worlds and new ways are
discovered. In Nicole Merola's reading, 'Winterson utilizes repetition,
intertexuality [*sic*], and palimpsest as formal strategies and thematic elements' and 'seems to propose that love – for human and nonhuman others
and for the planet – offers a prescription for setting a new, nondestructive
path'.[18] The novel thus consistently equates queer desire and discovery with
a greater ecological understanding. In other words, it aligns narrative,
erotic, romantic, and environmental receptivity at one stroke. At the
same time, however, this alternative futurity of openness comes into
conflict with the ethical effects of parental care, particularly maternal
care, on the child. The novel replays a set of conflicts in parallel modes:
unexpected sources of love and desire are offset by maternal care; a radical
ethics of openness is balanced against a relatively narrow ethics of human
posterity.

 *The Stone Gods* may be described as a set of 'novellas-in-a-novel' rather
than as a single narrative.[19] It is a collection in four chapters of three stories
that take place, respectively, in the distant future, the eighteenth century,

Jeanette Winterson's Post-Modernism', in Helena Grice and Tim Woods (eds.), *I'm Telling You
 Stories': Jeanette Winterson and the Politics of Reading* (Amsterdam: Rodopi, 1998), p. 53.
[16] Morrison, '"Who Cares about Gender at a Time like This?"', 170.  [17] Ibid., 177.
[18] Nicole M. Merola, 'Materializing a Geotraumatic and Melancholy Anthropocene: Jeanette
 Winterson's *The Stone Gods*', *Minnesota Review* 83 (2014), 125.
[19] Julie Ellam, *Love in Jeanette Winterson's Novels* (Amsterdam: Rodopi, 2010), p. 220.

and the near future; these revolve around three protagonists, each named Billie Crusoe (or Billy, where the protagonist is male in the second story). In all three stories, Billie/Billy makes a strong connection with a character called Spike (or Spikkers, in the second story) and witnesses unprecedented environmental destruction. In the first chapter, Billie and Spike are part of a reconnaissance crew that leaves the dying planet Orbus, which resembles a version of a future Earth, to establish the habitability of the newly discovered Planet Blue. The Billie of this first chapter is a scientist who despises her civilisation's Central Power for encouraging its citizens to stay in thrall to cosmetic surgery, celebrity culture, and artificial, climate-controlled environments, while it competes with the planet's other superpowers – the Sino-Mosco Pact and the Caliphate – to use up the last of the planet's resources; meanwhile, Spike is a type of advanced humanoid robot – a Robo *sapiens* – with evolutionary capabilities. Billy in the second chapter is a sailor on the second voyage of Captain Cook's *Resolution*, accidentally left behind on Easter Island, where he falls in love with a Dutchman called Spikkers, and – evoking the cultural common-place that the Easter Islanders sacrificed the viability of their ecosystem to their religious beliefs – witnesses the destruction of the island's last tree in a power struggle. The Billie of the third and fourth chapters lives on Earth in a near-future time known as 'Post-3 War' (158), the aftermath of a devastating world war amidst the ruins of a climate-changed planet. Her job involves educating Spike, this time a cyborg created to assist the government in making objective, rational policy decisions. Britain is run by a faceless corporation called MORE, which has rebuilt the war-torn economy and now asserts complete control over it. But MORE is also the name of the corporation behind the Central Power of the first chapter. Thus, Earth is committing identical, not merely similar, mistakes to those made by humans on Orbus, but – at the same time and in a piece of temporal illogicality – it is also revealed that Earth was once the Planet Blue of the first chapter. In this final story, too, hope and openness increasingly give way to resignation and regression, figured most of all by the last Billie's desire for a return to childhood.

The novel makes explicit early on the similarities between loving planets and loving people. Hearing of Planet White, destroyed when 'humans, or whatever they were, massively miscalculated and pumped so much $CO_2$ into the air that they caused irreversible warming' (68), Billie bemoans how humans 'keep making the same mistakes over and over again', to which Pink – a typically youth-obsessed, cosmetically enhanced citizen of Orbus – responds that 'Women are just planets that attract the wrong species' (69). Certainly, the unloved Orbus presents as the victim of an abusive relationship. Asks Billie of the planet: 'We didn't do anything, did we? Just fucked it to death and kicked it when it wouldn't get up' (8). Even as it is on the receiving end of exploitation, Orbus is also the setting for it, particularly of a shallow kind of masculinist exploitation – what Fiona McCulloch describes as a 'mutated form' of 'patriarchal gender dichotomies'.[20] On Orbus, men no longer need women for procreation, women resort to identikit, artificial beauty to achieve desirability, and men turn to young girls for 'something different when everything has become the same' (21). Planet Blue seems to prove this maxim. Advertised on Orbus with a line from John Donne's poetry ('*She is all States, all Princes I*', 6; original emphasis), it is construed as feminine and ripe for conquest. Those lines, we learn, have come from Captain Handsome, the man who discovers Planet Blue and later engineers what he calls 'species-control' (82), an asteroid collision to kill the planet's dinosaurs and to create conditions in which humans can live.

Planet Blue, however, turns out to evoke something other than masculinist domination; it becomes – and then stands in for – the object of queer desire. Billie's journey to Planet Blue coincides with the awakening of her desire for Spike. What is significant for Billie is not that she is falling in love with a woman (indeed, Billie's sexual orientation prior to joining the reconnaissance mission is never described) but that she is falling in love with a robot: 'My lover is made of a meta-material, a polymer tough as metal but pliable and flexible and capable of heating and cooling, just like human skin' (83). Billie's first sight of the unknown planet glosses the radically new experience opened up by Spike: 'I can't wipe out the yes. One word and a million million worlds close. One word, and for a while there's a planet in front of me, and I can live there' (83–4). Billie's lyrical description of the planet – 'But there she is, sun-warmed, rain-cooled, moon-worshipped, flanked by the stars. There she is. Planet Blue' (84) – provides an alternative version to Donne's verse adopted as advance publicity for the planet. In pointed contrast, Spike is desired by Handsome in precisely the masculinist terms of Donne's poetry; indeed, it is his discovery of those lines and use of them to describe Spike that subsequently informs the marketing of Planet Blue to Orbus. Billie's and Spike's romance thus explicitly queers desire beyond the hetero-normative and, indeed, into the post-human.[21]

Strikingly, the post-human, as a space beyond conventional forms of human domination, also opens up a kind of ecological humility. That is, it dislodges not just (hetero)sexist but anthropocentric power as well. Both Orbus and its oversexed men and women are being destroyed by a selfish anthropocentrism: 'Humans always assumed that theirs was the only kind that mattered. That's how you destroyed your planet' (79), says Spike. 'But', she continues, 'you have a second chance. Maybe this time . . . ' (80). Spike and Planet Blue represent that second chance for Billie and for the reader: 'I looked at Spike, unknown, uncharted, different in every way from me, another life-form, another planet, another chance' (90). Such renewability is exemplified by Spike's ability to evolve into something that unites the best of human and robot: 'We are solar-powered and self-repairing. We are intelligent and non-aggressive' (79). Little wonder that the vision she has for Planet Blue is 'to develop a hi-tech, low-impact society, making the best of our mistakes here, and beginning again differ-ently' (39). The embrace of others, of possibility, of difference is troped as a radical new ecological ethics for the future. Spike explains their first kiss in the context of a 'quantum universe' that 'is potential at every second' (75). And so Spike and Planet Blue function as sites of resistance not to masculinism as such but, simultaneously, to heteronormativity, technolo-gical aggression, and narrow visions of the future.

The correlation of masculinism and heterosexism with ecological irre-sponsibility, and the countermove that is Spike and Billie's post-human and cyborgian ethics, echoes Haraway's cyborgian feminist ethics.[22] For Haraway, after all, the cyborg privileges multiplicity of identity and rejects essentialism, gesturing to 'permanently partial identities and contradictory standpoints'.[23] Such a rejection of identity politics concurs with a queer acknowledgement of the contingency of gender: 'Cyborgs might consider more seriously the partial, fluid, sometimes aspect of sex and sexual

---

[21] As Louise Squire suggests, Billie and Spike can be interpreted as representing, loosely, 'the subject categories of "human" and "nonhuman"', and the consummation of their relationship can be read as signalling the possibility of, simultaneously, a 'love solution' and a 'posthuman solution' to the existential demands of the Anthropocene; Squire, 'The Subject Reconsidered: Death-Facing and its Challenges in Contemporary Environmental Crisis Fiction', PhD dissertation, University of Surrey, 2014, pp. 116, 133–4.

[22] For an extended reading of Spike as a Harawayan cyborg, see Sonia Villegas-López, 'Body Technologies: Posthuman Figurations in Larissa Lai's *Salt Fish Girl* and Jeanette Winterson's *The Stone Gods*', *Critique* 56.1 (2015), 26–41.

[23] Haraway, 'A Cyborg Manifesto', p. 154.

embodiment. Gender might not be global identity after all, even if it has profound historical breadth and depth'.[24] Spike possesses a cyborgian subjecthood (a fixture of cyberpunk science fiction, as Veronica Hollinger points out) that is uniquely placed to figure both technological promise and technological over-reaching, while, at the same time, dismantling the expectations of gender performance.[25] In this case, Billie and Spike's ethics of receptivity towards human and non-human others and, indeed, towards the biosphere at large is explicitly also a que(e)rying of the ideas of both progress, that narrative of consumerist mastery over the world's finite resources, and posterity, the retelling of the future as human procreation and lineage. The novel, according to Abigail Rine, 'locates the hope of humankind – minimal though it may be – in forging new kinds of love-relations that cultivate and thrive on difference, relations characterized by mutuality'.[26] That is, the queering impulse is a transgression not just of heteronormativity but of norms per se; as Rine states: 'Queerness, for Winterson, is not simply non-heterosexuality, but that which intentionally challenges and exceeds the constraints of the normal.'[27]

In Winterson's novel, the queer coincides with renewal – indeed, the cyborgian discourse seems to appropriate the privilege of new life and new beginnings from parenthood ethics and rhetorics. In the conclusion to the first vignette, Billie and Spike die soon after arriving on Planet Blue, victims of the asteroid impact facilitated by Handsome. As death approaches, hybridity between humanity and technology is achieved, as Billie and Spike make love. Billie experiences this as a journey of enlightenment: 'She is the missing map. She is the place that I am' (107). Meanwhile, Spike develops a heartbeat. That is, death brings not only love but rebirth. Love is, for Billie, 'a journey on foot to another place' (109) and, for Spike, 'the chance to be human' (110). The novel insists, almost mantra-like, on birth instead of death, dream instead of sleep, and beginnings instead of ends: Billie intones, 'Things dying . . . things newborn' (112) and 'Close your eyes and sleep. Close your eyes and dream. This is one story. There will be another' (113).

---

[24] Ibid., p. 180.
[25] Veronica Hollinger, '"Something like a Fiction": Speculative Intersections of Sexuality and Technology', in Wendy Gay Pearson, Veronica Hollinger, and Joan Gordon (eds.), *Queer Universes: Sexualities in Science Fiction* (Liverpool University Press, 2008), p. 150.
[26] Abigail Rine, 'Jeanette Winterson's Love Intervention: Rethinking the Future', in Ben Davies and Jana Funke (eds.), *Sex, Gender and Time in Fiction and Culture* (Basingstoke: Palgrave–Macmillan, 2011), pp. 83–4.
[27] Ibid., p. 77.

This sense of rebirth is taken up in the next chapter (and indeed in the very existence of 'another' chapter and 'another' story). The reader finds another journey outward, another opportunity to witness and resist the standard narrative of progress. Billy the sailor, the protagonist of the next chapter, understands the self as a ship and the soul as 'the seabird that ploughs the wake of a Ship and then flies away no man knows where' (131–2). This chapter juxtaposes once more the journey to and discovery of love by an enlightened pair with the destruction of ecosystems by ignorant others. This Billy also finds love with someone who is at once a hybrid figure and a protector of the environment: the half-Dutch, half-native Spikkers, a man intent on saving the ravaged island. The events on the island microcosmically replay the failures on planet Orbus. The devastation of Easter Island is explained as the result, in the first instance, of the use of timber to transport and erect the giant *moai* in a regime of ancestor worship.[28] Environmental exploitation is then exacerbated by corruption and resource war, laying waste to the entire island. Thus, both Billies' journeys of queer discovery coincide with love for another and love for the non-human environment. While the first Spike opens up for Billie a 'hi-tech, low-impact' future of possibility, Spikkers unfolds for Billy the island's 'ghastly history' (132) and then reveals his plan to usurp the current regime and to restore both civil and ecological stability. Moreover, just as the first Billie discovers her love for Spike as they approach a new world and a newly possible world view, Billy realises he is in love with Spikkers in the midst of Spikkers' attempt at overthrow.

At Spikkers' death, however, we must give pause. The chapter has continued the previous chapter's short circuiting of linear narratives and conventions of care with a queer, cyborgian openness, but at this point it complicates this. Spikkers introduces to Billy the wish for home, a desire that is both the openness of outer space and the closure of return to his father's homeland: in a gesture that combines both impulses and is overlaid by a further desire for Billy, 'Spikkers pointed up to a bright and steady star close to the moon . . . "Holland," he said, kissing my fingers, one by one by one, and until my hand became a five-pointed star' (129). This confuses Billy's ideas of home: he wonders if his home, Plymouth, is 'nearer than a Holland star – or easier to believe?' (130). He comforts the dying Spikkers

---

[28] The novel thus repeats the accepted (though now contested) version of Easter Island's history; however, that the people of Easter Island, or Rapa Nui, devastated their forests to assist in building the *moai*, or stone gods, has been recently challenged: see, for example, Christian M. Stevenson, Cedric O. Puleston, Peter M. Vitousek, *et al.*, 'Variation in Rapa Nui (Easter Island) Land Use Indicates Production and Population Peaks Prior to European Contact', *PNAS* 112 (2015), 1025–30.

with the thought of home, represented by the tall house on Spikkers' Delft tile but also signified by the night sky: 'In the sky there is a star called Holland and the tall wooden houses of Amsterdam are clear to be seen' (139). And this is Billy's journey too, for he looks forward, after Spikkers' death, to being reunited with him in such a house – or, rather, to their souls being reunited. The 'white Bird [that] opens its wings' (140) in the chapter's final line becomes a reference simultaneously to Spikkers' soul on its voyage of return to his fatherland and to Billy's soul in anticipation of his reunion with Spikker. The chapter ends, then, on a note of openness, but this openness is now mingled with a nostalgic longing.

This is also what happens in the third and fourth chapters. In the novel's final tale, set in London, the third Billie is defined not as a journeyer but as a castaway, and thus not as venturing into a queer future of potentiality and openness but as stranded in the present; here, Billie's surname of Crusoe finally comes into its own, as she is 'shipwrecked on the shore of human-kind' (148). This Billie is also figured not as a moral agent but as a moral patient; indeed, she is positioned as the child. She is in search not of queer love but of parental care, defined by the loss of her mother, who, young and unmarried, was forced to abandon her as a baby. Obsessively seeking this mother, Billie will 'never stop looking', and lives with the thought of her mother as though 'in an echo of another life' (149). She thus calls to mind less the impulse of queer love as signified by the previous incarnations of Billie and Spike and more the nostalgic desire of Spikkers for his father's home. One must note, too, that in evoking the continued longing of the child rather than the care of the parent, this Billie in particular constructs care and love as trapped within the dyadic dimensions of parent–child relationships.

In line with the intensity of Billie's filial yearning, the Spike of this vignette is hardly Billie's soulmate. Indeed, she could be regarded as inferior to the first Spike both physically and ethically. This Robo *sapiens* is nothing more than a robotic head, developed to provide advice to the MORE corporation: 'She has no body because she won't need one ... to take the planet-sized decisions that human beings are so bad at' (158–9); these are 'neutral, objective decisions ... for the global good' (198). Attuned to MORE's corporate goals, this Spike believes in the possibility of 'the transition from the economics of greed to the economics of purpose' and insists that the 'economics of purpose is not about making money: it is about realigning resources' (164). The 'economics of purpose', part of MORE's 'new world order' of 'modest and eco-conscious members' (165), comes suspiciously to sound like an anthropocentric narrative of progress, in which ecological and social justice is translated into environmental services and resource management. No surprise, then, that Billie is aware that 'Neither art nor love fits well into the economics of purpose, any more than they fitted into the economics of greed. Any more than they fit into economics at all' (169). This Spike does not offer Billie the intervention of queer love.

Alternative modes of desire and ethics do exist, but their potential is frustrated in this narrative. Beyond Tech City, the MORE-controlled zone where Billie and Spike live, is Wreck City, a 'No Zone – no insurance, no assistance, no welfare, no police' (179); if Tech City represents the economics of purpose, Wreck City promises something like openness. Wreck City's town centre – the Playa – is a carnivalesque space that serves as meeting place, market square, performance ring, 'fairground, bacchanal, dream' (224), and is home to 'twenty alternative communities' (207). Spike, having been taken to Wreck City by Billie on an educational and experiential excursion, decides to join a group of young lesbian vegans called Chic X (so-called because they regret the damage done by the asteroid at Chicxulub, and therefore regret, unwittingly and according to the novel's twisted timeline, Captain Handsome's anthropocentric geoengineering). But any possibility for queer transformation is half-hearted, to say the least. Spike's sexual encounter with one of the Chic Xs is a comic version of the cyborgian epiphany experienced by the first Billie and is dismissed sarcastically by the last Billie: 'Great. The robot that was designed to become the world-sage has had oral sex with a teenager called Nebraska and become a drop-out free-love silicon guru' (210).

This Billie's rejection of cyborgian love emphasises her longing for maternal love, and underlines this story's contrast between the two. Moreover, that this Billie wants a landing place rather than a journey suggests, correspondingly, a recursive movement rather than a trajectory of openness and possibility. Her default state, she recognises, is loneliness, and the 'opposite of loneliness isn't company, it's return. A place to return' (175). Then, later, she realises that the landing place she seeks 'isn't a place at all: it's a person, it's you' (200). In the first two stories, the free-floating second-person pronoun seems to represent the ultimate and unknown object of desire, before it is gradually revealed to be Spike or Spikkers. In this story, 'you' is the first object of desire, the mother. But, at the end of the story, when Billie is reunited with this original love, this union happens in death: return collapses into finality. Shot by MORE soldiers, Billie experiences a phantasmal out-of-body sensation of walking to the stone farmhouse to which her mother used to walk when pregnant with her and, at the gate to the farmhouse, she is met by her dead mother. At this point, it is difficult to read in the third Billie's death anything like openness, for it speaks primarily of return and regress.[29]

Nonetheless, Billie's reunion with the mother repays a closer reading. Just before she dies, Billie repeats the words of the first Billie and Spike:

> A quantum universe – neither random nor determined. A universe of potentialities, waiting for an intervention to affect the outcome.
> Love is an intervention.
> Why do we not choose it? (244)

Could it be that the discovery of the mother is as much an intervention as the first Billie's journey to openness and cyborgian love? Several critics have remarked on the novel's equivalence of maternal love and queer love, and the orientation of both towards the future: McCulloch finds that Billie's reunion with her mother is yet another example of 'the capacity of human love that transcends divisions' and Susana Onega proposes simply that the reunion is 'pregnant with possibilities'.[30] As Susan Watkins notes, the novel avoids 'the cliché of maternal salvation' by investing in 'cyclism'.[31] What these commentaries miss, however, is the complex way in which the narrative transforms nostalgic desire for the mother into a radical and future-oriented desire, and replaces the dyadic bond with a very different dynamic. What they miss, indeed, is the way in which the mother herself expresses a cyborgian rather than a closed and parochial form of care.

For this mother is the first Billie. The farm to which the third Billie returns, the home her mother used wishfully to label 'our house' (156), is

---

[29] Squire explicitly figures this as a retreat from the kind of posthuman solution proffered by the first Spike: 'The novel's sense of irresolution, as Billie withdraws from all networks into her narcissistic death, demonstrates a failure of the human to grasp the meanings of the posthuman'; Squire, 'The Subject Reconsidered', p. 149.

[30] McCulloch, *Cosmopolitanism in Contemporary British Fiction*, p. 72; Susana Onega, 'The Trauma Paradigm and the Ethics of Affect in Jeanette Winterson's *The Stone Gods*', in Susana Onega and Jean-Michael Ganteau (eds.), *Ethics and Trauma in Contemporary British Fiction* (Amsterdam: Rodopi, 2011), p. 297.

[31] Susan Watkins, 'Future Shock: Rewriting the Apocalypse in Contemporary Women's Fiction', *LIT: Literature Interpretation Theory* 23 (2012), 127. That this section of the novel is fixated on the abandoned child rather than on mature queer experience may be relatable to Winterson's belated search for her biological mother and her discovery in 2007, when she had just completed the novel, that her mother had nursed her till Winterson's adoption at the age of six months. Winterson herself relates the erotic desire of which she writes to time spent with her birth mother and her unconscious desire for her: 'I realised that what I had written in *The Powerbook* was not about a lover but someone else. I was effectively asking: "What have you done with my mother?"'; see Stuart Jeffries, 'Jeanette Winterson: I Thought of Suicide', *The Guardian* (22 February 2010).

identifiable – with its apple tree, water barrel, and gate – as the first Billie's. That farm was, for the original Billie, 'the last of its line – like an ancient ancestor everyone forgot . . . a message in a bottle from another time' (13). But, lest this return is read as a nostalgic embrace of an unfulfillable idyll of the past, it is worth recalling the extent to which the first Billie was troped by her ability to reach outward rather than back, defined by her inter-planetary voyage and transgressive relationship with Spike. Moreover, the first Billie had always looked forward, even in the guise of motherhood. Facing her own death, she had remembered 'Not the stories with a beginning, a middle and an end, but the stories that began again, the ones that twisted away, like a bend in the road' (106), and had mused, 'Much of what I have done lies unfinished . . . because it had a life of its own that continues without me. Children, I suppose, are always unfinished business: they begin as part of your own body, and continue as separate as another continent' (106). The first Billie's construction of maternal care points to the life of the child as a life that is inevitably independent of its mother, as a new world and a new story.

Much has been made of the effect of the novel's emphasis on repetition, what Watkins calls 'cyclism', with its suggestion of a closed loop rather than an opening up; however, I would contend that that repetition occurs in the spirit of acknowledgement and critique, and thus with regard for possibility and potential. The novel is, in Winterson's own words, about our 'endlessly making the same mistakes'.[32] Merola finds that, 'by utilizing the formal strategies of repetition and intertexuality [*sic*] and by construct-ing a looping narrative that offers no closure and no escape, Winterson positions the reader in a melancholy, dysphoric space'.[33] Nonetheless, what Merola characterises as melancholy need not be unproductive, and Winterson's demonstration of our tendency to repeat our mistakes is not an uncritical one. In displaying the third Billie's wish for the mother, the novel enables an acknowledgement of the power of the nostalgic yearning for return, while continuing to affirm the need for radical openness; most importantly of all, it points to the revelation of trauma and a breaking of the cycle. For the novel, it could be argued, points to an ethics of the Real in Sandilands's sense. As Rine suggests, the third Billie's longing for the mother situates her in the context of 'a Lacanian reading of split-subjectivity'.[34] Rine reads Billie's lack as productive of agency; yet, while

---

[32] Sonya Andermahr, *Jeanette Winterson* (Basingstoke: Palgrave–Macmillan, 2009), p. 131.

[33] Merola, 'Materializing a Geotraumatic and Melancholy Anthropocene', 130.

[34] Rine, 'Jeanette Winterson's Love Intervention', p. 83.

her interpretation depends on a straightforward connection of loss with desire and hence with creativity – the 'loss of the mother is what gives Billie desire and what allows her to write as an expression of that desire' – I would suggest instead that it is the delineation of the contours of loss and desire that is truly transformative.[35] Through Billie, the novel enacts and acknowledges the trauma that compels us to desire the future in very particular and nostalgic ways, but it does so in order to caution against the constant repetition that this engenders. It does so, in other words, to break the cycle and to practise the love interventions that are celebrated throughout the novel.

The novel's display of hybrid identity not only queers expectations of ethics of care; it also queers notions of reader identification and empathy. For one thing, the reader, initially invited to identify and sympathise with the first Billie, finds herself shifting identity as the novel shifts narrative, moving in and out of narrators and their experiences, and being further destabilised by the third Billie's position as both a character in the novel and as another reader of it – after all, this Billie discovers the manuscript of 'The Stone Gods' on the London Underground. For another, the plot proceeds not so much in terms of focalised or narrated experience but in lyrical intonations of desire, exhibiting what Jean-Michel Ganteau has perceptively labelled Winterson's 'baroque aesthetics'.[36] In keeping with her emphasis on transcendence, Winterson situates her stylistic experiments within an idealised notion of the power of story (as Andermahr notes, 'she disparages realism with its focus on narrative storytelling, yet extols storytelling as a human need and aesthetic principle').[37] The novel's descriptions of love read as free-floating assertions, rather than as plot- or character-driven expressions or opinions. Because they are statements about the power of literature and love together, they offer metatextual guidelines to the reader on how to experience the novel. So, for example:

> Every second the universe divides into possibilities and most of these possibilities never happen. It is not a uni-verse – there is more than one reading. The story won't stop, can't stop, it goes on telling itself, waiting for an intervention that changes what will happen next.
>
> Love is an intervention. (83)

---

[35] Ibid., p. 81.

[36] Jean-Michel Ganteau, '"Rise from the Ground like Feathered Mercury": Baroque Citations in the Fiction of Peter Ackroyd and Jeanette Winterson', *Symbolism: An International Journal of Critical Aesthetics* 5 (2005), 193.

[37] Andermahr, *Jeanette Winterson*, p. 27.

And:

> The problem with a quantum universe, neither random nor determined, is
> that we who are the intervention don't know what we're doing.
> *Love is an intervention.* (217; original emphasis)

Winterson's evocation of love as an intervention – a radical and quantum
ethics of care rather than a parental one – depends on the reader's invocation and internalisation of that line and, indeed, a participation in that
love. This is an invitation, as Rine notes, to 'a love between reader and text
that opens new worlds, new possibilities'.[38] The novel, that is, queries the
stability of not just identity but of identification as a mediator between the
reader and a textual portrayal of care or love. That care or love, moreover, is
itself radically unstable, itself an intervention with unpredictable consequences, rather than a stable ground from which to intervene.[39]

## Identity and the Agonal Moment

This echoes the Arendtian view of identity and agency, which, as we
have seen, is of identity as formed in coalitional and dialogic action, and
of such action as a space of (unpredictable) ethical potential. Sandilands,
paraphrasing Arendt, suggests that 'action is the capacity for speech and
deed', where speech and deed are productive of identity.[40] What is
revealed, then, is not an essential identity, lying passive or latent and
waiting to be expressed; identity is unknown prior to – and thus made
in – the expression of it. When Arendt states that in 'acting and
speaking, men reveal who they are, reveal actively their unique personal
identities', she is also at pains to clarify that such identity 'remains
hidden from the person himself' and is 'visible only to those he
encounters'.[41] This, then, is what allows her to declare: 'With word or
deed we insert ourselves into the human world, and this insertion is
like a second birth.'[42] Identity is not just disclosed but discovered –
including by the individual herself – in reaching out to others.

---

[38] Rine, 'Jeanette Winterson's Love Intervention', p. 78.
[39] That is, care here is ontological (agential) rather than ontic (the grounds on which agency occurs).
As Squire puts it, the novel 'may depict love as an intervention; nonetheless, this intervention
operates within an endless multiplicity of possible givens and outcomes, always contributing but
never occupying any single primacy'; Squire, 'The Subject Reconsidered', p. 142. For more on care
and love as ontological, see Adeline Johns-Putra, 'Environmental Care Ethics: Notes toward a New
Materialist Critique', *symplokē* 21.1–2 (2013), 125–35.
[40] Sandilands, *Good-Natured Feminist*, p. 155.    [41] Arendt, *The Human Condition*, pp. 179–80.
[42] Ibid., p. 176.

Nevertheless, Arendt's insistence that identity is made in the public act of disclosure and discovery should not be mistaken for a conception of identity formation in a moral or ethical vacuum. One need recall that, for Arendt, identity both emerges from and contributes to a public and communal realm. Thus, action results in 'power', a word that for Arendt has positive connotations and betokens the potential of social action for social good. Indeed, power is distinct from 'force', which is the monopolistic exercise of an individual's strength over others and thus involves 'violence'.[43] As Elisabeth Young-Bruehl explains, for Arendt, 'power and violence are *opposites*'.[44] The combination of force and violence are the markers of 'tyranny', a form of government that takes place in isolation from its people and is, hence, ultimately impotent.[45] That 'Tyranny prevents the development of power' means that, even while it diminishes or disables power among its citizens, it is also unable to accrue power to itself.'[46]

With such a conception of identity (as shaped in and by public action and conversation), the relationship of ethical agency (as concomitant with identity, since identity is always dialogic and coalitional) to the public and the private requires some reformulation. Identity on these terms is no private phenomenon awaiting its unveiling, but is equivalent to the agency initiated, declared, and practised in public; as Sandilands states: 'Action does not cement the private self but disrupts it in the creation of something entirely new, something that cannot be grounded or predicted in private life.'[47] As Sandilands explains the Arendtian view, 'in private life, the self is fragmented and conflicted. Only through performative appearance in public, in the presence of others, does it attain identity, a sense of who it is as distinct from the constraints of what one might call the identities of private life.'[48] One could, after Young-Bruehl, distinguish between public action and private behaviour; Young-Bruehl clarifies, 'action is quite different from behavior, which is repetitive and habitual, showing what people have become, not who they can become in the performance of action, which forces them to rise to an occasion'.[49] For this reason, Sherilyn MacGregor's analysis of ecofeminism and activism identifies the need for a 'feminist ecological citizenship' that is a reimagining rather than 'an

---

[43] Ibid., pp. 199–202.
[44] Elisabeth Young-Bruehl, *Why Arendt Matters* (New Haven, CT: Yale University Press, 2006), p. 90; original emphasis.
[45] Arendt, *The Human Condition*, p. 202.      [46] Ibid., p. 202.
[47] Sandilands, *Good-Natured Feminist*, p. 160.      [48] Ibid., p. 159.
[49] Young-Bruehl, *Why Arendt Matters*, p. 87.

extension of women's private roles'.[50] This suggests, among other things, the need to dislodge ecomaternalist positions grounded in domestic and familial care, positions that, as I have argued in chapters 2 and 3, are proximal to parochial and paternalistic attitudes that, when practised unreflectingly, might express themselves in resentment, self-interest, or possessiveness.

The Arendtian concept of identity also invites a closer scrutiny of the public and performative moments that are productive of identity – those points of self-declaration and exchange in the realm of public and political action. Sandilands posits an Arendtian-inflected model for ecofeminist identity-making in which the political subject attains a sense of self in performance, and clarifies: 'Arendt herself uses the word *performance* to describe the speech process by which the actor reveals her unique personal identity in relation to the common world.'[51] This revelatory instance, Sandilands reminds us, is 'the agonal moment of Arendt's public' (the agonal here referring to the contestatory nature of self- or, more accurately, identity-formation in relation to others).[52] In Young-Bruehl's words, the revelation of identity through action 'requires not skill or strength or application of violent force for achieving a result, but courage in the face of the unknown; action is risk'.[53] It is a risky because entirely radical undertaking – the bringing forth of an identity full of unpredictability and promise. According to Sandilands, the appeal of such an agonal vision is that it frees political and ethical agency from existing constraints, such as norms to do with gender, sexuality, or race (it allows for a 'noncorrespondence between social location and political action'), or business-as-usual, bureaucratised politics ('it does not respect existing boundaries').[54] It possesses, in other words, true democratic potential.

At the same time, however, what is risked in the agonal moment – conceived as identity (re)birth, and with it, uncertainty – deserves some comment. Following Seyla Benhabib, Sandilands identifies two tendencies in Arendtian theorisations of public life – what Benhabib calls the

---

[50] Sherilyn MacGregor, *Beyond Mothering Earth: Ecological Citizenship and the Politics of Care* (Vancouver: University of British Columbia Press, 2006), p. 5.

[51] Sandilands, *Good-Natured Feminist*, p. 159, citing Arendt, *The Human Condition*, p. 179; Sandilands makes clear that this conception of performativity differs from Judith Butler's: in Arendt, the performance is 'the only moment at which an individual can be said to exist (the rest of the time, she or he is defined by what, not who, she or he is), whereas, for Butler, parodic performance relies on the careful and conscious repetition of precisely the categories through which an individual is defined (the what) in order to disrupt them', *Good-Natured Feminist*, p. 160.

[52] Sandilands, *Good-Natured Feminist*, p. 159.   [53] Young-Bruehl, *Why Arendt Matters*, p. 89.

[54] Sandilands, *Good-Natured Feminist*, p. 16.

'agonistic' and the 'associational'.[55] Both seem compatible with Arendt's emphasis on the collaborative, dialogic, and coalitional nature of action, but, at the same time, each exists in tension with the other, to the point that, as Shmuel Lederman puts it, a 'heated controversy' exists in Arendtian studies over this apparent 'self-contradiction'.[56] While the agonal model privileges extraordinary, noteworthy, and, one might say, heroic entries into the public realm, the associational ideal also evident in Arendt's work focuses on commonplace and egalitarian participation for all; as Sandilands acknowledges, the agonal vision is vulnerable to charges of individualism and elitism.[57] Indeed, François Debrix and Alexander Barder have recently argued that Arendt's agonal politics, 'taking place in a space allegedly freed from sovereign decisionism and valued for its performative manifestation', lends itself to the logic of drastic and even brutal regime change and governance (even while they acknowledge that Arendt's chosen emphasis is on 'a public sphere that ... needs to remain plural, free and, more importantly, contingent').[58] For Debrix and Barder, the agonal model unwittingly 'reveals how tenuous the boundaries can be between maintaining or, in fact, inventing a political domain and destroying it (as well as others or enemies in the same process) by having recourse to the performative acts of heroic public agents who are left in charge, without any limitation or safeguard, of devising or realizing new political possibilities'.[59] What they call 'agonal sovereignty' names the latter, destructive scenario.[60] One could say that Arendt's agonal actor, in Debrix and Barder's analysis, while initially committed to the 'power' of public action, is not immune from a turn to 'violence', 'force', and, consequently, 'tyranny'.

To apply an Arendtian understanding of identity to ethical agency oriented towards the human and non-human future – a future consisting of moral patients that are necessarily public rather than private – is to recognise that such obligations might call forth an agonal moment in which a public identity is created that is distinct from the private self. Yet, it is also to perceive that the agonal moment – which I take to refer not just to the formulation of identity but the reformulation of private modes

---

[55] Ibid., p. 162; Seyla Benhabib, 'Models of Public Space: Hannah Arendt, the Liberal Tradition and Jürgen Habermas', in Craig Calhoun (ed.), *Habermas and the Public Sphere* (Cambridge, MA: MIT Press, 1992), pp. 77–8.

[56] Shmuel Lederman, 'Agonism and Deliberation in Arendt', *Constellations* 21.3 (2014), 327–8.

[57] Sandilands, *Good-Natured Feminist*, pp. 161–2.

[58] François Debrix and Alexander D. Barder, *Beyond Biopolitics? Theory, Violence, and Horror in World Politics* (London: Routledge, 2012), pp. 35, 38.

[59] Ibid., p. 38.        [60] Ibid., p. 38.

of behaviour often mistaken for identity – is inherently fraught. As an opportunity to build a publicly oriented ethical agency (or what Arendt calls power) beyond intimate emotions, feelings, and hopes, the agonal performance must ensure that it does not transform itself into the exercise of will over others (which Arendt believed to be power's very antithesis).

## The Carhullan Army

Hall's novel juxtaposes two utopian visions against each other, the first implying the kind of motherhood environmentalism or ecomaternalism described in detail in chapter 3 and the second requiring an ecological citizenship of political action and public commitment to a cause. In the shift from one to the other, the narrator not only experiences fluxes in identity but makes and unmakes identity in response to a very public call to act on behalf of an endangered future. In so doing, she risks surrendering agency altogether to a violent and militant tyranny disguised as an ethical call to arms.

Hall came to attention as a young British novelist of promise when her second book, *The Electric Michelangelo* (2004) was shortlisted for the Man Booker Prize; already, her first book, *Haweswater* (2003) had received critical praise. *The Carhullan Army* (2007), published in North America as *Daughters of the North* (2008), also won acclaim. Hall's current body of work is difficult to categorise, ranging as it does from the historical settings of her first two novels to the immediate political present of *The Wolf Border* (2015) and the temporal shifting of *How to Paint a Dead Man* (2009). *The Carhullan Army*, meanwhile, takes place in a dystopian future Britain; indeed, the prizes it has won – the James Tiptree, Jr. Award and a nomination for the Arthur C. Clarke Award – suggest its ready acceptance as science fiction. In general terms, Hall may be regarded as a writer of place and its effect on people, with all her novels – even *The Electric Michelangelo* with its evocation of Coney Island and *How to Paint a Dead Man* with its setting in mid-twentieth-century Italy – referencing the remote landscapes of Cumbria in northwest England, where she was born.

The action of *The Carhullan Army*, like *Haweswater*, is set almost entirely in Cumbria's mountainous Lake District, with its descriptions intended to be topographically accurate. It takes place in a future marked by food scarcity and rising water levels brought about by climate change, when, 'of all the English traditions to have been compromised, the weather was the saddest' (6). Hall has indicated that the novel was inspired by her experience of the 2005 Cumbrian floods centred on the town of Carlisle, an environmental disaster that, as she has noted, is part of the larger picture of global warming and rising temperatures: 'There are reasons for [the flooding]. The snow doesn't hold in the uplands. It melts very quickly because temperatures are slightly warmer, so we know that we're not going to have a gentle trickle down of snow into the rivers; we're going to have flash floods and overwhelming levels of thaw.'[61] In Hall's novel, the devastation and its impact on infrastructure and agriculture have led to the rise of a paranoid dictatorship known as the Authority. Citizens registered with the Authority live in impoverished, urban communities, circumscribed in all aspects of their private lives – housing, employment, mobility, and even reproduction. Meanwhile, those who have remained in the increasingly wild spaces without are disregarded as 'Unofficials' (15). The novel's narrator leaves her husband in the Authority settlement of Rith (based on the town of Penrith) to join an all-female community living in self-sufficient exile on a remote farm in the Cumbrian mountains called Carhullan. Carhullan is led by Jackie Nixon, a tough, mercurial figure who eventually inspires the women to launch a bold guerrilla attack on the Authority. Carhullan's appeal is crystallised through Jackie's charisma, and both are framed by the narrator's infatuation with the woman and her land. From the outset, the reader knows the narrator only as 'Sister', which is the name she is given in Carhullan, and knows also that the attack has failed, since the narrative is presented as Sister's fragmented and partially recovered confession to the Authority.

The novel posits two responses to the dystopian regime: both are, in their way, utopian, inasmuch as they are grounded in the belief in a better, alternative social order. Although they are premised on the same investment in living close to the land, eschewing technology and machinery, and – most of all – privileging (feminist) community over (masculinist) competition, their modes of execution differ, a difference that eventually places the two in conflict. The one, embodied in the Carhullan farm, is centred on withdrawal to an isolationalist retreat, on achieving a true utopia in the sense of a distinct topos or place; the other, expressed in Jackie's martial offence against the Authority, is premised on a sense of mission, the need to attack the dystopian state and replace it with a utopian one. They reiterate, then, a crucial distinction in commentaries on literary utopias (a difference I discuss further in chapter 5) between static and

---

[61] 'Sarah Hall – *The Carhullan Army*', *Bookclub*, BBC Radio 4, 9 December 2010; the floods were the worst seen in Carlisle since 1822, see 'Floods in Carlisle – January 2005', Met Office, 29 October 2012, www.metoffice.gov.uk/climate/uk/interesting/jan2005floods.

kinetic utopias, that is, between 'the classical utopia of static perfection and the "modern" utopia characterised by a continuous process of political and social improvement'.[62] In Iain Robinson's insightful reading of the novel, whereas the Carhullan community presents on the one hand as a 'flawed or failing utopia', Jackie's bellicose solution is 'a militant attempt to provide an alternative to the dystopian situation'.[63] The novel considers the ideological and geographical limits of its separatist utopia, and depicts the final dismantling of its borders as part of a wider strategic battle for not just survival but supremacy. Finally, then, having committed to a utopian ideology, Sister unwittingly participates in the tyrannical execution of this ideology.

Initially, Carhullan presents as a tempting vision of an alternative green utopia in the static, escapist sense, a stark contrast to the techno-dystopia that Sister flees. The Authority has chosen to concentrate its people in towns, all the better to control them and to use them as cheap industrial labour. Sister associates her once like-minded but now apathetic husband, Andrew, with the unremitting grind of living under the Authority and working in its factories: he has been 'reduced to the base mechanism of getting by' (30). When Sister finds her way to the open country of the Lake District, her sense of emancipation is more than just about liberty from the Authority; it is about the rediscovery of an emphatically 'natural' subjectivity and agency. The reader takes in the transition from urban devastation to pastoral idyll through Sister's eyes. Indeed, in their readings of the novel, Deborah Lilley and Astrid Bracke emphasise how the pastoral haunts and gives meaning to the dystopian landscape through which Sister travels.[64] The abandoned cars she passes while on the run have been reclaimed by animals, plants, and weather, the 'observances of airbags and seatbelts, stereo systems' and 'bright paint' defeated by rust, mildew, and nests in their engines. These corroded symbols of technological redundancy – 'husks of a privileged era' (20) of fuel and highway maintenance – are implicitly compared to both the government and her husband, and both are being left behind: 'I knew that I had done

[62] Patrick Parrinder, *Utopian Literature and Science: From the Scientific Revolution to* Brave New World *and Beyond* (Basingstoke: Palgrave–Macmillan, 2015), p. 4.

[63] Iain Robinson, '"You Just Know When the World is About to Break Apart": Utopia, Dystopia and New Global Uncertainties in Sarah Hall's *The Carhullan Army*', in Siân Adiseshiah and Rupert Hildyard (eds.), *Twenty-First Century Fiction: What Happens Now* (Basingstoke: Palgrave–Macmillan, 2013), p. 202.

[64] Deborah Lilley, 'Unsettling Environments: New Pastoral in Kazuo Ishiguro's *Never Let Me Go* and Sarah Hall's *The Carhullan Army*', *Green Letters* 20.1 (2016), 60–71; Astrid Bracke, *Climate Crisis and the Twenty-First-Century British Novel* (London: Bloomsbury, 2018).

the right thing by leaving Andrew, leaving the harsh orchestration of the town, the dismal salvaged thing that the administered country had become' (21).

Carhullan, according to this logic, is the locus of pastoral purity. The transition from dystopia to utopia is boosted by Sister's remembered experiences of the women of Carhullan. Sister knows of the farm as 'a truly green initiative' that 'had never been built with the outside world in mind' (54), an assessment founded on girlhood memories of the women of Carhullan, who used to visit her town to sell their produce – homegrown, wholesome vegetables, butter, and honey that are very different from the 'cubes of meat and fruit, from the shipments of tins sent from America' (31) sold by the Authority and unthinkingly consumed by Andrew. Each time Sister 'opened a tin and transferred the gelatinous contents into a bowl', she would think 'of the farm's bright vegetables on the market stall a decade before' (52). When she does reach the farm, her first proper meal is a hearty porridge and 'the most delicious fruit I had tasted for years' (83). Likewise, her adolescent infatuation with Jackie Nixon is based on Jackie's indigeneity: of old Cumbrian stock, 'the Border Nixons' (49), she appears in the photographs in Sister's saved newspaper cuttings as 'hard-cast, like granite' (49); upon their first meeting, her pale grey eyes seem to be 'the colour of slate riverbeds' and enforce the impression that 'that the territory had somehow gone into the making of her' (78). Most importantly of all, Carhullan's utopia is identified with both environmental sustainability and female agency. Sister thinks of it, with its waterwheel, vegetable gardens, orchard, and fishery, as 'grandly holistic, a truly green initiative' (54), while the news reports quote Jackie's beliefs that, too often, women 'endorse the manmade competition between ourselves that disunites us, stripping us of our true ability' and her declaration that 'It's time for a new society' (51). Sister's anticipation of, journey towards, and first experience of Carhullan establish a confluence of closeness to the land, authenticity of self, and pure womanhood.

Carhullan, as land that is solely and truly female, stands in juxtaposition with the masculinity of the Authority's towns, implied not just through the Authority's male leadership – a figurehead king and a 'dangerous' and 'power hungry' (25) man named Powell – but through the complicity of the unsympathetic and unquestioning Andrew. As Sister makes the arduous trek to Carhullan, she appears to travel from female objectification under a masculinist agenda to female subjectivity in kinship with a female landscape: the journey is troped as a rediscovery of the power of her body, in which the reader partakes, thanks to a slowly paced, lyrical vocabulary.

Sister describes the environment as endowing her with a heightened and corporeal experience of selfhood: first, 'I felt the arrival of a new calmness, an assurance of my own company ... I was aware of my own warm predominance in the environment, my inhabited skin, my being. I suddenly felt myself again, a self I had not been for so long' (41); then, 'as I stood and looked in the direction of the summits, I felt dressed in my own muscles, and ballasted by my sense of physicality' (42).

The female body – in this case, Sister's body – becomes the ground of a transformation in identity, as it moves from being the site of male control to female agency. The most damning motif of the Authority's power and Andrew's collusion with it is the government-issue contraceptive coil that is inserted in women, including Sister, in order to regulate reproduction and population. That it signifies the ultimate violation of Sister is made patently clear through a series of episodes: the painful fitting from a male doctor although Sister had asked to be seen by a woman; Andrew's arousal by the device and the unwelcome sex that follows; his dismissal of it as 'obsessing over [her] maternal rights' (33); and the humiliating spot check of Sister's device by government monitors in the back of an Authority cruiser, an incident whose lack of detail but considerable effect on Sister – it is what first inspires her to go to Carhullan – only heighten the sense of trauma and threat. When Andrew insists that she be 'complicit in Britain's attempts to rebuild herself', her angry rebuke presses home the point that the brutalisation of her body functions metaphorically to suggest the ecocidal degradation of the land: 'She's a female, is she, this country that's been fucked over' (31). The regulator takes on added poignancy as a contaminant to the apparently organic sense of self she develops at Carhullan. There, the device 'felt exactly as it was: an alien implant, an invader in my body' (90), and it is removed very soon after her arrival. The device, then, is an important part of the novel's presentation of Sister in both literal and figurative terms. The reader is invited to share Sister's experiences as both site and symbol of alternative powers, and to anticipate that her recuperation at Carhullan will present a utopian, (eco)feminist challenge to a broader agenda of exploitation.

For the device also raises the questions of motherhood and its conjunction with female autonomy. At a casual glance, Carhullan is a site of female control over reproduction, in keeping with the novel's initial identification of it as a utopian alternative. The Authority's regulation of reproduction – its infringement of Sister's 'maternal rights' and its rendering of her as a 'sterile subject' (41) – contrasts with Carhullan's ability to create and support new generations of its community. When Sister catches sight of a baby at the farm, the use of restricted point of view and gradual revelation of this information establishes it as climactic and significant: 'It took a moment for me to comprehend what I had seen. My eyes were still watery and smarting, but they were not mistaken. There was a newborn at Carhullan' (80–1). Sister then forms an immediate connection with a young woman called Megan, the oldest of Carhullan's second generation, whose pregnant mother had come to the farm to escape an abusive husband. Megan describes herself as 'multi-mothered' by the women, raised as 'an experiment . . . to see what they could do without the influence of nem' (107). The invented word 'nem' – 'men turned round and made to face the other way' (107) – is intended to reflect back onto men their exploitation of women. Both the description and the context of the 'experiment' confirm the marginalisation of men: the farm's other children are the offspring of Carhullan women and a small number of men, who are allowed to live on a satellite settlement and obtain food and fuel in exchange for doing odd jobs for Carhullan; any boys are sent to the men's crofts when they reach puberty. The community is, then, an insistently homosocial space, and – while it is not necessarily homo*sexual* – it is a space in which rich, loving relationships develop between women, whether romantic (as for Sister and her lover Shruti) or maternal (as with Megan's upbringing). This female-only space is correlative with women's care for the land. It is a version, that is, of an ecomaternalist utopia.

Ultimately, however, the novel suggests that this sanctuary of care cannot provide a long-term future in practical or political terms. An ecofeminist counter-ideology operates at Carhullan, one that requires open resistance to the Authority and active engagement with other communities. There occurs in the novel, as Robinson notes, 'a shift in the nature of the counter-narrative offered by Carhullan, from social experiment to martial resistance'.[65] This is already signalled in Jackie's warning to Sister on their first meeting that 'we're going to have to change' (98), and in Jackie's sarcasm about the settlement's utopian credentials: 'She did not try to describe Carhullan as any kind of Utopia' and 'when she had referred to Shangri-la . . . it had been with a note of irony', so that Sister wonders whether she 'might have failed in her original plan' (100). Gradually, both Sister and the reader realise that Jackie disparages the other women's wish to 'just bolt the door. Hole the fuck up. And pray to be left alone' (116); she intends to 'start again, but differently' (156). Indeed, the history of Carhullan, going back to its founding by Jackie and her lover Veronique,

---

[65] Robinson, '"You Just Know When the World is About to Break Apart"', p. 209.

suggests a split in its utopian personality – a contrast between Jackie's hardness and Veronique's warm 'optimism' (156), a difference that is part of an 'oppositional gravity' (115) in the community and that can be mapped onto the novel's two versions of utopia as private sanctuary and as political project. Having had to shoot Veronique in a violent act of mercy killing, Jackie has 'killed her love with her lover, and cured herself of human weakness' (158), and plans to create utopia anew, this time through the army of the novel's title. The Authority's decision to spread its jurisdiction to the country's unofficial zones only confirms Jackie's conviction that, in order truly to last, Carhullan's ethos must be defended and disseminated. This marks the narrative's transition from a tale of utopian retreat to one of utopian operation.

This militant brand of utopianism seems to promise an ethics for and on behalf of the future of the country, an ethics of public action rather than the insulated and interiorised care that would seem to be promised by the farm. It is based, then, not on an idea of the women's innate caring ability or identity but on an identity forged in the women's communal debates and responses to Jackie's fiery speeches as leader. What this requires is both the unmaking and making of identity, namely, Sister's.

Thus, from the point of Sister's arrival at the farm, Jackie works to disassemble her sense of a stable self. Jackie's confinement of her in the tiny, windowless 'dog box' (70) seems a shocking contradiction to the idyll that Sister had earlier imagined Carhullan to be, but it is also part of an initiation that completes the self-renewal that began with Sister's escape from the Authority. Sister realises, in her confinement, that the experience is 'letting me break apart, so I could use the blunt edges of my reason to stave in my mind, and the jagged ones to lance open the blisters of my insanity' (74); the result is 'a kind of suicide', the realisation that she is 'nothing', 'void to the core', and 'an unmade person' (94). All this is in keeping with the stripping away of her old name and imposition of the appellation of 'Sister'. Here, the breaking down of self is a prerequisite for the assumption of a new identity.

Sister's identity-making occurs in what might be read as an agonal moment. The farm holds regular 'formal debates and discussion that ran to order' (109), at which Jackie makes the case for dissolving the farm and initiating armed resistance to the Authority. She makes her argument, strikingly, by singling out Sister to decide in public if she will join the army's action. Of this moment, Sister states:

> I don't remember what I said. The words were lost to me even as I spoke
> them. I felt Jackie's arm on my shoulder, acknowledging my allegiance,
> binding me to her. I felt the flow of energy leaving her frame and filling
> mine, circulating with my own blood through the vessels of my body. She
> had always understood what my potential was, the apparatus she could work
> with. (162)

Sister's identity as a soldier for Carhullan's ideals is enacted in this instance,
and emerges both as a performance before the others and in coalition with
Jackie, a coalition emphasised by the image of corporeal intermingling.
This is, importantly, seen by Sister as both a dissolution and a constitution
of identity. Sister's initial feeling is that she is 'a piece in a game [Jackie] was
playing' (162) and her sense that she is 'the apparatus [Jackie] could work
with' (162) even echoes the Authority's dehumanisation of her. Eventually,
however, where Sister had been objectified by the contraceptive device
planted in her, she comes to feel, after this moment of public declaration,
and through the performance that is her army training, that her body is
a 'matchless device' (170). Sister then claims of Jackie: 'We knew she was
deconstructing the old disabled versions of our sex, and that her ruthless-
ness was adopted because those constructs were built to endure' (187).
The identity that Sister makes, in word and action, is the 'anima' (204) she
sees in her mirror, suggesting an activator of Carhullan's utopian ideals
rather than a passive consumer of them.

Here, the crucial apparatus in Sister's performance of identity is her
father's gun. It is taken by Sister to Carhullan as a sign of her willingness to
contribute to its cause and is returned to her when she is ready to play a role
in the army. The gun represents an adherence to Carhullan's principles of
female solidarity; it signals Sister's and the other women's willingness to
stand their ground and refusal 'to submit to survive' (116). In another
performance of action – an exchange with Jackie – Sister is asked if holding
her father's gun would have 'ma[d]e any difference' to her ability to prevent
the insertion of the contraceptive device. Sister's answer – 'Yes, it would'
(118) – underlines the gun's potential in her assumption of agency. But, of
course, the gun can be no innocent symbol of female agency; like the all-
female constitution of the Carhullan army, it serves to remind the reader of
the contingency of gender identities. The gun is a marker of patriarchy and
patrilineage – it is her great-grandfather's rifle – but, crucially, Sister
appropriates it. Similarly, she, Jackie, and the other Carhullan women
appropriate soldier identities to defeat the Authority.

All this, however, should alert the reader to another possibility, that
Sister's agonal moment is really subsumed into Jackie's supremely agonal

invention of herself as leader or, as Debrix and Barder might put it, 'agonal warrior'.[66] Jackie, more than Sister, shows how identity can be formed in the agonal moment and put to use as political agency. After all, Sister and her gun are really Jackie's apparatuses in her reinvention – tellingly, Sister cannot even remember the details of the speech and deed that constituted her entry into public action. The reader is reminded at several points in the novel that Jackie has 'many faces', that she 'passed through arrangements of humour and pragmatism, lightness and invective, as she presented herself, as she covered those matters she wanted to discuss' (86). With each 'rotation of her personality' (157), it is Jackie who shows how identity might be made out of public action and, more strikingly, performance.

The ethical potential for posterity that Jackie's identity offers wavers between what Arendt distinguishes as the opposite poles of power and tyranny. On the one hand, there are hints that the political vision of the Carhullan army encompasses an enlarged view of futurity, specifically, a desire to transmit and transfer its ecological feminist ideas to posterity. Built into the narrative is an insistence that it is something to be passed down. The text's prefatory paraphernalia identify it as Sister's incomplete statement as a prisoner of the Authority, a status that is clarified at the end of the narrative in Jackie's dying instructions to Sister: 'Tell them everything about us, Sister. Make them understand what we did and who we were' (207). The text is Sister's oral testimony to Carhullan's ethos, and thus available to be read metatextually as a record of a political and ethical effort to change the future for ecofeminist ends, a manifesto of Carhullan's utopian action. On the other hand, however, Jackie's ethos is hardly life-affirming in the present, as is demonstrated, for example, by her willingness to kill deserters in order to safeguard the military operation. The novel's conclusion also seems to undermine any sense of future potential – after the army's brave occupation of Rith for fifty-three days, it is defeated and Jackie killed. As Robinson notes: 'The possibility of utopia, or hope, in the brutal near future presented by Hall, gives way to fundamentalism and violence as an ideology, a response to oppression that is ultimately self-defeating'.[67] The agonal opportunity for ethical power becomes, instead, the exercise of what Debrix and Barder call agonal sovereignty; agonal sovereignty as violent tyranny is, as Arendt might argue, ultimately impotent.

This contrast between Jackie's utopian vision as one of power on the one hand and tyranny on the other pivots on whether Sister truly

---

[66] Debrix and Barder, *Beyond Biopolitics?*, p. 41.
[67] Robinson, '"You Just Know When the World is About to Break Apart"', p. 206.

assumes identity and agency. The agonal birth turns, tragically, into the destruction rather than constitution of identity – indeed, it recalls what Arendt famously recognised as the atomisation of individuals and the prevention of coalitional identity that precedes the totalitarian establishment of 'mass society'.[68] One could go so far as to argue that Jackie's ideology, resting on the eradication rather than coalitional creation of identity, comes to resemble not just the violence and force of tyranny, but the evil of what Arendt identified as totalitarianism. For Arendt, totalitarian movements depend on driving 'their members to the point of complete loss of individual claims and ambition . . . and succeed in extinguishing individual identity permanently and not just for the moment of collective heroic action'.[69] Sister's identity, and with it the potential for ethical agency for now and for posterity, flicker briefly as heroic endeavour but are subsumed into the instruments of ideology.

*The Stone Gods* and *The Carhullan Army* reflect on the partial and processual nature of identity as described by Sandilands: Winterson's novel focuses on hybridity and Hall's on – ultimately compromised – agonal processes. Winterson's narrative shows how belief in stable identity is driven by a quest to achieve wholeness and by a corresponding denial of the traumatic ruptures in that wholeness. The acknowledgement of that trauma, specifically, an awareness of the impossibility of achieving such perfect future knowledge, is part of what, following Sandilands, I would term a futural ethics of the Real. Meanwhile, Hall's narrative sheds a harsh spotlight on the ethical risks of identity-making, and is a cautionary tale of futural ethics turned violently ideological. Both novels also undermine the process of readerly identification in order to undermine the reader's investment in identity. In Winterson's *The Stone Gods*, the reader's slippery and ultimately fruitless identification with the three Billies enables the ironic awareness that there is no essential identity that performs the act of identification in which the reader is engaged. In Hall's *Carhullan Army*, in contrast, the reader is brought on a journey of identification with Sister only to be left, like Sister herself, bereft of identity as a result of the agonal contest for it; at the same time, the collapse of identity is also the collapse of utopian power into a tyrannical – even totalitarian – display of violence and force. Winterson's novel shows the possibilities for radical posterity when trauma is acknowledged and the desire for wholeness exposed, while

---

[68] Arendt, *The Origins of Totalitarianism* (first published 1951; New York: Shocken, 2004), p. 422.
[69] Ibid., p. 417.

Hall's novel cautions against the replacement of that desire for wholeness with a totalitarian ideology. As I suggest in the next chapter, possibilities for radical posterity might exist in the development of an ecocentric posterity that reconfigures not so much ideas of identity as notions of eudaemonia.

# CHAPTER 5

# Science, Utopianism, and Ecocentric Posterity: Kim Stanley Robinson's 'Science in the Capital' and Barbara Kingsolver's Flight Behaviour

Science and technology provided the methods, the content and the ideology to make a certain kind of future thinkable. It is a future deeply moulded by the belief in progress.

Helga Nowotny, 'Science and Utopia: On the Social Ordering of the Future'

I have an allegiance to community, which includes both my human community and the biological community that surrounds me in this habitat. And I have an allegiance to the possibility of their collective, maybe even collaborative survival into the future.

Barbara Kingsolver, in Stephen L. Fisher, 'Community and Hope: A Conversation'

Since science provides us with information on the causes, impacts, and extent of climate change, it is tempting to look to science too for information on how to mitigate its effects on, and prevent further damage to, an ecocentric posterity of humans and non-humans alike—to look to science, that is, for tools and concepts with which to create and maintain an ecologically sustainable future. The idea of the future within scientific practice, however, is not a straightforward one: on the one hand, science is a process-oriented—indeed, one could say, future-oriented – activity, inasmuch as it is predicated on advancement and enlightenment; on the other hand, science holds itself aloof from the ethical, psychological, and emotional decisions that inform what that future should look like.

Certainly, a particular construction of the future, or at least the idea of progress, is essential to the project of science. Progress in these terms signals an idealised, intellectual march towards the future – a collaboration of minds, aimed at ever greater knowledge about and discovery of the species, systems, and processes that make up the non-human world that interacts with, exists around, and even occurs within humans. Such progress, however, is essentially an 'objective' endeavour – it is value-free at the level of determining what that endeavour should achieve (though not at the level of whether that endeavour might be immediately harmful to humans and non-humans, as scientific ethics committees around the world would attest). This can be seen in the relationship between scientific progress and economic progress. On the one hand, science would seem to be opposed to the standard economic narrative of progress – ongoing economic growth, technological advancement, industrial expansion, and material comfort for humans. The scientific ideal of enhancing our understanding of the (non-human and human) world seems inimical to the economic story of human exceptionalism and the damage it is capable of inflicting on non-human organisms, systems, and environments, not to mention the harm that rebounds onto humans. On the other hand, scientific progress informs and makes possible the increased technological sophistication that underpins economic progress. Scientific knowledge is politically, morally, and ideologically appropriable, even to anthropocentric social practices and systems that might be egregious to science's objects of study.

In other words, the knowledge needed to meet present obligations to the humans and non-humans of the future is, in large part, granted by science, but for ethical guidance towards an explicitly better future one must look elsewhere. An ethical, hopeful version of scientific endeavour – what I call a utopian vision of science – requires a particular combination of science with values and practices extrinsic to it.

In this chapter, I discuss two climate change narratives with utopian views of science that are enabled by the practice of compassion or care. I begin with Kim Stanley Robinson's 'Science in the Capital' trilogy of *Forty Signs of Rain* (2004), *Fifty Degrees Below* (2005), and *Sixty Days and Counting* (2007).[1] Robinson's narrative combines science with the teachings of Buddhism to create a utopian project to mitigate against and even reverse some of the worst effects of global warming. With his focus on community, whether scientific or religious, Robinson usefully imagines a commitment to posterity outside the bounds of parent–child relations and ethics. Yet the scope of this posterity does not extend far, for it deals with human concerns and human futures. Thus, despite its engagement with science and notions of scientific progress, and, indeed, with Buddhism, the novel's eudaemonistic circle of concern is, broadly speaking, a human one. I then turn to Barbara Kingsolver's *Flight Behaviour*

---

[1] Kim Stanley Robinson, *Forty Signs of Rain* (first published 2004; London: HarperCollins, 2005); *Fifty Degrees Below* (first published 2005; London: HarperCollins, 2006); *Sixty Days and Counting* (London: HarperCollins, 2007). Subsequent page references to these texts are in parentheses.

(2012).[2] Kingsolver's novel, like Robinson's trilogy, attempts to leaven science with an ethical stance; in her case, however, this ethics is explicitly derived from parental care. Indeed, the novel clearly invites a eudaemonistic enactment of empathy and sympathy with the parental actions and disposition of its protagonist, and with the future of the humans and non-humans under her care. On one reading, Kingsolver's narrative, like Robinson's, is stubbornly anthropocentric, engendering a sympathy for the fate of non-human species and ecosystems but subsuming these within a greater sympathy for and interest in the future of the humans of the novel, particularly, the heroine and her family. However, on another reading, one that pays close attention to the novel's tragic conclusion, the novel ends on an insistently ecocentric note. Indeed, it does not simply widen the eudaemonistic circle of care; it shifts it from the human to the non-human. It does this on the basis of what Martha Nussbaum has called non-human 'wonder', a concept productively read in dialogue with Chris Cuomo's ethics of flourishing based on 'dynamic charm'.[3] In what follows, I set out the relationship between science and utopian hope, and show how this is framed by Robinson's novels. I then discuss and clarify the ecocentric possibilities of wonder or dynamic charm, as a prelude to two readings of Kingsolver – the anthropocentric celebration of parenthood and the ecocentric revelation of dynamic charm.

## The Utopianism of Science

Many scientists would agree that the aim of science is to move towards an understanding of the 'truth about physical reality', that is, rational and objective (or testable) truths about the state of the world.[4] Truth is the goal of the scientific method, by which I mean not just the empiricist conventions of observing, experimenting, and collecting data, but the practice of hypothesising – putting forward a hypothesis and then conducting empirical research in order to support or refute, that is, refine, this hypothesis.[5] As Karl Popper insisted, and Peter Medawar would go on to clarify, such 'hypothetico-deductive' refinement depends less on inductive reasoning

---

[2] Barbara Kingsolver, *Flight Behaviour* (London: Faber, 2012). Subsequent page references to this text are in parentheses.

[3] Martha C. Nussbaum, *Upheavals of Thought: The Intelligence of Emotions* (Cambridge University Press, 2001), p. 321; Chris J. Cuomo, *Feminism and Ecological Communities: An Ethics of Flourishing* (London: Routledge, 1998), p. 71.

[4] Hugh G. Gauch, *Scientific Method in Practice* (Cambridge University Press, 2003), p. 409.

[5] Ibid., pp. 406–9, citing G. E. P. Box, W. G. Hunter, and J. S. Hunter, *Statistics for Experimenters: An Introduction to Design, Data Analysis, and Model Building* (New York: John Wiley, 1978), p. 4.

(broadly definable as the drawing of conclusions based on observation) and more on deductive reasoning (the use of observations to refine a previous hypothesis).[6] This reasoning and refinement, moreover, is often imagined as a collective endeavour, as scientists build on the work of other scientists, and expect that at all times results will be disseminated widely. What I describe here is a deliberately forward-looking as well as collaborative activity. It imagines a longitudinal enterprise carried out by dispersed actors over time and space, whose ultimate goal – sought step by step – is truth. For this reason, as science studies pioneer Helga Nowotny reminds us, the refinement of the scientific method in the nineteenth century 'made a certain kind of future thinkable', a future 'deeply moulded by the belief in progress'.[7] In other words, science is driven by a notion that the future holds – indeed, is equivalent to – cumulative knowledge and enlightenment.

Science understood thus could be called a utopian project. Of course, such a claim depends much on how one defines science. I acknowledge that the conceptualisation of science I outline here is a particular view, subscribed to by scientists, but not necessarily born out in practice. One must be careful to distinguish between the ideology that undergirds scientific activities and the discrete activities themselves. For Thomas Kuhn, the everyday work of 'normal science' has little to do with the paradigm shifting of 'revolutionary science': the normal scientist solves relatively local problems within a given paradigm, and only a particularly stubborn problem or set of problems would result in a rethinking of the paradigm itself.[8] At this point, it must be said that the emphasis on revolutionary over normal science differs between scientific disciplines – for example, the biological sciences operate within what is accepted as the relatively durable paradigm of Darwinian theory while the expectation in physics, what with comparatively recent upheavals such as relativity and quantum mechanics, is that there may yet be more major shifts to come. Even so, many scientists across the fields – who can hardly be assumed to be working in ignorance of Popperian and Kuhnian descriptions of their endeavours – tend to see both the 'consensus' research of normal science and the major discoveries of

---

[6] Inductive reasoning might, however, play a part in the formulation of the earlier hypothesis; see Karl Popper, *The Logic of Scientific Discovery* (first published 1959; London: Routledge, 1992), pp. 3–7; Peter Medawar, *Induction and Intuition in Scientific Thought* (London: Methuen, 1969), p. 48.

[7] Helga Nowotny, 'Science and Utopia: On the Social Ordering of the Future', in Everett Mendelsohn and Helga Nowotny (eds.), *Nineteen Eighty-Four: Science between Utopia and Dystopia* (Dordrecht: Reidel, 1984), p. 8.

[8] Thomas S. Kuhn, *The Structure of Scientific Revolutions* (first published 1962; University of Chicago Press, 1996), pp. 52–76.

revolutionary science as differently sized – and sometimes 'tentative' and 'approximate' – steps towards truth.[9]

To describe science as utopian depends, too, on how one defines utopia. The idea of science as perfectibility is not readily compatible with the notion of utopia as perfection; the one suggests progress and the other attainment. Science, in utopian scholar Krishan Kumar's idealist description of it, 'knows no end. It has no point of rest or stability. It constantly undermines existing beliefs and practices'.[10] The utopia, in contrast, suggests just such an end. To be fair, this has led both writers and scholars of utopia to distinguish between the pure utopia and other forms, such as the 'critical utopia', whose narratives, according to Tom Moylan, 'reject utopia as blueprint while preserving it as a dream'.[11] In considering the utopianism of science, then, it pays to distinguish, as Patrick Parrinder does, citing the work of H. G. Wells, between 'the classical utopia of static perfection and the "modern" utopia characterised by a continuous process of political and social improvement'. For Parrinder, the modern utopia is more appropriately described as 'uchronia', so committed is it to a 'kinetic' mode of hopeful, forward movement.[12] Or, following Carl Freedman, one could distinguish between the traditional, topographical utopia inaugurated by Thomas More and the 'hermeneutic' utopia theorised by Ernest Bloch – a psychological and philosophical stance, rather than a place, 'to be found in the Not Yet, or the Not-Yet-Being, or the In-Front-of-Us'.[13] In referring to the utopianism of science, then, I am invoking not just the conventional conceptualisation of science as an aggregation towards truth, but also Wellsian and Blochian understandings of modern utopia as mobile. These are all relevant to the idea that underpins the scientific method – that science is a collaborative and gradual advancement of human knowledge.

For all this, however, science is not *overtly* utopian; that is, it is wary of advertising its efforts towards truth. As I have already suggested,

---

[9] Gauch, *Scientific Method in Practice*, p. 99, quoting from American Association for the Advancement of Science, *The Liberal Art of Science: Agenda for Action* (Washington, DC: American Association for the Advancement of Science, 1990), p. 20.

[10] Krishan Kumar, *Utopianism* (Milton Keynes: Open University Press, 1990), p. 59.

[11] Tom Moylan, *Demand the Impossible: Science Fiction and the Utopian Imagination* (New York: Methuen, 1986), p. 10.

[12] Patrick Parrinder, *Utopian Literature and Science: From the Scientific Revolution to Brave New World and Beyond* (Basingstoke: Palgrave-Macmillan, 2015), p. 4.

[13] Carl Freedman, 'Science Fiction and Utopia: A Historico-Philosophical Overview', in Patrick Parrinder (ed.), *Learning from Other Worlds: Estrangement, Cognition, and the Politics of Science Fiction and Utopia* (Liverpool University Press, 2000), p. 74.

objectivity, that mainstay of the Popperian scientific method, precludes the expression of wishfulness and the normative push towards what is ethically 'right' that some might associate with utopian thinking. For Popper, following Immanuel Kant, 'scientific knowledge should be *justifiable*, independently of anybody's whim: a justification is "objective" if in principle it can be tested and understood by anybody'.[14] One could say that the practitioners – and, with it, the practice – of the scientific method are to some degree informed by a utopian ideology, even if they do not explicitly espouse it. Ethical duty is, apparently, for others to impute to science, and not for science to ascribe to itself.

Such a task has often fallen to those who would communicate or popularise science, including the authors who employ scientific understandings in climate change novels. The utopian potential of science has been a theme in science fiction since the advent of modern science in the nineteenth century: novels such as Edward Bellamy's *Looking Backward* (1888) and Wells's *A Modern Utopia* (1905) have shaped their utopian worlds out of scientific and techno-logical advances.[15] This is not to suggest that there has been universal utopianism in science fiction: many twentieth-century dystopian fic-tions have associated scientific progress with psychological and cul-tural alienation, from Aldous Huxley's *Brave New World* (1932) to Margaret Atwood's *The Handmaid's Tale* (1985). Even in green uto-pian science fiction narratives, such as Ursula K. LeGuin's *The Dispossessed* (1974) and Ernest Callenbach's *Ecotopia* (1975), the potential gulf between naïve technological determinism and a just utopian society has continued to be a topic of concern and scrutiny. Nonetheless, this possibility of science as itself compromised has led to a distinctive recent brand of scientific utopianism, centred on the figure of the scientist as a lone heroic voice, a trend that Roslynn Haynes analyses as part of a late-twentieth-century stereotype of 'scientist as idealist'.[16] Haynes astutely ascribes the rise of the idealist scientist in literature towards the end of the century to a growing environmental awareness among authors and readers. Indeed, the type of the utopianist scientific hero becomes pertinent in a time of global ecological concerns.

---

[14] Popper, *The Logic of Scientific Discovery*, p. 22.
[15] Darko Suvin, *Metamorphoses of Science Fiction: On the Poetics and History of a Literary Genre* (New Haven, CT: Yale University Press, 1979), p. 4.
[16] Roslynn D. Haynes, *From Faust to Strangelove: Representations of the Scientist in Western Literature* (Baltimore, MD: Johns Hopkins University Press, 1994), pp. 311–12.

## 'Science in the Capital'

Perhaps the most rigorous literary defender of scientific utopianism in recent times is Robinson. A major science fiction writer, with both the Hugo and Nebula awards to his name, Robinson displays in his work a profound interest in science and politics. Many of his novels are explicitly utopian scenarios for environmental and social justice that successfully combine scientific technology and progressive politics. His first novels – the 'Three Californias' trilogy of *The Wild Shore* (1984), *The Gold Coast* (1988) and *Pacific Edge* (1990) – are experiments in narrating disaster, dystopia, and utopia respectively, ultimately imagining the successful green reconstruction of a devastated California. More sustained in its utopianism is Robinson's great critical and popular success, the Mars trilogy of *Red Mars* (1992), *Green Mars* (1993), and *Blue Mars* (1999), an elaborate narrative in which human colonisers on Mars successfully terraform the planet – that is, transform its biosphere into a version of Earth's – by living a kind of scientifically informed, ethically minded, green socialism called 'eco-economics'.[17] The utopian terraforming of Mars thus provides a space in which the physical alteration of the planet coincides with the political conversion of its new inhabitants, that is, 'humans are areoformed – shaped by Mars – even as Mars is terraformed'.[18] The 'Science in the Capital' trilogy might represent a rare foray for Robinson into near contemporary realism and away from the futuristic science fiction of much of his work, but it constitutes a high point in Robinson's environmental fiction inasmuch as it spells out, in a narrative space free of otherworldly distraction, his ideas for scientific utopianism in the service of environmentalism.[19]

Robinson explicitly identifies himself as a utopian science fiction writer, and, in doing so, demonstrates a scholarly awareness of its generic history. Speaking of the Mars trilogy, Robinson has employed a definition that echoes Parrinder's formulation of it as kinetic. He rejects static descriptions of 'Utopia as "pie-in-the-sky", impractical and totalitarian', and instead

---

[17] The idea of 'terraforming' was invented by science fiction writer Jack Williamson in 1942; see Brian Stableford, 'Science Fiction and Ecology', in David Seed (ed.), *A Companion to Science Fiction* (Malden, MA: Blackwell, 2005), p. 134, and Robinson, *Imagining Abrupt Climate Change: Terraforming Earth* (Seattle: Amazon Shorts, 2005), p. 1. For a description of 'eco-economics', see Robinson, *Red Mars* (New York: Bantam, 1993), p. 298.

[18] Frederick Buell, *From Apocalypse to Way of Life: Environmental Crisis in the American Century* (New York: Routledge, 2003), p. 279.

[19] Adam Trexler, focusing on the novels' politics, labels this a 'technocratic, even bureaucratic, utopianism', *Anthropocene Fictions: The Novel in a Time of Climate Change* (Charlottesville: University of Virginia Press, 2015), p. 155.

insists, 'Utopia has to be rescued as a word, to mean "working towards a more egalitarian society, a global society".'[20] Fredric Jameson writes of the Mars trilogy that, even in its conclusion, the reader is aware that the 'achievement' of utopia on Mars 'must constantly be renewed', so much so that 'utopia as a form is not the representation of radical alternatives; it is rather simply the imperative to imagine them'.[21] Robinson retains such an emphasis with the 'Science in the Capital' trilogy, remarking:

> I think of myself as a utopian novelist . . . Utopia is a name for one course of history, a progressive course in which things become more just and sustainable over the generations. We're not there now, but depending on what we do, and what our descendants do, we could still be said to be living in a utopian history, as being on the path. I prefer to work as if that were the case. And it seems to me the great work continues.[22]

Thus, for Robinson, goodness exists not as panoply, in a simple utopian sense, nor even as possibility, in Moylan's critical utopian sense, but as perfectibility, with that perfectibility premised on a mapping of scientific practice onto scientific ideals.

*Forty Signs of Rain* (2004), *Fifty Degrees Below* (2005) and *Sixty Days and Counting* (2007) acquired the informal label of the 'Science in the Capital' trilogy from the author's working title for the first novel in the sequence.[23] As with the 'Mars' trilogy, the three novels are ideally discussed together, as they resemble not just a trilogy but a single text in the style of a Victorian triple-decker, as Robinson has himself indicated.[24] Indeed, they have more recently been abridged and re-issued as a single novel, *Green Earth* (2015).[25] The scenario depicted in the novels is one of 'abrupt climate change', a term and concept Robinson borrowed from a 2002 report to the National Research Council that reconceptualised climate change as possible within three to five years.[26] The trilogy narrates global climate catastrophe from

[20] Bud Foote, 'A Conversation with Kim Stanley Robinson', *Science Fiction Studies* 21.1 (1994), 56.

[21] Fredric Jameson, '"If I Can Find One Good City, I Will Spare the Man": Realism and Utopia in the Mars Trilogy', in Patrick Parrinder (ed.), *Learning from Other Worlds: Estrangement, Cognition and the Politics of Science Fiction and Utopia* (Liverpool University Press, 2000), p. 231.

[22] Imre Szeman and Maria Whiteman, 'Future Politics: An Interview with Kim Stanley Robinson', *Science Fiction Studies* 31.2 (2004), 185.

[23] Robinson changed the names of his second and third novels, 'The Capital in Science' and 'Global Cooling', when his publisher insisted on more 'novelistic' titles; Moira Gunn, interview with Kim Stanley Robinson, *Tech Nation: IT Conversations*, 4 April 2007, http://itc.conversationsnetwork.org /shows/detail1773.html.

[24] Robinson, *Imagining Abrupt Climate Change*, p. 16; David Seed, 'The Mars Trilogy: An Interview', *Foundation* 68 (1996), 76.

[25] Robinson, *Green Earth* (New York: Del Rey, 2015).

[26] Robinson, *Imagining Abrupt Climate Change*, p. 6.

the perspective of a group of scientists and policy wonks in Washington, DC: biologist Frank Vanderwahl; Diane Chang, the director of the National Science Foundation, or NSF; fellow NSF scientist Anna Quibler; and Anna's husband, Charlie, environmental advisor to the ecologically committed Senator Phil Chase. Also depicted are the Quiblers' young children, Nick and Joe. In the course of events, Washington, DC, experiences extreme floods and record-breaking winters, with this microcosm dramatically emblematic of global chaos, climatic and otherwise: 'they were entangled in a moment of history when climate change, the destruction of the natural world, and widespread human misery were combining in a toxic and combustible mix' (*Fifty*, 4). Yet, the narrative's tone and dénouement are hopeful and happy: the scientists' lives acquire a spiritual depth thanks to their friendship with a group of political exiles from the fictional Buddhist island nation of Khembalung; lonely misfit Frank finds true – if unlikely – love with a government intelligence agent enmeshed in rogue secret service operations; and romance blossoms between Phil Chase and Diane Chang, who end the narrative as, respectively, President and Presidential Science Advisor. Diane and Phil's wedding is the comic happy ending of the trilogy, just as Anna and Charlie's marriage provides its ballast.

The trilogy's moral, then, is that science and politics in concord will save the day – such concord enables the narrative's large-scale scientific interventions, which ultimately mitigate and stabilise the many climate change disasters. But Robinson's scientists must learn not only to engage with policy but to refine and acknowledge their scientific aspirations, ensuring that 'normal science' is leavened with a compassionate outlook. This much is put into train when the Khembalis, whose home is affected by rising sea levels, establish an embassy in an office in the NSF building. When they are invited by Anna to give an NSF seminar on Buddhist ideas of knowledge and progress, they propose a marriage of scientific with Buddhist enlightenment, that is, the introduction of compassion to scientific ratiocination. As the Khembali spiritual leader Rudra Cakrin explains, compassion is definable as 'Right action. Helping others. . . . Reduce suffering' (*Forty*, 236). The knowledge gained by science and the compassionate wisdom of Buddhism make them 'parallel studies', according to Rudra Cakrin, in which science has 'specialized, through mathematics and technology, on natural observations, finding out what is, and making new tools', while 'Buddhism has specialized in human observations, to find out – how to become. Behave. What to do. How to go forward' (*Forty*, 236). That is, the two are complementary.

What is more, the novel frames the interweaving of Buddhism with science not as a simple ideological choice but as a biological imperative. Rudra Cakrin aligns the Buddhist concept of 'compassion' with scientific understandings of 'altruism' as the 'best adaptive strategy' (*Forty*, 238); that is, fellow feeling has been identified by behavioural ecologists as one way for species to ensure their survival: 'in Buddhism we have always said, if you want to help others, practice compassion; if you want to help yourself, practice compassion. Now science adds, if you want to help your species, practice compassion' (*Forty*, 238). This echoes Frank's conclusions in his ongoing sociobiological observations and analyses of fellow human beings. Earlier in the novel, when stuck in a queue of cars on the Beltway in Washington, DC, Frank reflects on how the merging of two lanes of traffic replicates the prisoner's dilemma – the game theory scenario in which, as discussed in chapter 1, two prisoners are kept separate and each is asked to inform against the other in order to gain his release. Assuming that the game is only played once, the best strategy is the selfish one of informing; if the game is played many times with the same opponent, the best strategy – and arguably the one that is eventually learned – is for both prisoners to cooperate and remain silent. Translated into the experience of driving in merging traffic on the Beltway, this predicts that if drivers base their decisions on individual good (with each vehicle cutting off merging traffic and trying to get ahead), delays result, but, if drivers act towards the common good (by taking turns), traffic flows more easily. Frank muses, 'In traffic, at work, in relationships of every kind – social life was nothing but a series of prisoner's dilemmas. Compete or cooperate? Be selfish or generous? It would be best if you could always trust other players to cooperate, and safely practise always generous' (*Forty*, 112). When translated into optimal behaviour in the Anthropocene, humans must learn the answer to the prisoner's dilemma. Frank realises, as he listens to Rudra Cakrin's lecture, that 'it is an invocation for all to make the "always generous" move, for maximum group return, indeed maximum individual return' (*Forty*, 238). As Timothy Morton notes, 'hyperobjects' have brought future humans 'into the adjoining prison cell'.[27] Climate change, according to Frank, the Khembalis, and indeed the trilogy, is the prisoner's dilemma writ large, while the union of politics and science – when science is a compassionate version of itself – is the intergenerational solution that humans have evolved to make.

[27] Timothy Morton, *Hyperobjects: Philosophy and Ecology after the End of the World* (Minneapolis: University of Minnesota Press, 2013), p. 123.

Following Frank's lead, the NSF enters a renewed phase of compassionate science, achieved through the cooperation of Diane, Frank, and Anna; here, Robinson's preference for detailed plot interactions and character ensembles plays out in terms of form the idea of collaboration that is at the heart of the novel in terms of theme. Through their actions, large-scale, international, geoengineering projects are enacted, including the salinisation of the Atlantic to reactivate the Gulf Stream and the use of genetically modified species of lichen to encourage tree growth in a massive carbon sequestration farm in Russia. And, when Phil Chase is elected president, his left-leaning, socially minded, long-termist policies provide the ideal context for a Buddhist-inflected scientific enlightenment to be translated into action. He negotiates, among other things, a deal with an environmentally devastated China in which the United States sends technological and financial aid to help build a greener Chinese economy in return for China's agreement to a carbon cap.

One might think that Robinson's foreshortened version of evolution, in which compassion emerges as an adaptive strategy, would place an emphasis on present obligations to future generations and specifically on parental care as a way of achieving this relatively short-term adaptation. Certainly, Robinson's public statements on climate change have focused on the importance of recognising our intergenerational legacy and invoked parenting as an analogy: climate change represents the utilitarian exploitation of future humans – 'the victims in this competition are the future generations to come' – and behavioural change as an adaptive strategy is akin to 'a mother–daughter chain, of generations holding hands'.[28] In Robinson's novels, however, posterity, as a joint concern of politics, science, and the spiritual expression of compassion, is a social and collaborative concern, rather than a familial one. That cooperation based not on 'kinship' but on 'empathy' might be beneficial to evolution is precisely what Frank reads in the science journal *Nature*, his conclusion being that this is 'group selection' but only if individuals realised that 'other groups' constituted a larger group: 'the story of human history so far [was] successive enlargement of the group' (*Fifty*, 282). Frank's sociobiological analysis of 'altruism-as-adaptation' (*Fifty*, 281) is increasingly refined, then, to encourage collaboration with, or being 'always generous' to, all humans. It would seem, then, that parent–child relationships are hardly the place to look in the novel for expressions of passing on environmental legacy; indeed, children are cared

[28] Robinson, 'Climate Change and the Pursuit of Happiness', lecture at Sustainable Actions for a Sustainable Future Conference, Missouri State University, 22 April 2009.

for and cared about outside domestic, secure spaces, as well as within them. Thus, when the Quiblers' young son, Joe, is suspected by the Khembalis to be an incarnation of Rudra Cakrin upon his death, Joe is closely watched, cared for, and, indeed, loved by that community; meanwhile, his brother, Nick, is mentored by Frank and encouraged in his scientific interests.

Moreover, parenting emerges, for the parental characters themselves, as one of many manifestations of the self. Near the end of the final novel, for example, Anna and Charlie take delivery of photovoltaic panels for their home; this is not framed as a domestic issue but, rather, occurs alongside the information they exchange and political actions that they make as a scientist and a policy advisor. Even Charlie's decision to give up working full time for Phil Chase is about assuming a range of roles and identities rather than defining himself as any one of these: his departure from Phil's staff is neither permanent nor total, as he promises it will be for a 'couple of years' (*Sixty*, 457) and he commits to daily phone conversations with the White House staff. After all, as Frank discovers in the second novel when he becomes homeless and divides his time between a neo-palaeolithic existence in Rock Creek Park and his work at the NSF, life is 'parcellated': 'No one saw enough to witness your life and put it all together' (*Fifty*, 74). Such a parcellated life is divided up among multiple and shifting identities.

Accordingly, the reader is not called on to identify with any one character, either for very long or in any strictly focalised way. Although it is possible to identify Frank as the central character, it is significant that his experiences do not come to the fore until the second novel; the first novel opens with Anna and expends narrative energy on the Quiblers, energy which is then diffused in subsequent instalments in the trilogy. Another, perhaps more obvious candidate for the role of hero is "*Unconventional, unpredictable, devil-may-care*" (*Sixty*, 49; original emphasis) Phil; yet, even this mercurial character enjoys only a brief moment of focalisation when he takes office at the start of the third novel. Finally, one might, as Adam Trexler does, focus on Diane as the initiator of the scientific and political collaborations and renegotiations – or 'boundary work' – that so dramatically resolve the novel's climate change crises, and identify her as the true 'embodiment of the NSF's power, will, and effectiveness'.[29] Even so, Diane is only one of many important actors in the drive to the plot's resolution (and her identity is, one might add, formed – in the Arendtian mode discussed in the previous chapter – in coalition and dialogue). It would

---

[29] Trexler, *Anthropocene Fictions*, p. 160.

seem, then, that the nature of Robinson's collaborative and coalitional utopian vision does not require exclusive reader identification.

That is, Robinson's trilogy eschews the usual patterns of identificatory plot and character development, and, along with this, subsumes parental care, attachment, activities, and identity within characters' public and communal roles, all under the rubric of a larger compassion and empathy. Intergenerational care is not only reassigned away from the private and domestic and towards the scientific and political, it is also concerned with non-human animals. It is not just that Frank's Palaeolithic experiment makes him aware of his status as a human animal – as 'Primate in forest' (*Fifty*, 40) – but it is also that the novel depicts the effects of the many extreme weather events on zoo animals, showing how many die or escape, as Frank comes to be involved with these animals as a volunteer tracker.

Yet, the trilogy's admirable version of posterity is not as radical as it could be, even as it gestures to the inclusion of the non-human, the need to redefine notions of compassion and care, and the instability of identity. In the final analysis, these are relayed as descriptions of the actions of a small group of people in a plot that, for all its mentions of nations and groups from elsewhere in the world, represents a heteronormative and mostly white version of American life and is focused on a narrowly American and anthropocentric solution – specifically, geoengineering projects initiated by top-down federal government – to a crisis of unprecedented spatial and temporal scale and complexity. Ursula Heise notes that the trilogy 'remains for the most part stuck in Washington and American government perspectives . . . and the omniscient narrator never relinquishes his grip of this local scene to let other perspectives and discourses percolate', a point echoed by Trexler.[30] Timothy Clark, citing 'the way Washington politics is simplified' and the presence of 'so US-centric a focus on a global issue' in the novels, concludes that 'even Robinson's ambitious project is a form of intellectual miniaturization'.[31] Moreover, Jeanne Hamming reads Robinson's attempt at rewriting the gender and racial norms that inform environmental attitudes as ultimately collapsing into a preoccupation with white, American masculinity: 'any attempt to articulate a post-national, post-global-warming subjectivity can only reproduce . . . the very power structures that continue to drive American identity and environmental

---

[30] Ursula K. Heise, *Sense of Place and Sense of Planet: The Environmental Imagination of the Global* (New York: Oxford University Press, 2008), p. 207; Trexler, *Anthropocene Fictions*, p. 166.

[31] Timothy Clark, *Ecocriticism on the Edge: The Anthropocene as a Threshold Concept* (London: Bloomsbury, 2015), p. 79.

politics'.[32] Similarly, the extent of the effect of biospheric devastation on ecosystems and species is reduced to particular types of charismatic animal experiences, a disregard for ecological complexity that is not helped by the novel's optimistic reading of evolutionary process.

## Radical Ecocentric Posterity

What possibilities might there be for a radical ethical concern for the future that includes non-human organisms, communities, and processes within the compass of moral considerability, not simply for their ability to increase humans' flourishing, but for their own and other non-human flourishing? Put another way, what might an ecocentric scientific utopianism look like? As I suggested in chapter 1, there is a useful distinction to be made between the two types of human ethical responses to the non-human put forward by Nussbaum. The first is a eudaemonistic account, which, in Nussbaum's terms, is a sympathetic response to a non-human animal in which its distress, suffering, or other non-flourishing suggests a 'common vulnerability' with the human witnessing that distress; it requires, therefore, a recognition of shared grounds of suffering between the human and non-human, such as pain and hunger.[33] The second is one of wonder at the marvellous complexity of the non-human animal.[34] For Nussbaum, the two are usually linked in some way (with wonder as a support and motivation for sympathy); crucially, however, Nussbaum speculates that they are separate emotions.[35] More importantly for my purposes here, Nussbaum clarifies elsewhere that wonder as the basis for an ethical attitude to non-human animals is not about the relevance of the non-human to human flourishing. She extends the capabilities approach of Amartya Sen (extrapolating from the concept of eudaemonia to argue that the capability, or freedom, to achieve eudaemonia is a fundamental freedom) to include human as well as non-human animals, and bases this measure of capability on the wonder of non-human animals: 'if we feel wonder looking at a complex organism, that wonder at least suggests the idea that it is good for that being to flourish as the kind of thing it is'.[36] This element of wonder asks for an understanding of non-human suffering as

---

[32] Jeanne Hamming, 'Nationalism, Masculinity, and the Politics of Climate Change in the Novels of Kim Stanley Robinson and Michael Crichton', *Extrapolation* 54.1 (2013), 42.

[33] Nussbaum, *Upheavals of Thought*, p. 319.    [34] Ibid., p. 321.    [35] Ibid., p. 322.

[36] Nussbaum, 'Beyond "Compassion and Humanity": Justice for Nonhuman Animals', in Cass R. Sunstein and Martha C. Nussbaum (eds.), *Animal Rights: Current Debates and New Directions* (Oxford University Press, 2004), p. 306.

appropriate to that organism and the system in which it exists, as far as possible: 'It wants to see each thing flourish as the sort of thing it is.'[37]

Nonetheless, Nussbaum's use of wonder in this way is limited by a need to draw the line of moral considerability somewhere: that is, not every organism is capable of invoking wonder. Building on Peter Singer's animal-rights utilitarianism, which proposes a calculus of moral inclusion for humans and non-humans based on sentience (the more sentient a being, the greater its rights and its importance in calculations of utility), Nussbaum adds, citing James Rachels, the criterion of complexity.[38] Both the ability to feel pain and the vulnerability to it, thanks to the diversity of harms that might occur in the life of a complex being, are thresholds to membership of this moral community of human and non-human beings: 'More complex forms of life have more and more capabilities to be blighted, so they can suffer more and different types of harm.'[39] Nussbaum's position, focused on individuals, precludes a consideration of the ecological interactions played by all organisms, missing, for example, the significant potential for harm to beings on the wrong side of the sentientist line to bring harm to those on the right side of it. Moreover, the judgement of moral considerability based on sentience and complexity is predicated on a very human understanding of pain and distress; certainly, to some extent, an ethical response to the non-human will always demand a human perception and calibration, but Nussbaum's account of the limits of wonder reproduces the limitations of eudaemonistic responses to non-human suffering: it is suffering when the human can imagine that it is.

Where, then, might a third response, more than either eudaemonism or wonder, come from? The ethical model put forward by Cuomo offers a promising set of proposals. Cuomo's work on environmental ethics stems from an ecofeminist concern, like that of Catriona Sandilands, with the risks of applying an identitarian and essentialist logic to terms such as 'women' and 'nature'.[40] Cuomo particularly cautions against 'representing humans, women or nature in ways that are static and bounded'.[41] At the

---

[37] Ibid., p. 306.

[38] Ibid., p. 308; Peter Singer, 'Animals and the Value of Life', in Tom Regan (ed.), *Matters of Life and Death: New Introductory Essays on Moral Philosophy*, 3rd edn. (New York: McGraw-Hill, 1993), pp. 280–321; James Rachels, *Created from Animals: The Moral Implications of Darwinism* (Oxford University Press, 1990).

[39] Nussbaum, 'Beyond "Compassion and Humanity"', p. 309.

[40] Catriona Sandilands, *The Good-Natured Feminist: Ecofeminism and the Quest for Democracy* (Minneapolis: University of Minnesota Press, 1999).

[41] Cuomo, *Feminism and Ecological Communities*, p. 34.

same time, Cuomo is mindful of the need to account for humans' ethical position vis-à-vis the non-human; as she reminds us: 'Although nature and human nature cannot provide universal, static norms, it is still meaningful to characterize the social/natural world as comprised of ethical agents and objects with interests and levels of well-being.'[42] Like Nussbaum, what Cuomo proposes is an ethics of flourishing, inspired in part by Aristotle's terms of *eudaimonia;* she contends that the value of the flourishing of non-human beings lies in their constitutive value to other beings, including – but not restricted to – humans. In a suggestive combination of Aristotelian and Leopoldian sensibilities, she states:

> The basic claim [of Aristotle's] is that we are political as surely as we are human, and so our social units ought to promote our flourishing as social selves, which in turn creates a stronger *polis.* What would follow from the observation that we are *ecological* beings – 'mere citizens of the biotic community', in Aldo Leopold's words – as surely as we are human? Perhaps social units ought to promote our flourishing as ecological selves, and therefore some degree of flourishing of nonhuman life, in order to create a stronger ecological community.[43]

In an argument that resembles Sandilands's Arendtian account of human agency as coalitional (discussed in the previous chapter), Cuomo develops such agency further as ecological.[44]

Importantly, Cuomo's model of flourishing finds moral positions for human and non-human organisms in a way that avoids assigning value to the non-human from a human perspective (while, importantly, not eroding human accountability to the non-human). Key to this is not just her analysis of flourishing as a criterion for moral considerability, but her location of the capacity for flourishing in an organism's 'dynamic charm'.[45] Writes Cuomo, 'it is an entity's *dynamic charm* – its diffuse, "internal" ability to adapt to or resist change, and its unique causal and motivational patterns and character – that renders it morally considerable, and that serves as a primary site for determining what is good for that being or thing'.[46] Dynamic charm describes a process both unique and intrinsic to an organism, and hence situates its moral value within it rather than in the (human) other. It references not just complexity but the

---

[42] Ibid., p. 34.

[43] Ibid., p. 69; original emphasis. See also Aldo Leopold, *A Sand County Almanac: With Essays on Conservation*, illustrated edn. (first published 1949; Oxford University Press, 2001) p. 171.

[44] Sandilands, *Good-Natured Feminist*, pp. 155–62.

[45] Cuomo, *Feminism and Ecological Communities*, p. 70.   [46] Ibid., p. 71; original emphasis.

unpredictability and mutability of all living entities in themselves and in interaction with the communities to which they belong.

Thus, Cuomo's conceptualisation of dynamic charm as the basis of moral considerability encompasses both the biocentric and ecocentric (where, as Robin Attfield explains, the ecocentric affords moral considerability to ecosystems or even the biosphere while the biocentric is concerned with individual organisms).[47] It avoids the holism of a Leopoldian 'land ethic', yet it captures a moral attitude to ecosystems.[48] Moreover, it is distinct from Nussbaum's extreme biocentric and individualist emphasis on an organism's complexity and sentience. Drawing in part on the work of Jon Moline, Cuomo explains that the idea of dynamic charm:

> gives us reason to 'count' some individuals in the moral universe, without committing ethics to promoting the individual interests of protozoa or plants, while still appreciating the value of plants and other members of biotic communities: individual members of 'higher' (sentient, conscious) species are capable of response in ways not exhibited by individual plants, for example, so some sentient animals might be morally valuable as individuals, while plants are only valuable as members of species, populations, or communities.[49]

Aside from the questionability of some of Cuomo's plant/animal boundaries in the light of some startling recent findings in botany (investigations into plant intelligence, for example), her consideration of biotic membership as well as individual sentience allows the moral inclusion of all organisms, without necessarily emphasising non-complex beings as individuals.[50]

Cuomo's ethical framework has two important corollaries for scientific utopianism. First, her invocation of charm is no unquestioning or unscientific account of the mystery of nature, for it acknowledges that a degree of comprehension is crucial to achieving an ethical attitude: 'science and other empirical inquiries can, in theory, give us the kind of information we need to proceed with as much respect as possible with regard to living systems'.[51] After all, scientific comprehension of ecological processes would

---

[47]  Robin Attfield, *Environmental Ethics: An Overview for the Twenty-First Century*, 2nd edn. (London: Polity, 2014), p. 39.

[48]  Leopold, *Sand County Almanac*, p. 171.

[49]  Cuomo, *Feminism and Ecological Communities*, p. 71; see Jon N. Moline, 'Aldo Leopold and the Moral Community', *Environmental Ethics* 8.3 (1986), 99–120.

[50]  See, for example, Stefano Mancuso and Alessandra Viola, *Brilliant Green: The Surprising History and Science of Plant Intelligence* (Washington, DC: Island Press, 2015), and Anil Ananthaswamy, 'Roots of Consciousness', *New Scientist* 224 (6 December 2014), 34–7.

[51]  Cuomo, *Feminism and Ecological Communities*, p. 71.

shed light on the workings and extents of dynamic charm. In this under-standing of the relationship of science to wonder, Cuomo productively foreshadows Lisa Sideris's recent defence of the place of wonder (defined differently from Nussbaum's concept of wonder) in scientific investiga-tion; wonder, suggests Sideris, is often accompanied by 'modest habits of mind' – as opposed to celebratory and even hubristic proclamations of science's achievements – and can thus 'encourage deeper reflection on which paths we ought and ought not to pursue'.[52] 'Genuine wonder', Sideris proposes, 'is the grounding for intellectual virtues and habits of mind'.[53]

Second, the idea of dynamic charm suggests not only that some organ-isms have moral worth in and of themselves, but that, for all organisms, moral worth emerges as part of a larger whole; importantly, this whole includes the human and non-human. By its logic, 'nature' is constituted by non-human and human beings, each possessed of an internal dynamic charm but all linked by a mutually constitutive flourishing – or, in the case of humans, by the ethical imperative to participate in such a flourishing. An ecocentric scientific utopianism, one that lends a moral purpose to science, would complement the scientific understanding of the workings of dynamic charm and the ways of flourishing with the impetus to maintain that flourishing.

## Flight Behaviour

Kingsolver's treatment of climate change sees a fuller exploration of the need for science to develop a more hopeful and compassionate sense of its responsibility to the future. It effects this through identification with a central character, who bridges two communities – a scientific research group and a rural township – and their two perspectives. This bridging enables the incorporation of science with an ethics of parental care, even as it introduces ecological insights to protagonist and reader. Yet, the human exceptionalism of care threatens to turn this novel into a deeply anthro-pocentric exercise, in which non-human organisms and their ecological habitats are placed at the eudaemonistic service of humans. Still, the novel, I argue, makes possible an alternative and radically ecocentric reading, in which the flourishing of the non-human is of ultimate significance.

---

[52] Lisa H. Sideris, *Consecrating Science: Wonder, Knowledge, and the Natural World* (Oakland, CA: University of California Press, 2017), p. 26.
[53] Ibid., p. 27.

Novelist and essayist Kingsolver has enjoyed popular and critical acclaim as a writer of contemporary American life, as well as a reputation as a proponent of a strongly ecological worldview; all her novels – from *The Bean Trees* (1988) onwards – demonstrate the interconnectedness of human and non-human communities. Over the course of her career, she has become ever more committed, as she puts it, to the 'collaborative survival' of both human and non-human species; that is, she imagines a future not merely constituted of – but achieved through – ecological cooperation.[54] Many of her novels are concerned with the struggle of rural families and communities (often with women at their centre), and with the way in which such dramas play out against wider issues of environment-alism. Often setting her narratives in the southern United States (though the African context of her best-known work, *The Poisonwood Bible* of 1998, is a marked departure from this), Kingsolver has increasingly become identified with the Appalachian region.[55]

Her seventh novel, *Flight Behaviour*, brings together all these themes in its story of Dellarobia Turnbow, a young woman living in the deprived agricultural belt of east Tennessee, who unwittingly finds herself at the centre of climate change crisis when its ecological effects unfold in her backyard. Intelligent but undereducated, mother-of-two Dellarobia is trapped in a loveless marriage to the well-meaning but unambitious Cub. The couple live in financial dependence on Cub's overbearing parents, sheep farmers who are themselves struggling with debt as a result of a precarious side-venture. As the novel opens, Dellarobia is on the verge of throwing away this unfulfilling life for a tryst with a handsome tele-phone repairman. But, on her way to a rendezvous in a hunting hide on the Turnbow property, she encounters the impressive sight of millions of monarch butterflies in diapause, or hibernation: in this ecologically plau-sible (though so far, fortunately, unrealised) scenario, the butterflies have been thrown off their migratory path by the increasingly wild weather events wrought by climate change and forced to overwinter in Appalachia rather than their customary destination of the Michoacán highlands in Mexico. The sight of the roosting monarchs not only inspires Dellarobia to return to her family, it is hailed as a miracle by her God-fearing Southern Baptist community and divides the Turnbow family, who had planned to sell their land to loggers in an attempt to evade bankruptcy. It also attracts

[54] Stephen L. Fisher, 'Community and Hope: A Conversation', *Iron Mountain Review* 28 (Spring 2012), 32.
[55] Robert H. Brinkmeyer, *Remapping Southern Literature: Contemporary Southern Writers and the West* (Athens: University of Georgia Press, 2000), pp. 98–9.

the notice of a scientific team led by an eminent entomologist named Ovid Byron, whose investigations reveal that not only deforestation but the onset of winter could wipe out the entire species, as the planet's unsettled weather patterns have effectively reduced the monarchs to this one eastern migrating population.

The novel's setting is a notoriously conservative and economically disadvantaged region of the United States; its context is the encounter between climate change denialism and the hard evidence of climate change's ecological impact. As Kingsolver has put it, her novel tackles the 'culture war' of climate change where the stakes are highest: 'I live in southern Appalachia … the people most affected by climate change already are people among whom I live: rural conservative farmers. And it strikes me that these are the same people who are least prepared to understand and believe in climate change and its causes.'[56] In the novel, the ideological gulf between the scientists and the locals is focalised through Dellarobia: her assessment is expressed in pithy descriptions of the two sides. In conversation with her sceptical husband, Dellarobia realises: 'Teams had been chosen, and the scientists were not *us*, they were *them*' (231; original emphasis). As she explains it to Ovid, the 'environment got assigned to the other team. Worries like that are not for people like us. So says my husband' (445). The 'teams' that Dellarobia identifies are defined by whether they treat the world as an opportunity for investigation and deductive reasoning or approach it as a matter of faith. The scientific method, captured in Ovid's simple explanation to Dellarobia's son, means that 'a scientist doesn't just make a wild guess. … He measures things. He does experiments'; in order to 'discover the truth', scientists 'ask' (164). The townspeople of Feathertown, in contrast, take 'the Word on faith' (83) and are passive consumers of mass media; Cub maintains that 'Weather is the Lord's business' (361). Dellarobia's analysis, as paraphrased by Ovid's folklorist wife, is of a 'territorial divide' (543) that only deepens as markers of difference reflexively shape identity.

Dellarobia is able to evaluate this divide, for both herself and her reader, because she is able to cross it. Born and raised in Feathertown, she is also possessed of a scientific mind, what Ovid calls 'a talent for this endeavour' (392). It is Dellarobia, who, for example, finds that she alone of the Turnbow family is capable of understanding the behaviour of sheep by dint of attentive observation, that is, by her commitment to the deductive reasoning that defines the scientific method. Set apart from her community

---

[56] Bryan Walsh, 'Barbara Kingsolver on *Flight Behavior*', *Time* (8 November 2012).

by her inherent inquisitiveness – she recalls being kicked out of Bible class for 'her many questions' (83) – Dellarobia feels inexplicably at ease with the scientists when she starts helping them. She thus not only straddles the two communities; she facilitates the reader's sympathy with both sides, as she expresses this sympathy herself. Indeed, as Axel Goodbody points out, Kingsolver depicts conservative denialism 'with sympathy and understanding'.[57] Dellarobia realises that Cub's annoying habit of channel surfing, which she derides as 'ADHD TV' (154), echoes a wider community strategy of ignoring bad news: 'If people played their channels right, they could be spared from disagreement for the length of their natural lives' (357). This is an understandable response, Goodbody reminds us, from a marginalised and underprivileged people who inhabit 'a world over which they have little control' and who therefore seek to 'avoid confrontation with inconvenient truths'.[58] At the same time, as the scientists interact with Dellarobia, they command sympathy too: 'We are scientists. Our job here is only to describe what exists', Ovid explains, 'But we are also human. We like these butterflies, you know?' (204). Moreover, his deep grief at their impending extinction – expressed in Dellarobia's realisation that 'the one thing most beloved to him was dying' (315) – reveals that, for all their earnestly spouted dispassion, the research team, particularly Ovid, are motivated by something like love for the butterflies.

While Dellarobia fulfils an important intermediary function for the reader (not to mention for other characters in the novel), she also, importantly, transforms into an apprentice ecologist over the course of the narrative. The novel is, as commentators have noted, her *Bildungsroman*.[59] Dellarobia becomes Ovid's research assistant, and eventually separates from Cub and enrols on a college degree with the intention of becoming 'Some kind of scientist' (587); that her scientific awakening constitutes a kind of rebirth is even implied by the internet meme brought

---

[57] Axel Goodbody, 'Risk, Denial and Narrative Form in Climate Change Fiction: Barbara Kingsolver's *Flight Behavior* and Ilija Trojanow's *Melting Ice*', in Sylvia Mayer and Alexa Weik von Mossner (eds.), *The Anticipation of Catastrophe: Environmental Risk in North American Literature and Culture* (Heidelberg: Universitätsverlag Winter, 2014), p. 50.

[58] Ibid., pp. 50–1.

[59] Sylvia Mayer, 'Explorations of the Controversially Real: Risk, the Climate Change Novel, and the Narrative of Anticipation', in Mayer and Alexa Weik von Mossner (eds.), *The Anticipation of Catastrophe: Environmental Risk in North American Literature and Culture* (Heidelberg: Universitätsverlag Winter, 2014), p. 30. However, Linda Wagner-Martin's analysis of the novel as *Bildungsroman* concludes – not entirely convincingly – that Dellarobia does not develop and that even 'her personal thirst for knowledge' is 'given to her' by Ovid; Wagner-Martin, *Barbara Kingsolver's World: Nature, Art, and the Twenty-First Century* (New York: Bloomsbury, 2014), pp. 196–7.

about by the brief media interest in her story – Photoshopped onto Botticelli's famous painting, Dellarobia becomes 'the Butterfly Venus' (294). Dellarobia's entry into the scientific community has several ramifications. First, it enables the relaying of scientific information from Ovid to Dellarobia and sometimes her son, and from Dellarobia to friends and family, not to mention to the reader; these ecological findings reveal both the dynamic charm of the monarch butterflies and the damage being done to their ability to flourish. As Ovid explains, the monarchs perform several long migrations over the course of a year: hatched in Canada, they winter in Mexico because of their vulnerability to the cold; they then fly north to Texas for the milkweed plants that are their larval food; the hatched caterpillars journey further north, repeating the process, till three spring generations have fed and migrated northwards; then, after this, the third generation flies to Mexico to winter and repeat the process. The butterflies possess a complexity that gives them dynamic charm. And, not only are the distance and pattern of migration impressive, but the question of how successive generations are able to return to the very same trees as previous ones, never having been there, is a mystery or, to invoke Nussbaum, an object of wonder. It is not, however, any individual butterfly but the butterflies as a 'complicated system' (200) that warrants such wonder. What Dellarobia also learns, however, is that the wonder of their migration has been disrupted by human destruction of the environment, a disruption that could spell the death of this particular population and the near extinction of the species.

Furthermore, Dellarobia's initiation into science is not just a journey of discovery for her; it allows her to bring something of her own to the scientific endeavour. This something is the exercise of parental care. Dellarobia's experience of parenting is depicted as consumed by anxiety about her children's limited future: living a subsistence existence, she finds herself refraining from 'counting on things being fine. Meaning her now-living children and their future, those things' (320). Ovid's concerns for the future of the butterflies are focalised through Dellarobia as a luxury in contrast with the 'real' fears of a parent whose children's future seems hopeless: 'If Ovid Byron was torn up over butterflies, he should see how it felt to look past a child's baby teeth into this future world he claimed was falling apart' (320). Eventually, however, her concerns become a heightened version of Ovid's, a fear for the loss of the future for the sake of her son: 'Dellarobia felt an entirely new form of panic as she watched her son love nature so expectantly, wondering if he might be racing toward a future like some complicated sand castle that was

crumbling under the tide' (341). That is, Dellarobia combines her experience of poverty-stricken parenthood with her new ecological understanding of the threatened global environment into a very particular view of
posterity.

Dellarobia – and the reader with her – develops an enhanced understanding of the future predicated on parental care. More than that,
Dellarobia specifically employs this to redress what she comes to see as
the shortcoming of science: its objectivity. In a pivotal conversation
between Ovid and Dellarobia, the 'febrile biosphere' is brought into the
same frame as a sick child. Ovid compares the warming planet to
a child developing a fever: a small change of two degrees creates 'a low-
grade fever' that makes Dellarobia think of her 'children's cheeks hot to
the touch, their racked sobs that wrenched her will for living' (386);
with a further rise of two and a half degrees, Dellarobia would 'head for
the emergency room' (386). As Ovid reveals, these are the same tem-
perature rises that create the grim scenario of the latest report from the
Intergovernmental Panel for Climate Change; thus 'we are headed for
the ER' (386). Moreover, Ovid compares the seemingly invisible phenomenon of climate change to the growth of a child: '"A trend is
intangible, but real," he said calmly, "A photo cannot prove a child is
growing, but several of them show change over time. Align them, and
you can reliably predict what is coming … "' (387). Thus, imagining
the climate-changed future should be no less difficult than imagining
'Your children's adulthood' (389). It would seem that what is being
asked for is the response of a caring parent. Importantly, Dellarobia
takes this further, and translates parental care into an ethical stance
based primarily on hope. She concludes to Ovid, 'I'm not saying I *don't*
believe you, I'm saying I *can't*' (392; original emphasis).
Misunderstanding this as a statement of intellectual rather than ethical
or psychological inability, Ovid praises her talent for science but warns,
'For scientists, reality is not optional' (392). Yet, Dellarobia continues
to express 'hope': 'Are we at least allowed to hope that the butterflies
will make it through this winter?' (392). Later, she objects to his
pessimism, 'Don't say that, "too late." I hate that. I've got my kids to
think about' (443). Where Robinson presents a utopian view of
a science of compassionate Buddhist enlightenment, Kingsolver's
novel, through Dellarobia, seems to suggest that science should be
imbued with parental hope and care: as Goodbody puts it, Dellarobia
comes to possess a 'blend of cognitive knowledge, ethical commitment

to future generations, and faith in the ability of people to change things'.[60]

At this point, the novel's scientific utopianism is capable of offering either an anthropocentric or ecocentric account of posterity. That is, on the one hand, it is concerned with the biosphere and the butterflies that represent it synecdochically for the sake of human well-being, and, in comparing responsibility to the biosphere to parental obligations to children, it implies that this is where the ethical response lies; on the other hand, however, the butterflies exhibit a dynamic charm in and of themselves. Much, then, depends on the narrative's treatment of the butterflies and, particularly, of their future relative to human futures.

On one reading, the butterflies act as pointers to Dellarobia's identity, particularly, her maternal identity. She is aligned with the bright orange monarchs not just by her 'flame-coloured hair' (1), but by her recurring need for a 'flight path' out of her narrow life.[61] The colour of the butterflies also brings to mind Dellarobia's first child, stillborn with a 'fine hair all over its body that was red like hers' (14), who is further united with the butterflies as something to be mourned 'while most people paid no attention' (316). Dellarobia explicitly connects this baby with the butterflies, thanks to the poignant Mexican belief that the monarchs are the souls of dead children; she tells Preston that 'one of those [butterflies] is ours' (583). This belief links Dellarobia's first child with the unfortunate Michoacán children who have been killed in mudslides caused by excessive rainfall and deforestation. It thus identifies the butterflies with all children, including Dellarobia's surviving children, and potentially, with children of the future. Whether this aligns the monarchs with future children in an expression of hope (since Dellarobia herself, identifiable with the butterflies, has a hopeful future ahead of her) or as potential victims of climate change and other anthropogenic environmental crises is a moot point. What is clear, on this reading, is that the monarchs are enablers of a human story of loss, determination, and hope.

At the same time, the butterflies, in the novel's ecological explanations, are shown to possess a charm and complexity unknown to and seemingly aloof from humans; indeed, they represent an ability to flourish that is oddly superior to that of humans'. The 'complicated system' (200) of monarchs elucidated by Ovid is, after all, a compressed statement of intergenerational dynamics; because it lives only six weeks, no single

---

[60] Goodbody, 'Risk, Denial and Narrative Form', p. 48.

[61] Wagner-Martin, *Barbara Kingsolver's World*, p. 4.

monarch makes the annual migration from Mexico to Canada and back, which must thus occur in several generational stages. What the monarch provides in the novel, then, is an ironic comment on humanity: the monarch trajectory, one species' elegant exercise in intergenerational coop-eration, stands in stark contrast to humans' failure to maintain such cooperation themselves. That the monarch is also in danger of being extinguished by humans' failure has the potential to render that contrast tragic.

The narrative's conclusion holds the novel's two possibilities – the anthropocentric and the ecocentric – in delicate balance. Dellarobia sepa-rates from her well-meaning but ineffectual husband, enrols into college, and encourages her son to follow in her footsteps, all of which promises to end the novel on a deeply anthropocentric note of scientific utopianism. Such a dénouement would turn the fate of the monarchs into a metaphor for a happy ending of human triumph. Yet, something very different – and potentially profoundly ecocentric – happens instead. The freakishly wet and snowy weather that has dominated the narrative from the outset results in unprecedented flooding across the county, as wild weather events occur throughout the world. As the waters rise around her home, Dellarobia is alone: her children are at school or with her in-laws. Thus, she takes in the enormity of the situation alone and with a sense of fascinated calm: 'She comprehended the terms of what she saw, but couldn't turn away from it' (594). She witnesses the butterflies emerge from their hibernation, for the monarchs, it seems, have survived in sufficient numbers to recommence their migration for now. Yet, the reader is ignorant of whether or not Dellarobia, on the brink of embarking on her own journey, will also manage to take flight, and, indeed, it seems likely that the novel ends with her impending death or, at the very least, the devastation of both the life that she has and the new one she anticipates. It seems, then, that she is witness to the environmental disaster that will lead to her destruction, on the one hand, and the awakening of the butterflies in a miraculous survival for this remnant of the species, on the other.

The novel's ending has puzzled commentators. According to Sylvia Mayer, it 'can be ambiguously read: either as a sign of destruction, or as a sign of cleansing and renewal'.[62] That depends, indeed, on whether one's empathy and sympathy stay with Dellarobia or shift entirely to the butter-flies (when, up till now, attention had been directed at the butterflies through sympathy with Dellarobia). Curiously, readers on both sides

---

[62] Mayer, 'Explorations of the Controversially Real', p. 31.

have mistaken this, for different reasons, as a tragic ending. In Linda Wagner-Martin's anthropocentric reading, the monarchs and Dellarobia are all doomed, so that this 'last irretrievable chapter' shows that 'Dellarobia, like the butterflies, has no more choices'.[63] Meanwhile, Clark seeks, but does not find, an ecocentric reading; elsewhere so keen to examine Anthropocene novels for the possibility of a scalar shift away from the human, he interprets this novel's conclusion as one in which Dellarobia survives, and in which the butterflies 'have come almost entirely to symbolize a positive turning point in one character's life', a symptom of the novel's tendency to engage the reader in an 'individualizing way'.[64] He particularly opines that 'a pointed *disjunction* between the individual character's story and the fate of the insects would have made the text more provocative as a climate change novel . . . the survival of the butter-flies could have been juxtaposed with some personal defeat or resignation'.[65] And yet, such a disjunction is precisely what has happened, for there occurs a significant 'defeat' of some kind for Dellarobia; thus, the novel does indeed end with a provocative version of the future in ecocentric terms. The fate of the monarchs, that is, takes precedence over any eudaemonistic investment in or by Dellarobia.

Such misapprehension on Clark's part, however, is telling, for it has to do with the novel's destabilisation of identification and empathy at this point, specifically, the abruptness of the turn away from Dellarobia as the facilitator of an overwhelmingly conservative and conventional set of readerly sympathies and parental ethics, towards a distinctly unconventional and radical kind of posterity. The novel shocks the reader out of an emotional connection with Dellarobia. So much is this so that it ends on a note of emotionlessness. Dellarobia's response to her impending death involves neither alarm and therefore disaster and tragedy, nor sadness and with it melancholy and lament. This is not the tragic spectatorship demanded by a eudaemonistic reading; it is, rather, a critically reflective spectatorship in appreciation of the monarchs' flourishing.

Kingsolver's novel facilitates what Robinson's scientific utopianism fails to achieve: the ultimate reversal of what Nussbaum, after Frans de Waal, calls 'anthropodenial', that is, the wilful denial of our animality and the arrogant claim to human transcendence.[66] With the monarchs' survival, it is less that we progress towards a tragic sympathetic understanding of our

---

[63] Wagner-Martin, *Barbara Kingsolver's World*, p. 197.        [64] Clark, *Ecocriticism on the Edge*, p. 177.
[65] Ibid., p. 178; original emphasis.
[66] Nussbaum, *Political Emotions: Why Love Matters for Justice* (Cambridge, MA: Belknap Press, 2013), p. 184.

embeddedness in the biosphere and more that we are dropped abruptly into the revelation of the insignificance of our place within it. The reader is effectively displaced from the insects' ecosystem, but, at the same time, called on to inhabit the same moral universe, thanks to their inherent dynamic charm.

# *The Sense of No Ending*

The method of analysis employed in this book has focused on readers' journeys of identification, sympathy, and empathy, in order to show how some of those journeys might be derailed, destabilised, or otherwise disrupted, and expectations, norms, and ethics built on identity, emotion, and knowability might be held up to scrutiny. In the age we now call the Anthropocene, such ontological certainties should not be taken for granted. What this has meant, among other things, is a critical awareness of endings, for even *critical* readerly journeys must end: they may not always be resolved, but they necessarily reach the final page.

The authoritative – perhaps, one should say, the last – word on literary endings has long been identified as belonging to Frank Kermode, who mused, in *The Sense of an Ending* (1967), on the reasons we expect narratives to end the way they tend to do, with finality, resolution, and a sense of a higher meaning. According to Kermode, we render human existence and time significant by suggesting to ourselves that it is how everything ends (everything being existence, time, and so on) that gives it meaning. Specifically, Kermode distinguishes between two attitudes to time – *chronos* and *kairos*, where '*chronos* is "passing time" or "waiting time"' and '*kairos* is the season, a point in time filled with significance, charged with a meaning derived from its relation to the end'.[1] We prefer, says Kermode, kairotic preoccupations with meaning over the merely chronological experience of life – indeed, such kairotic concerns make the mundanity of the chronological bearable. It is this preference that drives the production, communication, and reception of narrative. The process of narrative, in Kermode's formulation, is simply the chronological space between beginning and end; as he puts it somewhat aphoristically, though we know that 'tick' must be followed by 'tock', the gap

---

[1] Frank Kermode, *The Sense of an Ending: Studies in the Theory of Fiction* (first published 1967; Oxford University Press, 2000), p. 47.

between them must be filled, even as the importance of that gap is determined solely by tick's leading to tock. But it is how the narrative ends that gives all its events a kairotic dimension. Indeed, says Kermode, it is the need for kairotic meaning-making that drives Judaeo-Christian myths of apocalypse, for this most important and enormous of endings gives sense and significance to the everyday of life. Kermode's analysis highlights the psychological impulse that fuels the reader's desire for the end and its meaning. The result is an important recognition, which Peter Brooks would go on to develop in his psychoanalytical studies of the 'masterplot', that the desire for deferral, with its prolongation of enjoyment, is nothing without the desire for dénouement, with its satisfaction and its rendering of meaning.[2]

Yet, many of the novels discussed in this book interrogate, scrutinise, and even resist 'happy' endings, that is, endings that are definitive, satisfying, or kairotic. For example, the last paragraph of *The Road* ends the novel with a pastoral vision in the present tense, so that destruction is replaced with a disjunction that the reader might interpret as memory, eulogy, or even simply hallucination. The dénouement of *The Carhullan Army* takes place offstage, as it were, so that what is highlighted instead is the novel's metatextual status as unfinished testimony and manifesto. Similarly, *Flight Behaviour* ends ambiguously, shifting focus away from the human protagonist and refusing to confirm her fate. Meanwhile, *The Stone Gods* loops back to its start, and insists on beginnings rather than endings; indeed, it rejects the return to the known for the embrace of the unknown, brought on by love as an intervention. Why, in the Anthropocene, when humans are threatened by a physical but not cosmological end times, is narrative dominated not by the sense of an ending but by the wish for no ending? This is, I argue, no simple denial or avoidance of anxiety. This is an active critique of the kairotic wish for endings as ultimately unproductive, a critique emboldened by the concerns of the Anthropocene.

This is because *kairos* in Kermode's terms describes not simply the wish for endings but the need for meaning; specifically, it references, paradoxically, the desire for continuity. Simon Scheffler has described the extent to which philosophical well-being in the present depends on the guarantee of a continued human existence into the future; this girds, says Scheffler, our very purpose and will – the longevity of the human species is part of the value we place on the smallest and most prosaic daily activities.[3] And, as Lee

---

[2] Peter Brooks, *Reading for the Plot: Design and Intention in Narrative* (Oxford: Clarendon Press, 1994).
[3] Samuel Scheffler, *Death and the Afterlife* (Oxford University Press, 2013).

Edelman suggests, the child is a convenient mascot for these existentialist longings for continuity.[4] To read Edelman and Scheffler in Kermodian terms is to recognise that the happy ending is also the promise of posterity: it is not the 'after' in 'happily ever after' that matters so much as it is 'ever' (and, certainly, 'happily' helps). Edelman, after all, aligns readerly and romantic impulses to show that the desire for endings – what in Kermode's terms is our kairotic desire for narrative 'concordance' – is part of a heteronormative sexual desire for dynastic stability and continuity; he goes as far as to castigate happy endings not as moments of closure per se but as fulfilments of nuclear family fantasies. In other words, Edelman's analysis suggests that what we ask of our stories and of our lives are endings (for which, read *versions of the future*) that look like us.

In the Anthropocene, that wish for a recognisable and knowable future looks futile, its ethics appear suspect, and its fears – that the end of human procreation is the end of the world – are rendered absurd. The radical endings of many of the climate change novels discussed in this book, in contrast, offer up possibilities for different kinds of posterity. That is, these novels end with the awareness that endings do not bring neatly resolved meanings, that the future need not resemble us, and that it is, indeed, unknowable. Some invite us to consider not just the contingency and radical unknowability of our own identities, but, as in *The Stone Gods*, to consider the trauma that makes us seek stability and knowability, including our desire to render the future knowable. Some express, too, the unknowability of (non-human) others, though they invite no less a sense of wonder at their flourishing. It is towards such radical versions of posterity that the deceptively conventional form of the climate change novel beckons. And it is such a critical awareness of our empathetic and emotional impulses, and their role in an ethics of an unknowable future, that this book has attempted to foster.

---

[4] Lee Edelman, *No Future: Queer Theory and the Death Drive* (Durham, NC: Duke University Press, 2004).

# Works Cited

Alaimo, Stacy. *Bodily Natures: Science, Environment and the Embodied Self.* Bloomington: Indiana University Press, 2010.

Alaimo, Stacy, and Susan Hekman. 'Introduction: Emerging Models of Materiality in Feminist Theory'. In Stacy Alaimo and Susan Hekman (eds.), *Material Feminisms*. Bloomington: Indiana University Press, 2008, 1–19.

Ananthaswamy, Anil. 'Roots of Consciousness'. *New Scientist* 224 (6 December 2014), 34–37.

Andermahr, Sonya. *Jeanette Winterson.* Basingstoke: Palgrave–Macmillan, 2009.

Andre, Claire, and Manuel Velasquez. 'Justice and Fairness'. *Issues in Ethics* 3.2 (1990). https://legacy.scu.edu/ethics/publications/iie/v3n2

Arendt, Hannah. *Between Past and Future: Eight Exercises in Political Thought.* First published 1954; Harmondsworth: Penguin, 1977.

*The Human Condition*, 2nd edn. First published 1958; Chicago University Press, 1998.

*The Origins of Totalitarianism.* First published 1951; New York: Shocken, 2004.

Ariès, Philippe. *Centuries of Childhood: A Social History of Family Life.* Trans. Robert Baldick. New York: Vintage, 1962.

Aristotle. *The Nicomachean Ethics.* Trans. David Ross and rev. J. L. Ackrill and J. O. Urmson. Oxford University Press, 1980.

Armstrong, Nancy. *Desire and Domestic Fiction: A Political History of the Novel.* New York: Oxford University Press, 1987.

Asher, Kenneth. *Literature, Ethics, and the Emotions.* Cambridge University Press, 2017.

Attfield, Robin. *Environmental Ethics: An Overview for the Twenty-First Century*, 2nd edn. London: Polity, 2014.

'Non-Reciprocal Responsibilities and the Banquet of the Kingdom'. *Journal of Global Ethics* 5.1 (2009), 33–42.

Atwood, Margaret. *MaddAddam.* New York: Nan A. Talese–Doubleday, 2013.

*Oryx and Crake.* First published 2003; London: Virago, 2004.

*The Year of the Flood.* First published 2009; London: Virago, 2010.

Barad, Karen. *Meeting the Universe Halfway: Quantum Physics and the Entanglement of Matter and Meaning.* Durham, NC: Duke University Press, 2007.

'Posthumanist Performativity: Toward an Understanding of How Matter Comes to Matter'. *Signs* 28.2 (2003), 801–31.

Barnes, Brookes. 'Winner in the Amazon War'. *New York Times* (3 July 2014).

Barnes, Elizabeth. *States of Sympathy: Seduction and Democracy in the American Novel.* New York: Columbia University Press, 1997.

Barry, Brian. 'Humanity and Justice in Global Perspective'. In J. Roland Pennock and John W. Chapman (eds.), *Ethics, Economics, and the Law.* New York University Press, 1982, 219–52.

Benhabib, Seyla. 'Models of Public Space: Hannah Arendt, the Liberal Tradition and Jürgen Habermas'. In Craig Calhoun (ed.), *Habermas and the Public Sphere.* Cambridge, MA: MIT Press, 1992, 73–98.

Berry, Wendell E. 'The One-Inch Journey'. *Audubon* (May 1971): 4–11.

*The Unforeseen Wilderness: An Essay on Kentucky's Red River Gorge.* Lexington: University of Kentucky Press, 1971.

Blackmore, Tim. 'Life of War, Death of the Rest: The Shining Path of Cormac McCarthy's Thermonuclear America'. *Bulletin of Science, Technology and Society* 29 (2009), 18–36.

Booth, Wayne. *The Company We Keep: An Ethics of Fiction.* Berkeley: University of California Press, 1988.

Boxall, Peter. *The Value of the Novel.* Cambridge University Press, 2015.

Bracke, Astrid. *Climate Crisis and the Twenty-First-Century British Novel.* London: Bloomsbury, 2018.

Brassier, Ray. *Nihil Unbound: Enlightenment and Extinction.* Basingstoke: Palgrave–Macmillan, 2007.

Brinkmeyer, Robert H. *Remapping Southern Literature: Contemporary Southern Writers and the West.* Athens: University of Georgia Press, 2000.

Brooks, Peter. *Reading for the Plot: Design and Intention in Narrative.* Oxford: Clarendon Press, 1994.

Brown, Gillian. *Domestic Individualism: Imagining Self in Nineteenth-Century America.* Berkeley: University of California Press, 1990.

Buell, Frederick. *From Apocalypse to Way of Life: Environmental Crisis in the American Century.* New York: Routledge, 2003.

Carson, Rachel. *Silent Spring.* First published 1962; London: Penguin, 2000.

Chabon, Michael. 'Dark Adventure: On Cormac McCarthy's *The Road*'. *Maps and Legends: Reading and Writing along the Borderlands.* San Francisco: McSweeney's, 2008, 107–20.

Clark, Timothy. *Ecocriticism on the Edge: The Anthropocene as a Threshold Concept.* London: Bloomsbury, 2015.

Clarke, Jim. 'Reading Climate Change in J. G. Ballard'. *Critical Survey* 25 (2013), 7–21.

Cohen, Tom, ed. *Telemorphosis: Essays in Critical Climate Change.* Ann Arbor, MI: Open Humanities Press, 2012.

Cohen, Tom, Claire Colebrook, and J. Hillis Miller. *Theory and the Disappearing Future: On De Man, on Benjamin.* New York: Routledge, 2012.

Colebrook, Claire. *Death of the Posthuman: Essays in Extinction*. Ann Arbor, MI: Open Humanities Press, 2014.

Collado-Rodríguez, Francisco. 'Trauma and Storytelling in Cormac McCarthy's *No Country for Old Men* and *The Road*'. *Papers on Language and Literature* 48 (2012), 45–69.

Collard, Andrée, with Joyce Contrucci. *Rape of the Wild: Man's Violence against Animals and the Earth*. London: Women's Press, 1988.

Coole, Diana. 'Too Many Bodies? The Return and Disavowal of the Population Question'. *Environmental Politics* 22.2 (2013), 195–215.

Cooper, Lydia. 'Cormac McCarthy's *The Road* as Apocalyptic Grail Narrative'. *Studies in the Novel* 43 (2011), 218–36.

Cuomo, Chris J. *Feminism and Ecological Communities: An Ethics of Flourishing*. London: Routledge, 1998.

Daly, Mary. *Gyn/Ecology: The Metaethics of Radical Feminism*. London: Women's Press, 1978.

Dawkins, Richard. *The Selfish Gene*. First published 1976; Oxford University Press, 1989.

Debrix, François, and Alexander D. Barder. *Beyond Biopolitics? Theory, Violence, and Horror in World Politics*. London: Routledge, 2012.

De Bruyn, Ben. 'Borrowed Time, Borrowed World and Borrowed Eyes: Care, Ruin and Vision in McCarthy's *The Road* and Harrison's *Ecocriticism*'. *English Studies* 91 (2010), 776–89.

De-Shalit, Avner. *Why Posterity Matters: Environmental Policies and Future Generations*. London: Routledge, 1995.

Dillon, Sarah. 'Imagining Apocalypse: Maggie Gee's *The Flood*'. *Contemporary Literature* 48 (2007), 374–97.

'Literary Equivocation: Reproductive Futurism and *The Ice People*'. In Sarah Dillon and Caroline Edwards (eds.), *Maggie Gee: Critical Essays*. Canterbury: Gylphi, 2015, 101–32.

Eaubonne, Françoise d'. *Féminisme ou la Mort*. Paris: Femme et Mouvement, 1974.

Edelman, Lee. *No Future: Queer Theory and the Death Drive*. Durham, NC: Duke University Press, 2004.

Edwards, Tim. 'The End of the Road: Pastoralism and the Post-Apocalyptic Waste Land of Cormac McCarthy's *The Road*'. *Cormac McCarthy Journal* 6 (2008), 55–61.

Ehrlich, Paul R. *The Population Bomb*. 1968; London: Pan, 1971.

Ehrlich, Paul, and Anne Ehrlich. 'The Politics of Extinction'. *Bulletin of the Atomic Scientists* 37.5 (1981), 26.

Ellam, Julie. *Love in Jeanette Winterson's Novels*. Amsterdam: Rodopi, 2010.

Estes, Andrew Keller. *Cormac McCarthy and the Writing of American Spaces*. Amsterdam: Rodopi, 2013.

Estrin, Barbara L. 'Mutating Literary Form and Literalizing Scientific Theory in Liz Jensen's *Ark Baby*'. *Critique* 47 (2005), 41–56.

Fisher, Stephen L. 'Community and Hope: A Conversation'. *Iron Mountain Review* 28 (Spring 2012), 26–32.

'Floods in Carlisle – January 2005'. Met Office. 29 October 2012. www.metoffice.gov.uk/climate/uk/interesting/jan2005floods

Foote, Bud. 'A Conversation with Kim Stanley Robinson'. *Science Fiction Studies* 21.1 (1994), 51–60.

Freedman, Carl. 'Science Fiction and Utopia: A Historico-Philosophical Overview'. In Patrick Parrinder (ed.), *Learning from Other Worlds: Estrangement, Cognition, and the Politics of Science Fiction and Utopia.* Liverpool University Press, 2000, 72–97.

Ganteau, Jean-Michel. '"Rise from the Ground like Feathered Mercury": Baroque Citations in the Fiction of Peter Ackroyd and Jeanette Winterson'. *Symbolism: An International Journal of Critical Aesthetics* 5 (2005), 193–211.

Gardiner, Stephen. *The Perfect Moral Storm: The Ethical Tragedy of Climate Change.* Oxford University Press, 2011.

Gates, Barbara T. 'A Root of Ecofeminism: *Ecoféminisme*'. In Greta Gaard and Patrick D. Murphy (eds.), *Ecofeminist Literary Criticism: Theory, Interpretation, Pedagogy.* Urbana: University of Illinois Press, 1998, 15–22.

Gauch, Hugh G. *Scientific Method in Practice.* Cambridge University Press, 2003.

Gee, Maggie. *The Ice People.* First published 1998; London: Telegram, 2008.

Ghosh, Amitav. *The Great Derangement: Climate Change and the Unthinkable.* University of Chicago Press, 2016.

Gilligan, Carol. *In a Different Voice: Psychological Theory and Women's Development.* Cambridge, MA: Harvard University Press, 1982.

Godfrey, Laura Gruber. '"The World He'd Lost": Geography and "Green" Memory in Cormac McCarthy's *The Road*'. *Critique* 52 (2011), 163–75.

Goodbody, Axel. 'Risk, Denial and Narrative Form in Climate Change Fiction: Barbara Kingsolver's *Flight Behavior* and Ilija Trojanow's *Melting Ice*'. In Sylvia Mayer and Alexa Weik von Mossner (eds.), *The Anticipation of Catastrophe: Environmental Risk in North American Literature and Culture.* Heidelberg: Universitätsverlag Winter, 2014, 39–58.

Goodpaster, Kenneth E. 'On Being Morally Considerable'. *Journal of Philosophy* 75 (1978), 308–25.

Gosseries, Axel. 'The Egalitarian Case against Brundtland's Sustainability'. *GAIA* 14.1 (2005), 40–6.

Graulund, Rune. 'Fulcrums and Borderlands: A Desert Reading of Cormac McCarthy's *The Road*'. *Orbis Litterarum* 65 (2010), 57–78.

Griffin, Susan. *Woman and Nature: The Roaring inside Her.* New York: Harper and Row, 1979.

Grindley, Carl. 'The Setting of McCarthy's *The Road*'. *The Explicator* 67 (2008), 11–13.

Griswold, Robert L. *Fatherhood in America: A History.* New York: Basic Books, 1993.

Groves, Christopher. *Care, Uncertainty, and Intergenerational Ethics.* Basingstoke: Palgrave–Macmillan, 2014.

Gunn, Moira. Interview with Kim Stanley Robinson. *Tech Nation: IT Conversations*. 4 April 2007. http://itc.conversationsnetwork.org/shows/detail1773.html

Gwinner, Donovan. '"Everything Uncoupled from Its Shoring": Quandaries of Epistemology and Ethics in *The Road*'. In Sara L. Spurgeon (ed.), *Cormac McCarthy: All the Pretty Horses, No Country for Old Men, The Road*. New York: Continuum, 2011, 137–56.

Haldane, J. B. S. *The Causes of Evolution*. London: Longmans, Green and Co., 1932.

Hall, Dennis. 'The Land Is Borrowed from Our Children'. *Michigan Natural Resources* 44.4 (1975), 2–3.

Hall, Sarah. *The Carhullan Army*. London: Faber, 2007.

Hamming, Jeanne. 'Nationalism, Masculinity, and the Politics of Climate Change in the Novels of Kim Stanley Robinson and Michael Crichton'. *Extrapolation* 54.1 (2013), 21–45.

Hansen, James. *Storms of My Grandchildren: The Truth about the Coming Climate Catastrophe and Our Last Chance to Save Humanity*. London: Bloomsbury, 2009.

Haraway, Donna J. 'A Cyborg Manifesto: Science, Technology, and Socialist-Feminism in the Late Twentieth Century'. *Simians, Cyborgs and Women: The Reinvention of Nature*. London: Free Association Books, 1991, 149–81.

Hardin, Garrett. 'The Tragedy of the Commons'. *Science* 162 (13 December 1968), 1243–8.

Haynes, Roslynn D. *From Faust to Strangelove: Representations of the Scientist in Western Literature*. Baltimore, MD: Johns Hopkins University Press, 1994.

Heise, Ursula K. *Sense of Place and Sense of Planet: The Environmental Imagination of the Global*. New York: Oxford University Press, 2008.

Held, Virginia. *The Ethics of Care: Personal, Political, and Global*. Oxford University Press, 2005.

Hendrixson, Anne, and Erica Gies. 'If You Care about Climate Change, Should You Have Children?' *New Internationalist* 480 (March 2015). http://newint .org/sections/argument/2015/03/01/climate-change-children

Heyd, David. 'A Value or an Obligation? Rawls on Justice to Future Generations'. In Axel Gosseries and Lukas H. Meyer (eds.), *Intergenerational Justice*. Oxford University Press, 2012, 168–89.

Hollinger, Veronica. '"Something like a Fiction": Speculative Intersections of Sexuality and Technology'. In Wendy Gay Pearson, Veronica Hollinger, and Joan Gordon (eds.), *Queer Universes: Sexualities in Science Fiction*. Liverpool University Press, 2008, 140–60.

Honeyman, Susan. *Elusive Childhood: Impossible Representations of Childhood in Modern Fiction*. Columbus: Ohio University Press, 2006.

Hume, David. *An Enquiry Concerning Human Understanding*. Ed. Stephen Buckle. First published 1748; Cambridge University Press, 2007.

*An Inconvenient Truth*. Dir. David Guggenheim, perf. Al Gore. Lawrence Bender Productions, 2006.

James, Erin. *The Storyworld Accord: Econarratology and Postcolonial Narratives.* Lincoln: University of Nebraska Press, 2015.

Jameson, Fredric. "'If I Can Find One Good City, I Will Spare the Man'": Realism and Utopia in the Mars Trilogy'. In Patrick Parrinder (ed.), *Learning from Other Worlds: Estrangement, Cognition and the Politics of Science Fiction and Utopia.* Liverpool University Press, 2000, 208–33.

Jeffries, Stuart. 'Jeanette Winterson: I Thought of Suicide'. *The Guardian* (22 February 2010).

Jensen, Liz. *The Rapture.* London: Bloomsbury, 2009.

Johns-Putra, Adeline. 'Climate Change in Literature and Literary Studies: From Cli-Fi, Climate Change Theater and Ecopoetry to Ecocriticism and Climate Change Criticism'. *WIREs Climate Change* 7 (2016), 266–82.

'Environmental Care Ethics: Notes toward a New Materialist Critique'. *symplokē* 21.1–2 (2013), 125–35.

'A New Critical Climate'. *symplokē* 21.1–2 (2013), 9–12.

Jones, ed. 'Saving the Soil – by Private Initiative'. *Christian Science Monitor* (5 January 1983), 23.

Josephs, Allen. 'What's at the End of *The Road?*', *South Atlantic Review* 74 (2009), 20–30.

Kaufman, Gayle. 'The Portrayal of Men's Family Roles in Television Commercials'. *Sex Roles* 41 (1999), 439–58.

Keen, Suzanne. *Empathy and the Novel.* Oxford University Press, 2007.

Kellogg, Carolyn. 'Edan Lepucki Thanks Colbert Nation for Making *California* a Hit'. *Los Angeles Times* (22 July 2014).

Kelly, Janice, and Laura Tropp. 'Introduction: Changing Conceptions of the Good Dad in Popular Culture'. In Laura Tropp and Janice Kelly (eds.), *Deconstructing Dads: Changing Images of Fathers in Popular Culture.* Lanham, MD: Lexington, 2016, xi–xx.

Kermode, Frank. *The Sense of an Ending: Studies in the Theory of Fiction.* First published 1967; Oxford University Press, 2000.

Keyes, Ralph. 'Some of Our Favorite Quotations Never Quite Went that Way: Did They REALLY Say It?' *Washington Post* (16 May 1993), L10.

Kılıç, Mine Özyurt. *Maggie Gee: Writing the Condition-of-England Novel.* London: Bloomsbury, 2013.

Kingsolver, Barbara. *Flight Behaviour.* London: Faber, 2012.

Kollin, Susan. '"Barren, Silent, Godless": Ecodisaster and the Post-Abundant Landscape in *The Road*. In Sara L. Spurgeon (ed.), *Cormac McCarthy: All the Pretty Horses, No Country for Old Men, The Road.* New York: Continuum, 2011, 157–71.

Kuhn, Thomas S. *The Structure of Scientific Revolutions.* First published 1962; University of Chicago Press, 1996.

Kumar, Krishan. *Utopianism.* Milton Keynes: Open University Press, 1990.

Kunsa, Ashley. '"Maps of the World in Its Becoming": Post-Apocalyptic Naming in Cormac McCarthy's *The Road*. *Journal of Modern Literature* 33 (2009), 57–74.

'Landmark U.S. Federal Climate Lawsuit'. Our Children's Trust. www
.ourchildrenstrust.org/us/federal-lawsuit

LaRossa, Ralph. 'The Culture of Fatherhood and the Late-Twentieth-Century
New Fatherhood Movement: An Interpretive Perspective'. In Laura Tropp
and Janice Kelly (eds.), *Deconstructing Dads: Changing Images of Fathers in
Popular Culture*. Lanham, MD: Lexington, 2016, 3–30.

 *The Modernization of Fatherhood: A Social and Political History*. University of
Chicago Press, 1997.

Lederman, Shmuel. 'Agonism and Deliberation in Arendt'. *Constellations* 21.3
(2014), 327–37.

Leopold, Aldo. *A Sand County Almanac: With Essays on Conservation*, illustrated
edn. First published 1949; Oxford University Press, 2001.

Lepucki, Edan. *California*. First published 2014; London: Abacus, 2015.

Lilley, Deborah. 'Unsettling Environments: New Pastoral in Kazuo Ishiguro's
*Never Let Me Go* and Sarah Hall's *The Carhullan Army*'. *Green Letters* 20.1
(2016), 60–71.

Lovelock, James. *The Revenge of Gaia: Why the Earth Is Fighting Back—and
How We Can Still Save Humanity*. First published 2006; London:
Penguin, 2007.

Lupton, Deborah, and Lesley Barclay. *Constructing Fatherhood: Discourses and
Experiences*. London: Sage, 1997.

MacGregor, Sherilyn. *Beyond Mothering Earth: Ecological Citizenship and the
Politics of Care*. Vancouver: University of British Columbia Press, 2006.

Maczynska, Magdalena. 'This Monstrous City: Urban Visionary Satire in the
Fiction of Martin Amis, Will Self, China Miéville, and Maggie Gee'.
*Contemporary Literature* 51 (2010), 58–86.

Mancuso, Stefano, and Alessandra Viola. *Brilliant Green: The Surprising History
and Science of Plant Intelligence*. Washington, DC: Island Press, 2015.

Mangrum, Benjamin. 'Accounting for *The Road*: Tragedy, Courage, and Cavell's
Acknowledgement'. *Philosophy and Literature* 37 (2013), 267–90.

Mayer, Sylvia. 'Explorations of the Controversially Real: Risk, the Climate
Change Novel, and the Narrative of Anticipation'. In Sylvia Mayer and
Alexa Weik von Mossner (eds.), *The Anticipation of Catastrophe:
Environmental Risk in North American Literature and Culture*. Heidelberg:
Universitätsverlag Winter, 2014, 21–37.

McCarthy, Cormac. *The Road*. First published 2006; London: Picador, 2007.

McCaulay, Diana, Michael Mendis, and Maggie Gee. 'The Untold Story:
The Environment in Fiction'. *Hay Festival*, 29 May 2014.

McCulloch, Fiona. *Cosmopolitanism in Contemporary British Fiction: Imagined
Identities*. Basingstoke: Palgrave–Macmillan, 2012.

McKay, Margaret. 'An Interview with Maggie Gee'. *Studia Neophilogica* 69.2
(1997), 213–21.

Meadows, Donella H., Dennis L. Meadows, Jorgen Randers, and William
W. Behrens. *The Limits to Growth: A Report on the Club of Rome's Project
for the Predicament of Mankind*. New York: Universe Books, 1972.

Medawar, Peter. *Induction and Intuition in Scientific Thought*. London: Methuen, 1969.

Mehnert, Antonia. *Climate Change Fictions: Representations of Global Warming in American Literature*. London: Palgrave–Macmillan, 2016.

Meillassoux, Quentin. *After Finitude: An Essay on the Necessity of Contingency*. Trans. Ray Brassier. London: Continuum, 2010.

Mellor, Mary. 'Ecofeminist Political Economy and the Politics of Money'. In Ariel Salleh (ed.), *Eco-Sufficiency and Global Justice: Women Write Political Ecology*. London: Pluto, 2009, 251–67.

*Feminism and Ecology*. London: Polity Press, 1997.

Merchant, Carolyn. *The Death of Nature: Women, Ecology, and the Scientific Revolution*. First published 1980; San Francisco: Harper Collins, 1990.

*Earthcare: Women and the Environment*. London: Routledge, 1995.

Merola, Nicole M. 'Materializing a Geotraumatic and Melancholy Anthropocene: Jeanette Winterson's *The Stone Gods*'. *Minnesota Review* 83 (2014), 122–32.

Moline, Jon N. 'Aldo Leopold and the Moral Community'. *Environmental Ethics* 8.3 (1986), 99–120.

Monbiot, George. 'Civilisation Ends with a Shutdown of Human Concern: Are We There Already?' *The Guardian* (30 October 2007).

Morrison, Jago '"Who Cares about Gender at a Time like This?" Love, Sex and the Problem of Jeanette Winterson'. *Journal of Gender Studies* 15 (2006), 169–80.

Morton, Timothy. *The Ecological Thought*. Cambridge, MA: Harvard University Press, 2010.

*Hyperobjects: Philosophy and Ecology after the End of the World*. Minneapolis: University of Minnesota Press, 2013.

Moylan, Tom. *Demand the Impossible: Science Fiction and the Utopian Imagination*. New York: Methuen, 1986.

*Scraps of the Untainted Sky: Science Fiction, Utopia, Dystopia*. Boulder, CO: Westview, 2000.

Murtaugh, Paul A., and Michael Schlax, 'Reproduction and the Carbon Legacies of Individuals'. *Global Environmental Change* 19.1 (2009), 14–20.

Næss, Arne. 'The Shallow and the Deep, Long-Range Ecology Movement: A Summary'. *Inquiry* 16.1–4 (1973), 95–96.

Næss, Arne, and David Rothenberg. *Ecology, Community, and Lifestyle: Outline of an Ecosophy*. Cambridge University Press, 1989.

Noddings, Nel. *Caring: A Relational Approach to Ethics and Moral Education*, updated edn. First published 1984; Berkeley: University of California Press, 2013.

Nowotny, Helga. 'Science and Utopia: On the Social Ordering of the Future'. In Everett Mendelsohn and Helga Nowotny (eds.), *Nineteen Eighty-Four: Science between Utopia and Dystopia*. Dordrecht: Reidel, 1984, 3–18.

Nussbaum, Martha C. 'Beyond "Compassion and Humanity": Justice for Nonhuman Animals'. In Cass R. Sunstein and Martha C. Nussbaum (eds.), *Animal Rights: Current Debates and New Directions*. Oxford University Press, 2004, 299–320.

'Compassion and Terror'. *Daedalus* 132.1 (2003), 10–26.

*Cultivating Humanity: A Classical Defense of Reform in Liberal Education*. Cambridge, MA: Harvard University Press, 1997.

*Love's Knowledge: Essays on Philosophy and Literature*. Oxford University Press, 1990.

*Political Emotions: Why Love Matters for Justice*. Cambridge, MA: Belknap, 2013.

*Upheavals of Thought: The Intelligence of Emotions*. Cambridge University Press, 2001.

Onega, Susana. 'The Trauma Paradigm and the Ethics of Affect in Jeanette Winterson's *The Stone Gods*'. In Susana Onega and Jean-Michael Ganteau (eds.), *Ethics and Trauma in Contemporary British Fiction*. Amsterdam: Rodopi, 2011, 265–98.

O'Neill, Brian C., Michael Dalton, Regina Fuchs, *et al*. 'Global Demographic Trends and Future Carbon Emissions'. *PNAS* 107 (2012), 17521–6.

O'Neill, John. *Ecology, Policy and Politics: Human Well-Being and the Natural World*. London: Routledge, 1993.

Ortner, Sherry B. 'Is Female to Male as Nature Is to Culture?' In Michelle Zimbalist Rosaldo and Louise Lamphere (eds.), *Woman, Culture, and Society*. Stanford University Press, 1974, 67–87.

O'Toole, Garson. 'We Do Not Inherit the Earth from Our Ancestors; We Borrow It from Our Children'. *Quote Investigator: Exploring the Origins of Quotations*. http://quoteinvestigator.com/2013/01/22/borrow-earth/#;note -5296–1

Otto, Eric C. '"From a Certain Angle": Ecothriller Reading and Science Fiction Reading *The Swarm* and *The Rapture*'. *Ecozon@* 3 (2012), 106–21.

Padel, Ruth. 'Slices of Toast'. *London Review of Books* 29.5 (8 March 2007), 31.

Parfit, Derek. *Reasons and Persons*. Oxford University Press, 1986.

Parrinder, Patrick. *Utopian Literature and Science: From the Scientific Revolution to Brave New World and Beyond*. Basingstoke: Palgrave–Macmillan, 2015.

Plumwood, Val. *Feminism and the Mastery of Nature*. London: Routledge, 1993.

Popper, Karl. *The Logic of Scientific Discovery*. First published 1959; London: Routledge, 1992.

Proctor, Robert. *Value-Free Science? Purity and Power in Modern Knowledge*. Cambridge, MA: Harvard University Press, 1991.

Pykett, Lyn. 'A New Way with Words? Jeanette Winterson's Post-Modernism'. In Helena Grice and Tim Woods (eds.), *'I'm Telling You Stories': Jeanette Winterson and the Politics of Reading*. Amsterdam: Rodopi, 1998, 53–60.

Rachels, James. *Created from Animals: The Moral Implications of Darwinism*. Oxford University Press, 1990.

Rawls, John. *Justice as Fairness: A Restatement*. Cambridge, MA: Harvard University Press, 2001.

*Political Liberalism*. New York: Columbia University Press, 1993.

*A Theory of Justice*. Cambridge, MA: Harvard University Press, 1971.

Reese, Diana. 'Michael Brown's Mother Inspires Controversial Artwork by Mary Engelbreit'. *Washington Post* (25 August 2014).

Riley, Frank. 'John Muir's Legacy Still Strong in Glacier Country'. *Los Angeles Times* (14 August. 1988), 5.

Rine, Abigail. 'Jeanette Winterson's Love Intervention: Rethinking the Future'. In Ben Davies and Jana Funke (eds.), *Sex, Gender and Time in Fiction and Culture*. Basingstoke: Palgrave–Macmillan, 2011, 70–85.

Robinson, Iain. '"You Just Know When the World is About to Break Apart": Utopia, Dystopia and New Global Uncertainties in Sarah Hall's *The Carhullan Army*'. In Siân Adiseshiah and Rupert Hildyard (eds.), *Twenty-First Century Fiction: What Happens Now*. Basingstoke: Palgrave–Macmillan, 2013, 197–211.

Robinson, Kim Stanley. 'Climate Change and the Pursuit of Happiness' [lecture]. Sustainable Actions for a Sustainable Future Conference, Missouri State University, 22 April 2009.

*Fifty Degrees Below*. First published 2005; London: HarperCollins, 2006.

*Forty Signs of Rain*. First published 2004; London: HarperCollins, 2005.

*Green Earth*. New York: Del Rey, 2015.

*Imagining Abrupt Climate Change: Terraforming Earth*. Seattle: Amazon Shorts, 2005.

*Red Mars*. New York: Bantam, 1993.

*Sixty Days and Counting*. London: HarperCollins, 2007.

Rosenblatt, Louise M. *The Reader, the Text, the Poem: The Transactional Theory of the Literary Work*. Carbondale, IL: Southern Illinois University Press, 1978.

Salleh, Ariel. 'Class, Race, and Gender Discourse in the Ecofeminism/Deep Ecology Debate'. In Max Oelschlaeger (ed.), *Postmodern Environmental Ethics*. Albany: State University of New York Press, 1995, 79–100.

Sánchez-Eppler, Karen. *Dependent States: The Child's Part in Nineteenth-Century American Culture*. University of Chicago Press, 2005.

Sandilands, Catriona. *The Good-Natured Feminist: Ecofeminism and the Quest for Democracy*. Minneapolis: University of Minnesota Press, 1999.

'Sarah Hall – *The Carhullan Army*'. *Bookclub*, BBC Radio 4, 9 December 2010.

Scheffler, Samuel. *Death and the Afterlife*. Oxford University Press, 2013.

Sears, John. '"Making Sorrow Speak": Maggie Gee's Novels'. In Emma Parker (ed.), *Contemporary British Women Writers*. Cambridge: D. S. Brewer, 2004, 55–67.

Seed, David. 'The Mars Trilogy: An Interview'. *Foundation* 68 (1996), 75–80.

Sellars, Wilfred. 'Philosophy and the Scientific Image of Man'. In Robert Colodny (ed.), *Frontiers of Science and Philosophy*. University of Pittsburgh Press, 1962, 35–78.

Seymour, Nicole. *Strange Natures: Futurity, Empathy, and the Queer Ecological Imagination*. Urbana: University of Illinois Press, 2013.

Sideris, Lisa H. *Consecrating Science: Wonder, Knowledge, and the Natural World*. Oakland, CA: University of California Press, 2017.

Sidgwick, Henry. *Practical Ethics: A Collection of Addresses and Essays*. First published 1898; Oxford University Press, 1998.

Singer, Peter. 'Animals and the Value of Life'. In Tom Regan (ed.), *Matters of Life and Death: New Introductory Essays on Moral Philosophy*, 3rd edn. New York: McGraw-Hill, 1993, 280–321.

Snyder, Phillip A. 'Hospitality in Cormac McCarthy's *The Road*'. *Cormac McCarthy Journal* 6 (2008), 69–86.

Solomon, Robert C. *In Defense of Sentimentality*. Oxford University Press, 2004.

Squire, Louise. 'Death and the Anthropocene: Cormac McCarthy's World of Unliving'. *Oxford Literary Review* 34.2 (2012), 211–28.

'The Subject Reconsidered: Death-Facing and Its Challenges in Contemporary Environmental Crisis Fiction'. PhD dissertation. University of Surrey, 2014.

Stableford, Brian. 'Science Fiction and Ecology'. In David Seed (ed.), *A Companion to Science Fiction*. Malden, MA: Blackwell, 2005, 127–41.

Stark, Hannah. '"All These Things He Saw and Did Not See": Witnessing the End of the World in Cormac McCarthy's *The Road*'. *Critical Survey* 25.2 (2013), 71–84.

Stein, Rachel. Introduction. In Rachel Stein (ed.), *New Perspectives on Environmental Justice: Gender, Sexuality, and Activism*. New Brunswick, NJ: Rutgers University Press, 2004, 1–17.

Stevenson, Christian M., Cedric O. Puleston, Peter M. Vitousek, *et al*. 'Variation in Rapa Nui (Easter Island) Land Use Indicates Production and Population Peaks Prior to European Contact'. *PNAS* 112 (2015), 1025–30.

Sturgeon, Noël. *Environmentalism in Popular Culture: Gender, Race, Sexuality, and the Politics of the Natural*. Tuscon: University of Arizona Press, 2009.

Sunderland, Jane. '"Parenting" or "Mothering"? The Case of Modern Childcare Magazines'. *Discourse and Society* 17.4 (2006), 503–27.

Suvin, Darko. *Metamorphoses of Science Fiction: On the Poetics and History of a Literary Genre*. New Haven, CT: Yale University Press, 1979.

Szeman, Imre, and Maria Whiteman. 'Future Politics: An Interview with Kim Stanley Robinson'. *Science Fiction Studies* 31.2 (2004), 188–99.

Talbot, Lee M. 'A World Conservation Strategy'. *Journal of the Royal Society of Arts* 128.5288 (July 1980).

Thant, U. Statement at Presentation of Declaration on Population Growth, 10 December 1967. www.un.org/en/development/desa/population/theme/rights

Trexler, Adam. *Anthropocene Fictions: The Novel in a Time of Climate Change*. Charlottesville: University of Virginia Press, 2015.

Trexler, Adam, and Adeline Johns-Putra. 'Climate Change in Literature and Literary Criticism', *WIREs Climate Change* 2.1 (2011), 185–200.

Tronto, Joan C. *Moral Boundaries: A Political Argument for an Ethic of Care*. New York: Routledge, 1993.

Tronto, Joan, and Berenice Fisher. 'Towards a Feminist Theory of Caring'. In Emily K. Abel and Margaret K. Nelson (eds.), *Circles of Care: Work and*

*Identity in Women's Lives*. Albany: State University of New York Press, 1990, 36–54.

United Nations Environment Programme. *Annual Review 1978*. London: UNEP Earthprint, 1980.

United Nations General Assembly. *Universal Declaration of Human Rights*. New York: United Nations, 1967.

Villegas-López, Sonia. 'Body Technologies: Posthuman Figurations in Larissa Lai's *Salt Fish Girl* and Jeanette Winterson's *The Stone Gods*'. *Critique* 56.1 (2015), 26–41.

Vrousalis, Nicholas. 'Intergenerational Justice: A Primer'. In Iñigo González-Ricoy and Axel Gosseries (eds.), *Institutions for Future Generations*. Oxford University Press, 2016, 49–64.

Wagner-Martin, Linda. *Barbara Kingsolver's World: Nature, Art, and the Twenty-First Century*. New York: Bloomsbury, 2014.

Wall, Glenda, and Stephanie Arnold. 'How Involved Is Involved Fathering?' *Gender and Society* 21.4 (2007), 508–27.

Walsh, Bryan. 'Barbara Kingsolver on *Flight Behavior*'. *Time* (8 November 2012).

Watkins, Susan. 'Future Shock: Rewriting the Apocalypse in Contemporary Women's Fiction'. *LIT: Literature Interpretation Theory* 23.2 (2012), 119–37.

Weik von Mossner, Alexa. *Affective Ecologies: Empathy, Emotion, and Environmental Narrative*. Columbus: Ohio State University Press, 2017.

Winterson, Jeanette. *The Stone Gods*. First published 2007; London: Penguin, 2008.

Wong, Sam. 'Baby Emissions Fuel Global Warming', *The Guardian* (5 August 2009).

Woodson, Linda. 'Mapping *The Road* in Post-Postmodernism'. *Cormac McCarthy Journal* 8 (2010), 87–97.

World Commission on Environment and Development. *Our Common Future*. Oxford University Press, 1987.

Young-Bruehl, Elisabeth. *Why Arendt Matters*. New Haven, CT: Yale University Press, 2006.

Zibrak, Arielle. 'Intolerance, A Survival Guide: Heteronormative Culture Formation in Cormac McCarthy's *The Road*'. *Arizona Quarterly* 68 (2012), 103–28.

# Index